THE ATHENIAN AGORA

ISBN 960–7067–00–2

Cover: aerial view of the west side of the Agora.
Balloon photograph by Will and Ellie Myers.
Back: *watercolor view of the Agora area in 1834*
by J. J. Wolfensberger.

THE
ATHENIAN AGORA

A GUIDE TO THE EXCAVATION
AND MUSEUM

Fourth Edition Revised

1990

Publication and design: Lucy Braggiotti

Proof reading: Leslie Becker
Photo reproduction: K. Adam
Printing: Epikoinonia
Binding: Sp. Sgardelis

Foreward

This new edition of the Agora guide takes account of the important recent excavations which have taken place since 1976, the year of publication of the third edition. In addition, this version has been directed specifically toward those actually visiting the site: it is somewhat more compact than its predecessor and the illustrations have been chosen to help the visitor recreate the site in his mind's eye. Two narrative accounts of the monuments of the Agora are now available for those interested: The Agora of Athens by H. A. Thompson and R. E. Wycherley (Princeton 1972) and The Athenian Agora by J. Camp (London 1986). Other Agora publications are listed on pp. 13-16.

Many parts have been retained as they were written for earlier editions by Mabel Lang and C. W. J. Eliot (1954) and H. A. Thompson (1962, 1976). New drawings by the late W. B. Dinsmoor, Jr. have been added, as have several new photographs by Craig and Marie Mauzy. The recent field work has been carried out under the direction of Prof. T. L. Shear, Jr. and has been made possible with the support of the David and Lucile Packard Foundation. For help with the manuscript I am indebted to P. Felsch-Niterou, Anne Stewart, and Tracey Cullen.

As in the previous editions the views expressed here are based on the combined thinking of the many scholars who have worked together in the Agora over the past sixty years.

John McK. Camp II
Resident Director

CONTENTS

SOME LANDMARKS
IN THE HISTORY OF ATHENS
AND THE ATHENIAN AGORA

ca. 3000 B.C.	Earliest recorded habitation in Athens on the Acropolis slopes (Neolithic or Late Stone Age)
1550 - 1100 B.C.	Mycenaean Period (Late Helladic or Late Bronze Age)
1100 - 600 B.C.	Protogeometric, Geometric and Orientalizing Periods
ca. 600 B.C.	First democratic city organization, under Solon (594 B.C.)
560 - 510 B.C.	Rule of Peisistratos and his sons
508 B.C.	Democratic reforms under Kleisthenes
490 - 479 B.C.	The Persian Wars (sack of Athens by the Persians, 480/79 B.C.)
460 - 429 B.C.	Age of Perikles
431 - 404 B.C.	Peloponnesian War (Peace of Nikias, 421 - 415 B.C.)
399 B.C.	Death of Sokrates
338 B.C.	Supremacy of Macedon (Battle of Chaironeia); Lykourgos in charge of Athenian finances, 338 - 326 B.C.
323 B.C.	Death of Alexander the Great
322 B.C.	Macedonian occupation of Athens
3rd - 2nd centuries B.C.	Hellenistic Period
146 B.C.	Ascendancy of Rome (sack of Corinth by Mummius)
86 B.C.	Siege of Athens by Sulla
27 B.C. - 14 A.D.	Reign of Augustus
117 - 138 A.D.	Reign of Hadrian
138 - 161 A.D.	Reign of Antoninus Pius (visit of Pausanias to Athens, ca. 150 A.D.)
267 A.D.	Buildings in the Agora burned by the Herulians
396 A.D.	Invasion by Visigoths under Alaric

11

529 A.D.	Schools of Athens closed by the Emperor Justinian
582/3 A.D.	Devastation probably caused by Slavs
1204 A.D.	Lower city of Athens devastated by Leon Sgouros from Nauplia
1456 - 1458 A.D.	Capture of Athens by the Turks (lower city, 1456 A.D.; Acropolis, 1458 A.D.)
1821 - 1828 A.D.	Greek War of Independance
1834 A.D.	Athens becomes the capital of modern Greece

PUBLICATIONS
BY THE AMERICAN SCHOOL OF CLASSICAL STUDIES
AT ATHENS
RELATING TO THE ATHENIAN AGORA

Hesperia: the Journal of the American School of Classical Studies since 1932; contains annual reports on the progress of the excavations and many special studies.

Supplements to Hesperia: issued at irregular intervals in the same format as *Hesperia*. Quarto. Paper.

I   *Prytaneis: A Study of the Inscriptions honoring the Athenian Councillors.* By Sterling Dow. 1937.

II   *Late Geometric Graves and a Seventh Century Well in the Agora*, with an Appendix on the Skeletal Remains by J. Lawrence Angel. By Rodney S. Young. 1939.

IV   *The Tholos of Athens and its Predecessors.* By Homer A. Thompson. 1940.

V   *Observations on the Hephaisteion.* By William B. Dinsmoor. 1941.

VII   *Commemorative Studies in Honor of Theodore Leslie Shear.* 1949.

IX   *Horoi: Studies in Mortgage, Real Security, and Land Tenure in Ancient Athens.* By John V. A. Fine. 1951.

XII   *The Athenian Constitution after Sulla.* By Daniel J. Geagan. 1967.

XIII   *Marcus Aurelius: Aspects of Civic and Cultural Policy in the East.* By James H. Oliver. 1970.

XIV   *The Political Organization of Attica.* By John S. Traill. 1975.

XVII   *Kallias of Sphettos and the Revolt of Athens in 286 B.C.* By T. Leslie Shear, Jr. 1978.

XIX   *Studies in Attic Epigraphy, History and Topography Presented to Eugene Vanderpool.* 1982.

XX   *Studies in Athenian Architecture, Sculpture and Topography presented to Homer A. Thompson.* 1982.

XXII   *Attic Grave Reliefs that Represent Women in the Dress of Isis.* By Elizabeth J. Walters. 1988.

The Athenian Agora: series of monographs on the results of the excavations.

I   *Portrait Sculpture.* By Evelyn B. Harrison, xiv, 114 pp., 49 pls. Quarto. 1953.

II   *Coins from the Roman through the Venetian Period.* By Margaret Thompson. viii, 122 pp., 4 pls. Quarto. 1954.

III   *Literary and Epigraphical Testimonia.* By R. E. Wycherley. vii, 259 pp., 4 pls. Quarto. 1957. Reprinted 1973.

IV   *Greek Lamps and their Survivals.* By Richard Hubbard Howland. ix, 252 pp., 56 pls. Quarto. 1958. Reprinted 1966.

V   *Pottery of the Roman Period: Chronology.* By Henry S. Robinson. xiv, 149 pp., 76 pls. Quarto. 1958. Reprinted 1966.

VI   *Terracottas and Plastic Lamps of the Roman Period.* By Clairève Grandjouan. Quarto. 1961.

VII   *Lamps of the Roman Period.* By Judith Perlzweig. xiv, 240 pp., 53 pls. Quarto. 1961. Reprinted 1971.

VIII   *Late Geometric and Protoattic Pottery.* By Eva T. Brann. xiv, 134 pp., 46 pls. Quarto. 1962. Reprinted 1971.

IX   *Islamic Coins.* By George C. Miles. viii, 62 pp., 6 pls. Quarto. 1962.

X   *Weights, Measures and Tokens.* By Mabel Lang and Margaret Crosby. xii, 146 pp., 36 pls. Quarto. 1964.

XI   *Archaic and Archaistic Sculpture.* By Evelyn B. Harrison. xix, 192 pp., 68 pls. Quarto. 1965.

XII   *Black and Plain Pottery of the 6th, 5th and 4th Centuries B.C.* By Brian A. Sparkes and Lucy Talcott. Part 1: xix, 382 pp.; Part 2: ix, 90 pp., 100 pls. Both Quarto. 1970.

XIII   *The Neolithic and Bronze Ages.* By Sara Anderson Immerwahr. xx, 286 pp., 92 pls. Quarto. 1971.

XIV   *The Agora of Athens.* By Homer A. Thompson and R. E. Wycherley. xiii, 257 pp., 112 pls. Quarto. 1972.

XV   *Inscriptions. The Athenian Councillors.* By Benjamin D. Meritt and John S. Traill. xii, 486 pp., 2 pls. Quarto. 1974.

XVII   *Inscriptions. The Funerary Monuments.* By Donald W. Bradeen. xi, 240 pp., 85 pls. Quarto. 1973.

15

15   *Greeks and Roman Coins in the Athenian Agora.* By Fred S. Kleiner. 1975.

16   *The Athenian Agora: A Short Guide.* By Homer A. Thompson 1976. Also available in Greek, German and French.

17   *Socrates in the Agora.* By Mabel L. Lang. 1978.

18   *Mediaeval and Modern Coins in the Athenian Agora.* By Fred. S. Kleiner. 1978.

19   *Gods and Heroes in the Athenian Agora.* By John McK. Camp II. 1980.

20   *Bronzeworkers in the Athenian Agora.* By Carol C. Mattusch. 1982.

21   *Ancient Athenian Building Methods.* By John McK. Camp II and William B. Dinsmoor, Jr. 1984.

22   *Birds of the Athenian Agora.* By Robert D. Lamberton and Susan I. Rotroff. 1985.

All the above publications may be obtained from:
American School of Classical Studies at Athens
Souidias 54, Athens 10676, Greece

or: *American School of Classical Studies at Athens*
Publications Office
c/o Institute for Advanced Study
Princeton, New Jersey, 08540, U.S.A.

This guide book and the picture books are also available in the Sales Office on the ground floor of the Stoa of Attalos at Athens.

THE ATHENIAN AGORA

INTRODUCTION

Classical Athens saw the rise of an achievement unparalleled in history. Pericles, Aeschylus, Sophocles, Plato, Demosthenes, Thucydides and Praxiteles represent just a few of the statesmen and playwrights, historians and artists, philosophers and orators who flourished here during the 5th and 4th centuries B.C. when Athens was the most powerful city-state in Greece. Collectively they were responsible for sowing the seeds of western civilization. Even when her influence waned, Athens remained a cultural Mecca, a center for the study of philosophy and rhetoric until the 6th century A.D. Throughout antiquity Athens was adorned with great public buildings, financed first by its citizens, and later with gifts from Hellenistic kings and Roman emperors. Nowhere is the history of Athens so richly illustrated as in the Agora, the marketplace which was the focal point of life.

A large open square, surrounded on all four sides by public buildings, the Agora was in all respects the center of town. The excavation of buildings, monuments and small objects has illustrated the important role it played in all aspects of civic life. The senate chamber (*bouleuterion*), public office buildings (Royal Stoa, South Stoa I) and archives (*metroon*) have all been excavated. The law courts are represented by the discovery of bronze ballots and a water clock used to time speeches. The use of the area as a market place is suggested by the numerous shops and workrooms where potters, cobblers, bronzeworkers and sculptors made and sold their wares. Long stoas, or colonnades, provided shaded walkways for those wishing to meet friends to discuss business, politics or philosophy, and statues and commemorative monuments reminded citizens of former triumphs. A library and concert hall met cultural needs, and numerous shrines and temples received regular worship in the area. Thus administrative, political, judicial, commercial, social, cultural and religious activities all found a place here together in the heart of ancient Athens.

The many parts played by the Agora in the lives of the Athenians are reflected in the works of those ancient authors who frequented the Agora themselves. The mixture of political and commercial activity which characterized the heart of Athens is perhaps best described by the comic poet Euboulos:

> You will find everything sold together in the same place at Athens: figs, witnesses to summonses, bunches of grapes, turnips, pears, apples, givers of evidence, roses, medlars, porridge, honeycombs, chickpeas, lawsuits, beestings-puddings, myrtle, allotment machines, irises, lambs, water clocks, laws, indictments.
>
> (Athenaeus, *Deipnosophistai* XIV, 640b-c)

And for the Agora as the repository for reminders of former greatness:

> You will find that in other cities statues of athletes are set up in the agora, in Athens statues of good generals and of the Tyrannicides.
>
> (Lykourgos, *In Leokratem*, 51)

Even those with no particular business to transact would find in the Agora some entertainment to pass the time:

> And yet at Athens lately, in front of the Painted Stoa, with these two eyes I saw a conjuror devour a cavalry sword sharpened to a very keen point; and presently, with the inducement of a small payment, he also swallowed a hunting spear, point first, till it penetrated deep into his vitals... And all of us who witnessed the performance wondered.
>
> (Apuleius, *Metamorphoses* I, 4)

In its buildings and monuments the Agora came to be a cumulative record of past achievements and history and here the visitor to Athens can recapture at least part of the richness and diversity of life in the ancient city.

An asterisk here and elsewhere in the text indicates the presence of a note at the back of the book: pp. 273 ff.
The numbers in parenthesis, e.g. (Plan, 1), refer to the folding plan at the back of the book.

HISTORY OF THE AGORA*

The excavations, which cover an area of about thirty acres northwest of the Acropolis, have brought to light remains from all periods of the city's history, from Neolithic times to the present, a span of some five thousand years.

On the slopes of the Acropolis, just below the Klepsydra spring, twenty shallow wells or pits of the Late Neolithic period (ca. 3000 B.C.) have been discovered. The handmade pottery from these deposits is of excellent quality and shows that even at this remote period Athens had a settled population with high artistic standards. Scattered remains (wells and graves) of the Early and Middle Helladic periods (3000-1550 B.C.) have also been found.

The remains of the Late Helladic or Mycenaean period (1550-1100 B.C.) are more extensive (Fig. 1). Two large chamber tombs, the first to be found in Athens, were located on the north slope of the Areopagus, while many smaller tombs and simple graves of the same period were dotted throughout the area. Household wells dating from the late Mycenaean and the Submycenaean periods attest habitation in the level area as early as the 12th century B.C.

The early Iron Age, comprising the Protogeometric and Geometric periods (1100-700 B.C.), is well represented (Fig. 2). Many richly furnished graves have been found. No remains of houses have come to light, but numerous wells containing domestic refuse show that settlement was expanding in this direction.

Early in the 6th century B.C., in the time of Solon the Lawgiver, the gently sloping area northwest of the Acropolis and east of Kolonos Agoraios was designated as the site of the main square of the city, the Agora. (There may have been an earlier, less formal Agora perhaps just outside the entrance to the Acropolis.) Burials ceased to be made in this area and some private houses were demolished to make more open space for public needs. The first public buildings of which foundations have been discovered stood along the west side of the area and appear to have been intended for the needs of the Council (Fig. 3). (For a list of numbered buildings see the space adjoining the General Plan at the end of the book.)

During the half century (566-510 B.C.) when Athens was dominated politically by the tyrant Peisistratos and his family, limited building

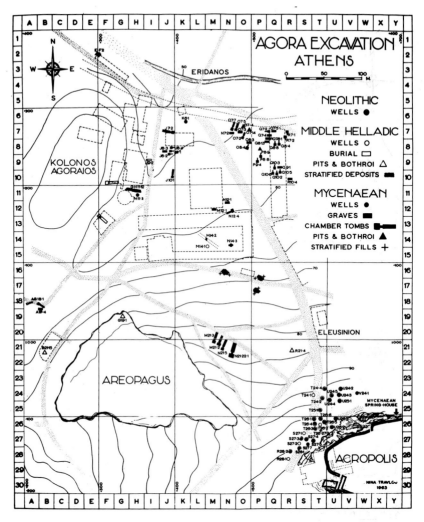

1. Plan of the Agora area in prehistoric times, showing Neolithic and Bronze Age wells and graves. (3000-1100 B.C.).

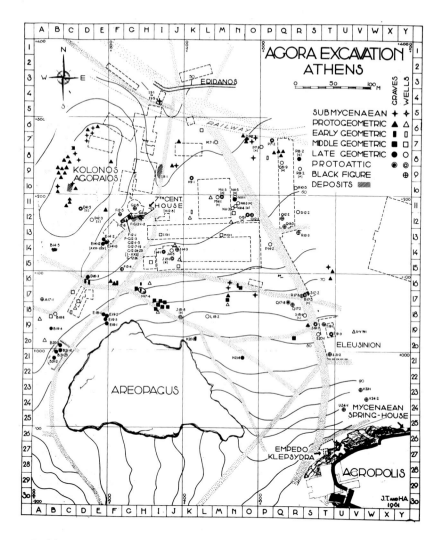

2. Plan of the Agora area, showing Iron Age wells and graves (1100-600 B.C.).

occurred in the Agora. Peisistratos was preoccupied primarily with great building programs elsewhere in the city, notably on and south of the Acropolis. A large house-like building dating from the early period of the tyrants preceded the Tholos at the southwest corner of the Agora; in later times it appears to have served the domestic needs of the Council, but it may have been built originally as a palace for the tyrants. A fountain house, supplied by a terracotta aqueduct, was built at the southeast corner of the square (Plan, **62**). The grandson and namesake of Peisistratos established the Altar of the Twelve Gods (Plan, **31**) and the family encouraged the development of the national festival of Athens, the Panathenaia, many events of which occurred in the Agora.

The increased tempo of civic life that followed the constitutional reforms of Kleisthenes at the end of the 6th century is reflected by considerable building activity in the early years of the following century (Fig. **3**). Many of the earliest substantial structures clearly designed for the needs of civic life seem to date to ca. 500 B.C. An area along the south side of the square was terraced and enclosed by a stone wall, apparently to accommodate the principal lawcourt, the Heliaia (Plan, **68**). The southwest corner of the square was leveled and a great stone drain was built to carry northward the surface water from the slopes of the Areopagus and from the valley between the Areopagus and the Pnyx (Plan, **11**). The small early buildings between this drain and Kolonos Agoraios were now demolished to make way for the Old Bouleuterion (Council House) (Plan, **14**). A small temple to the north of and slightly later than the Old Bouleuterion may have housed the cult of the Mother of the Gods. The Royal Stoa (Plan, **26**) also seems to date from the turn of the 6th to 5th century; though much smaller in scale it is comparable in quality to the Heliaia and Old Bouleuterion. The assembly of the citizens for political purposes (*Ekklesia*), which had previously met in the Agora, now found a more quiet meeting place on the Pnyx Hill, a 10-minute walk to the southwest. In keeping with this general trend toward more specialized facilities, some of the theatral gatherings likewise gave up the Agora in favor of a more sheltered site at the south foot of the Acropolis.

The excavations have produced much evidence of the widespread damage done by the Persians who occupied Athens in 480/79 B.C.

3. Plan of the Agora, ca. 500 B.C.

Private houses were destroyed and their wells filled with debris; sanctuaries such as those of Apollo and of the Twelve Gods were left desolate. The Heliaia, the Old Bouleuterion and the Royal Stoa presumably suffered as well but were subsequently repaired and continued in use.

To the 460's, i.e. to the time of Kimon, are to be dated new civic buildings in the area of the Agora: the Tholos (Plan, **5**) for the convenience of the Councillors and the Painted Stoa to serve as a pleasant promenade for the citizens. Kimon himself is reported to have adorned the Agora with plane trees.

Soon after the establishment of peace with the Persians in the mid-5th century, the Athenians began to restore their ruinous sanctuaries. Among the first of the new buildings was the Temple of Hephaistos (Plan, **1**). Work on the temple was interrupted, however, by the Periclean program on the Acropolis and was not resumed until the Peace of Nikias (421-415 B.C.). Other small sanctuaries and shrines were also repaired at this time (the Altar of the Twelve Gods, the Altar of Aphrodite, the Crossroads Enclosure). There was only limited civic building in the Agora during the Periclean period, the Strategeion or headquarters of the generals (Plan, **7**) being one of the few exceptions. As though to compensate for this neglect, a burst of activity followed in the last thirty years of the century (Fig. **4**); the Stoa of Zeus (Plan, **25**), South Stoa I (Plan, **64**), the New Bouleuterion (Plan, **13**) and the Mint (Plan, **61**) all appear to date from this time even while Athens was engaged in the Peloponnesian War and its aftermath. Another civic improvement was the remodeling of the Assembly Place on the Pnyx at the end of the 5th century.

After a half century of no building activity, the second half of the 4th century saw a capacious new fountain house erected at the southwest corner of the Agora (Plan, **70**) and the Monument of the Eponymous Heroes moved to a convenient location in front of the Bouleuterion (Plan, **19**). The period when Lykourgos controlled the city's finances (338-326 B.C.) witnessed many more improvements in the facilities for civic life (Fig. **5**). The shrine of Zeus Phratrios and Athena Phratria was erected on the west side of the Agora (Plan, **24**), to be followed shortly by the construction of the Temple of Apollo Patroos (Plan, **23**). A group of buildings for the use of the Lawcourts which had grown up at the northeast corner of the Agora in the later 5th and early 4th centuries was now replaced with a large cloister-like building which we shall call the Square Peristyle (Plan, **44**). Work on this structure was halted toward the close of the 4th century by the deteriorating military situation which ushered in an unsettled period of over a century during which little or no building occurred in the Agora.

An improvement in the city's economy, combined with the benevolent attitude of the eastern monarchies, led to a renewal of building activity in the 2nd century B.C. The whole aspect of the Agora was changed in the course of the second and third quarters of the century

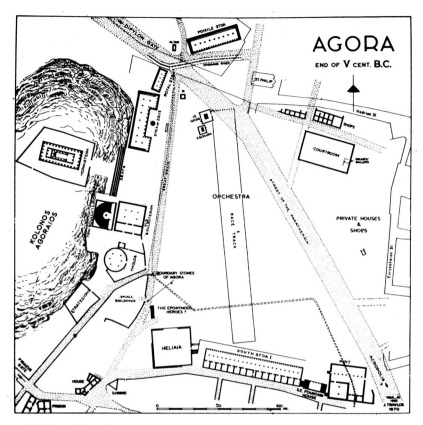

4. *Plan of the Agora, ca. 400 B.C.*

by the erection of the Middle Stoa (Plan, **67**), the East Building (Plan, **66**) and South Stoa II (Plan, **65**). The South Square thus formed took the place of several earlier buildings. The east side of the main square was now closed by a two-story colonnade (Plan, **46**), the gift of Attalos II, King of Pergamon (159-138 B.C.). The modernization was completed through the construction of the Metroon on the west side of the square (Plan, **14**). This building replaced the Old Bouleuterion which, after the construction of the New Bouleuterion late in the 5th century, appears to have housed both the

25

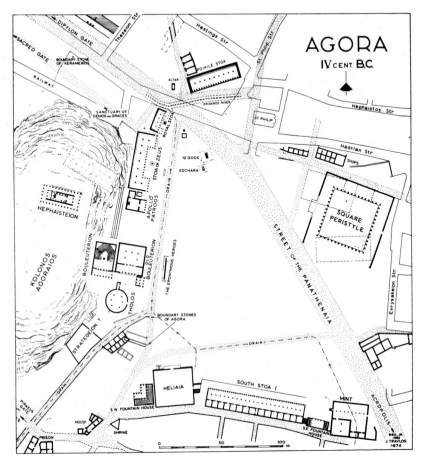

5. *Plan of the Agora, ca. 300 B.C.*

state archives and a sanctuary of the Mother of the Gods; the Hellenistic building served the same dual purpose. This remodeling of the 2nd century B.C. fixed the main lines of the Agora for the rest of antiquity (Fig. **6**). The area of the square and of the surrounding buildings was now about 50,000 square meters (12 acres).

In 88 B.C. the Athenians espoused the cause of Mithradates VI, King of Pontos, against Rome. After a long and bitter siege a Roman army

26

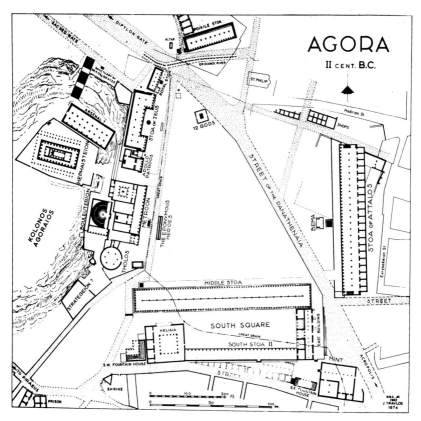

6. *Plan of the Agora, ca. 100 B.C., showing Hellenistic additions.*

under Sulla broke through the western wall of the city on March 1, 86 B.C. and stormed into the area of the Agora. A great slaughter followed and many private houses were destroyed. A number of public buildings were damaged, among them the Tholos (Plan, **5**), the Southwest Fountain House (Plan, **70**), the Heliaia (Plan, **68**), South Stoa II (Plan, **65**) and the East Building (Plan, **66**). The Tholos was soon repaired, and the south side of the Agora, after a period of desolation, was reoccupied by private industrial establishments which were built among the ruins of the old buildings; the remains attest to marble workers, iron foundries and potteries. Only in the time of Hadrian was this area cleaned up and restored to public use.

Meanwhile, and especially during the reign of Augustus, much had happened in the northern part of the Agora. A concert hall, named after its builder the Odeion of Agrippa, rose on the axis of the square (Plan, **41**). The Temple of Ares, a building of the 5th century B.C., was transplanted from somewhere in Attica to the northwest corner of the Agora (Plan, **38**) and the cult was apparently shared by Gaius Caesar, the adopted son of the Emperor. At some time in the 1st century A.D. the Southwest and Southeast Temples, both made largely of reused material, were erected (Plan, **20, 52**). An annex was built behind the Stoa of Zeus (Plan, **25**) probably to receive an imperial cult, and the Civic Offices at the southwest corner of the square were designed to relieve pressure on the old administrative buildings (Plan, **21**). A columnar porch was added to the Tholos, and the entrance to the forecourt to the Strategeion was adorned with a Doric propylon. Along the north side of the Agora, in its eastern part, a row of modest shops of the classical period was now supplanted by a large building which is known as yet only by its deep Ionic porch facing south on the open square. With the aid of grants from Julius Caesar and the Emperor Augustus the Athenians were able to erect a splendid colonnade around an old market place a hundred meters to the east of the classical Agora (Fig. **8**).

The 2nd century (Fig. **7**) opened with the construction of a small public library near the southeast corner of the Agora; the building is known by the name of its founder, Titus Flavius Pantainos (Plan, **48**). The construction of the Library was soon followed by the reorganization on a monumental scale of the roadway between the classical Agora and the Market of Caesar and Augustus to the east (Plan, **47**). Around the middle of the 2nd century a commercial building was erected on the east side of the Panathenaic Way to the south of the Library (Plan, **51**); its eleven shops were fronted by a deep Ionic porch which was aligned with a similar porch on the Library to create a street colonnade of a type much in vogue at that time. The appearance of the northeast corner of the square was also altered radically in the middle of the 2nd century by the construction of a basilica which presented its south end to the Agora; the colonnade of the earlier building to the west was now extended around the end of the basilica. The completion in 140 A.D. of an aqueduct begun by the Emperor Hadrian permitted the erection of a semicircular fountain

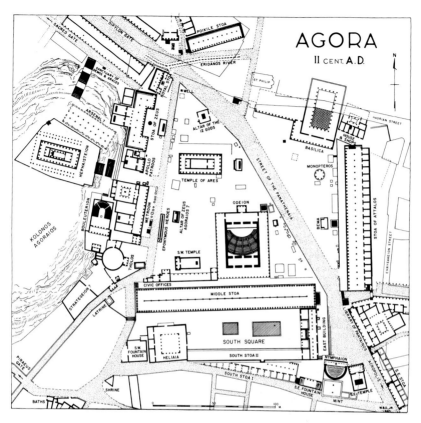

7. Plan of the Agora in ca. 150 A.D., the period of greatest expansion and the time of the traveler Pausanias.

house (*nymphaion*) at the extreme southeast corner of the Agora (Plan, **60**). Also to the Antonine period may be dated a charming round building, built perhaps to shelter a statue, in front of the Stoa of Attalos (Plan, **43**). At about this time also occurred a radical reconstruction of the Odeion of Agrippa (Plan, **41**). Among the last great architectural additions to the civic center was the library erected by the Emperor Hadrian (117-138 A.D.) to the east of the Stoa of Attalos (Fig. **8**).

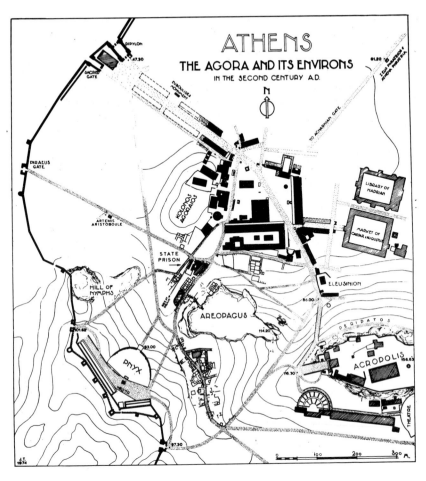

8. *Agora and environs, 2nd century A.D.*

In 267 A.D. the Herulians, a barbarian tribe from the north, invaded Greece. They sacked and burned several of the old cities including Athens. This raid was a turning point in the history of the city, the significance of which has beeh made clear for the first time by the Agora excavations. Most of the buildings in the region of the Agora, both public and private, were damaged. Public buildings elsewhere in the city and possibly even the temples on the Acropolis were burned.

Under the Emperor Valerian (253-260 A.D.) and shortly before the raid, the outer defences of the city were partially reconstructed on the line established by Themistokles. But the outer circle could no longer be maintained, and so was temporarily abandoned. A much smaller inner circuit, which we shall refer to as the Post-Herulian Wall, was now erected. It enclosed the Acropolis and the area immediately to the north, but not the Agora (Plan, 49). This new wall was under construction during the reign of Probus (276-282 A.D.). It was built entirely of reused material, much of it from the shattered buildings of the Agora.

The one building which certainly survived the holocaust of 267 A.D. was the Temple of Hephaistos (Plan, 1), and evidence from the excavations now seems to show that several of the civic buildings on the west and north sides of the square, though perhaps damaged in 267 A.D., also continued to stand. Among these were the Tholos, the Temple of Apollo, the Stoa of Zeus, the Royal Stoa and the Painted Stoa. During the 4th century the wall of the Tholos was strengthened, part of the Metroon seems to have been restored to use on a modest scale, and a good many of the large houses to the south and southwest of the Agora were reoccupied.

Disaster appears to have struck again toward the end of the 4th century. The excavations indicate that the Tholos, the Temple of Apollo, the Stoa of Zeus and the stoas bordering the road from the Dipylon Gate were destroyed at this time and abandoned. The probable culprit was Alaric at the head of a horde of Goths who appeared before the walls of Athens in 396 A.D. The literary evidence is divided regarding the damage done at this time to Athens and Attica, but the evidence of coins and pottery found in the debris overlying the floors of these buildings points to extensive destruction in the closing years of the 4th century.

Yet even at this late date the city showed remarkable powers of recuperation (Fig. 9). Throughout the 4th century the philosophical schools of Athens had attracted scholars, both pupils and teachers, from far and near, and the fame of the schools continued through the following century. Already in the early years of the 5th century considerable building occurred in the area of the old Agora. Above the middle of the ancient square arose a huge new complex, the most conspicuous feature of which was the so-called Porch of the Giants

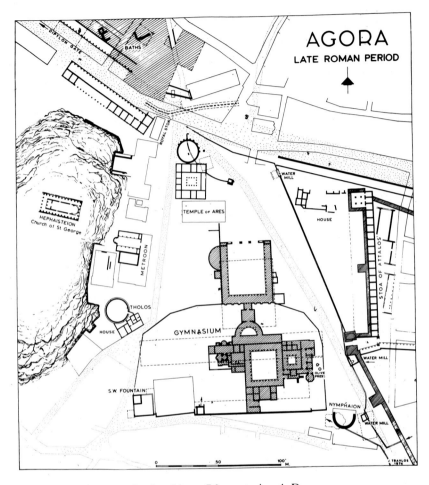

9. *The Agora area in the 5th to 7th centuries A.D.*

(Plan, **41**). Also of early 5th century date is a large square building with a colonnaded central court near the northwest corner of the Agora and north of that a round building of uncertain purpose. Toward the middle of the century colonnades were erected along the street bordering the north side of the area. In the same period a series of three water mills was installed along the east side of the Panathenaic Way in such a way that they were all turned in succession by the same water (Plan, **50**).

The area suffered once again from barbarian incursions in the 580's, and the continuing threat of further attacks led to the gradual abandonment of the area outside, i.e. to the west of the Post-Herulian Wall. Within the shelter of that wall stratified deposits record the continuance of community life into the 8th century, followed by a dark interval and then a general revival in the 10th century.

In later Byzantine, Frankish and Turkish times the area of the old Agora was chiefly a residential district. Large complexes of house foundations of the 11th and 12th centuries were encountered at a level high above the old classical floors; after being recorded they were removed to permit the study of earlier periods. Already by the early 7th century the ancient Temple of Hephaistos had been adapted to the needs of Christian worship. But the first church built as such within the area of the Agora dates from about 1000 A.D.; it is the graceful little church of the Holy Apostles that still stands above the southeast corner of the ancient square. In 1204 the area suffered once more when much of the lower city was devastated by Leon Sgouros, dynast of Nauplion. The floors of the houses destroyed at this time were covered by a deep layer of silt pointing to several centuries of comparative desolation.

During the Greek War of Independence (1821-1828) most of the houses then existing in the area were destroyed, particularly during the second siege of the Acropolis in 1827. One of these houses, situated a little to the southeast of the "Giants," belonged to the French consul Fr. S. Fauvel (1753-1838); some remnants of his large collection of antiquities were discovered when the area was excavated. After 1834, when Athens became the capital of the independent modern Greek state, the area was again developed as a residential district. The houses that were torn down to make way for the recent excavations were built for the most part about the middle of the 19th century (Figs. **10, 11**).

10. Area of the Agora in 1930, before the excavations. View from the west.

11. Same view as above, taken after excavations and the reconstruction of the Stoa of Attalos, in 1959.

34

HISTORY OF THE EXCAVATIONS

In 1832, immediately after the War of Independence, two distinguished architects, S. Kleanthes and E. Schaubert, were commissioned by the Greek government to prepare a plan for the development of Athens as the capital of the new kingdom. They recommended that the new development be kept well to the north of the Acropolis so that "the area of the ancient cities of Theseus and of Hadrian" might be available for eventual exploration. Although this far-sighted plan was upset by economic pressure, the Greek Archaeological Society took advantage of opportunities as they arose to explore individual monuments. Thus the Stoa of Attalos was cleared in a long series of campaigns (1859-1862, 1874 and 1898-1902). The "Porch of the Giants" was opened up (1859, 1871 and 1912), and parts of the west side of the Agora were brought to light (1907-1908). On the west side the Greek archaeologists had taken over an area that was first excavated by the German Archaeological Institute in the years 1896-1897 as part of an extensive program for the exploration of the Agora area. In 1890-1891 a deep trench cut through the north part of the area for the Athens - Peiraeus Railway brought to light extensive remains of ancient buildings and sculpture; measured sketches were made by German archaeologists.

The great influx of refugees from Asia Minor after 1922 compelled the Greek state to consider the alternatives of proceeding with large-scale excavation or of relaxing restrictions and permitting the redevelopment of the area. With the financial backing of the late John D. Rockefeller, Jr., the American School of Classical Studies was able to propose excavation. Legislation was passed by the Greek parliament whereby the School, having compensated the property owners, was entitled to excavate the area and to publish the results; on completion of excavation the area was to be landscaped. In accordance with existing Greek law antiquities found by the excavators were to remain in Greece as the property of the Greek state. At this time the area was almost entirely covered by modern houses, over 300 in number, which sheltered some 5000 persons (Fig. 10). Excavation began on May 25, 1931 and was continued in annual campaigns of four or five months each year through 1940. Before the outbreak of World War II most of the area had been opened up and the outline of the ancient square had been established. After the war field work was resumed with the object of clearing the whole area down to the level of classical antiquity. This second series of campaigns extended from 1946 through 1960, by which time all the major buildings within the original concession had been explored, and numerous soundings had been made in the deeper levels.

The original concession had permitted the exploration of most of the west side of the Agora and the whole of both the east and the south sides. The north side of the ancient square was still to be found. It obviously lay to the north of the Athens - Peiraeus Railway which had been accepted as the northern limit of the first concession. The search for the north side was begun in 1969 with the cooperation of the Greek state and with the financial support of the Ford Foundation and the Rockefeller Brothers Fund. The recent excavations in this area have brought to light the Royal Stoa at the extreme northwest corner of the square (Plan, **26**) and a large basilica at its northeast corner (Plan, **33**). New excavations begun in 1980 along the north side of Hadrian Street have brought to light the sanctuary of Aphrodite and the Stoa Poikile (pp. 101 ff.) to the north of the Agora square. Excavation of this area is expected to take several more years, with help of the David and Lucile Packard Foundation.

As the historical and architectural development of the Agora of classical times became clearer, the problem of the relationship between the old square and the great Roman buildings to the east, namely the Market of Caesar and Augustus and the Library of Hadrian, became increasingly intriguing. Here again, thanks to the collaboration of the Greek state in making available the necessary property, excavation on a significant scale was carried out from 1971 to 1976 (pp. 135 ff.).

To help the visitor in visualizing the physical effort involved in the excavation of the Agora it may be noted that the accumulation above the ancient ground level varied from one or two meters on the slopes of the hills to a maximum of 12 meters in the low-lying areas. The pre-excavation ground level along the north side is indicated by the bridges across the railway trench. The surface of the ancient street that borders the south side of the Agora lay about one meter below its modern successor. The great part of the accumulated deposit consisted of silt carried down by water wash from the neighboring hill slopes, but from top to bottom this deposit was sprinkled with ancient marbles, pottery and coins in such a way that it could be removed only by hand, i.e. with pick and shovel, and under close supervision. As the excavation of the original concession neared an end, conservation and landscaping were put in hand. Many of the early and less substantial foundations, after recording, were reburied. Exposed foundations were reinforced where necessary for their preservation. Open areas among the buildings were leveled, and paths were laid out for the convenience of visitors. Trees and shrubs have been planted, partly to beautify the area, partly to remind the visitor of an essential though seldom remembered element in the ancient setting. In the years 1953-1956, thanks again to the generous support of the late John D. Rockefeller, Jr., the Stoa of Attalos, which had closed the east side of the square, was reconstructed to house the finds from the excavation and to provide a base of operations for further archaeological work in the area. In June 1957 the Greek Archaeological Service assumed responsibility for maintaining and guarding the archaeological area and the Stoa of Attalos. The American School retains working facilities in the Stoa, and here are kept all the records of the excavation.

TOUR OF THE SITE

IDENTIFICATION

The location of the Agora in the area to the northwest of the Acropolis had been hesitantly inferred from references in the ancient authors; it was confirmed in 1938 by the discovery of a boundary marker of the Agora in its original position along the west side of the square (Plan, **10**).

The identification of several of the individual monuments is made certain by inscriptions: the Sanctuary of the Twelve Gods (Plan, **31**), the Stoa of Attalos (Plan, **46**) and the Library of Pantainos (Plan, **48**). The Tholos (Plan, **5**) was at once recognized from its round shape and early date; the Odeion of Agrippa (Plan, **41**) is the only odeion-like building in an area where the existence of an odeion is testified by the ancient authors.

The only consecutive literary account of the Agora that has come down to us occurs in the first book of Pausanias' *Description of Greece*, written about the middle of the 2nd century A.D. when the Agora was near the height of its development. Pausanias, proceeding from the Dipylon Gate, entered the square at its northwest corner. He was particularly interested in monuments that had religious and mythological associations, and in general he preferred the old to the new. Hence his treatment is selective, and his failure to note omissions has sometimes disturbed the modern reader; nevertheless, his account is now recognized as conscientious, trustworthy and invaluable.

ROUTE

The archaeological area may be entered through any one of three gates, one in the north side, one in the west side and one at the southeast corner of the square. The Southeast Gate, near the Church of the Holy Apostles, is convenient for those approaching on foot from the Acropolis. Those coming on foot from the middle of the modern city may enter through the North Gate near St. Philip's

Church. Those arriving by taxi should direct the driver to Monastiraki Square and thence proceed westward on foot, a five-minute walk, to the North Gate. Alternatively, one may take a taxi to the "Theseion", which continues to be the popular name for the Temple of Hephaistos, and enter by the West Gate which opens off the Plateia Theseiou.

An excellent overall view of the site is to be had either from the railway bridge inside the North Gate or from the east end of the Temple of Hephaistos. The tour described below begins from the Temple. Thence we shall proceed through the principal northern square of the Agora to the Stoa of Attalos (Plan, **46**) in which is housed the Agora Museum. After visiting the Museum we resume the tour, covering the southern part of the excavation.

A general plan is folded at the back of the book.

1. Temple of Hephaistos* (Figs. **12-17**)

Crowning Kolonos Agoraios, the Market Hill, is the Temple of Hephaistos, with which Athena was also associated; the two gods were worshipped here by the Athenians as patron divinities of the arts and crafts. The identification is based chiefly on Pausanias' account, reinforced by what is known from other authors and inscriptions about the cult statues and by the discovery around the temple of much evidence of metal-working. Other identifications which have been proposed include Theseus (hence the popular name, Theseion) and Artemis Eukleia. Construction of the temple seems to have been begun near the middle of the 5th century B.C.

A Doric peristyle surrounds a cella with pronaos and opisthodomos, each of which has its own inner porch of two columns. The bottom step is of poros; above this level all was of white marble: Pentelic for the building, Parian for the sculpture.The style of the outside is clearly earlier than that of the Parthenon, but there is reason to believe that the architect inserted an interior colonnade within the cella as a result of seeing the designs by Iktinos for the Parthenon, the construction of which was begun in 447 B.C. The name of the Hephaisteion architect is unknown.

Bronze cult statues of Hephaistos and Athena were made by

12. The Hephaisteion: temple of Hephaistos, god of the forge, and Athena, goddess of arts and crafts. Doric order, Pentelic marble, mid-5th century B.C.

13. Conjectural restoration of the interior of the Hephaisteion.

Alkamenes between the years 421 and 415 B.C.; these have perished (Fig. **13**). Of particular interest are the sculptures which remain on the outside of the building. Emphasis was placed on the ends of the temple, especially on the east front which was so prominent from the market place. Of the metopes, only those above the east porch are carved. The ten panels on the east front illustrate nine of the labors of Herakles; from left to right they show the Nemean Lion, the Hydra of Lerna, the Hind of Keryneia, the Boar of Erymanthos, the Mares of Diomedes, Kerberos, the Queen of the Amazons, Geryon (2 metopes), the Golden Apples of the Hesperides. Four of the labors of Theseus are represented on the north flank; from right to left appear the Sow of Krommyon, Skiron, Kerkyron and Prokrustes; another four on the south side show, from left to right, Periphetes, Sinis, the Bull of Marathon and the Minotaur (Fig. **14**). Because of their prominence the Theseus metopes suggested the name

14. Theseus and the Minotaur at the southeast corner of the Hephaisteion.

"Theseion" for the temple in modern times. A ninth labor of Theseus was depicted on the continuous frieze above the inner porch of the pronaos. This frieze completed the rectangle, the other three sides of which were adorned by the sculptured metopes. The theme of the inner frieze is identified as the battle between Theseus and the sons of Pallas, his rivals for the throne, in the presence of six divinities seated three on either side: Athena, Hera and Zeus on the left, Hephaistos, Hippodameia and Poseidon on the right. In the middle Theseus battles against his stone-throwing enemies. A corresponding frieze above the porch of the opisthodomos at the other end of the temple represents the battle between the Lapiths and the Centaurs. In the middle of the frieze Theseus is again prominent as he rushes to the aid of the Lapith, Kaineus, who is being hammered into the ground by two Centaurs (Fig. **15**).

Shallow sockets in the floors of the triangular gable spaces at the ends of the temple attest to the existence of groups of pedimental sculpture. A few fragments of sculpture which have been found in the environs of the temple and which are suitable in scale, quality and

15. Centaurs versus Kaineus, west frieze of Hephaisteion, 5th century B.C.

date may be attributed to these groups. All are of Parian marble like the metopes and the inner friezes. The best preserved of the pedimental pieces is a group of one woman supporting another on her back (Museum, p.202);this was found in a well on the slope of the hill to the east of the temple. A torso of a thinly clad female figure, though found on the floor of the Agora some 90 meters to the east, may be an akroterion from the building (Museum, p. 199).

The excavations produced evidence of a formal garden around the

16. Planting pits along south side of Hephaisteion, Hellenistic and Early Roman periods, at the time of excavation.

temple in Hellenistic and early Roman times (Fig. **16**). Rows of rectangular pits bordering the south, north and west sides of the building contained flower pots for the setting out of shrubs or small trees. The garden has been replanted with pomegranates next to the temple and myrtle in the outer rows. The flower pots are in the Museum storerooms.

Having survived the disasters both of 267 A.D. and of the end of the 4th century, the temple was converted into a Church of St. George, probably in the 7th century (Fig. **17**). The entrance was shifted from the east to the west end; two smaller doorways were opened in each of the side walls; the pronaos was replaced by an apse, and a barrel vault was erected over the cella. Many burials were made below the floors in the later Byzantine and Turkish periods, and a number of distinguished Protestant visitors who died in Athens in the 18th and early 19th centuries were buried within the building. The cover stone from one of these graves, that of George Watson (died 1810), has

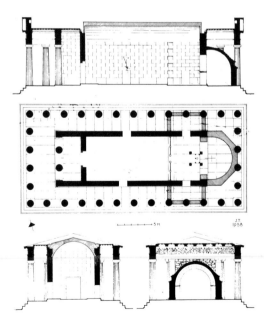

17. Conversion of Hephaisteion into church of St. George, 7th century A.D.

been set against the inner face of the north wall; it bears an epigram in Latin by Lord Byron.

At the beginning of December 1834, King Otho entered Athens, the newly established capital of his kingdom; he was greeted by the local clergy with a *te deum* in the Church of St. George. This was the last occasion on which the building was used as a church. Thereafter it served as a local museum until the excavation of the 1930's.

2, 3. Buildings to North and South of the Temple of Hephaistos* (Fig. 18)

North of the Temple of Hephaistos are remains of a number of buildings not sufficiently preserved to allow certain identification or detailed restoration. The first of these, of which only a few foundation cuttings and blocks are now visible, was a large structure of the early 3rd century B.C. with buttressed walls; the interior was divided into three aisles. Water from the roof was carried under the foundations into cisterns at the southwest corner and near the middle of the north side of the interior. The massive construction of the building and its proximity to the city administrative buildings, to the Temple of Hephaistos and to the quarter of the metal-workers suggest that it may have been a state arsenal* (Plan, 2).

At the north foot of Kolonos Agoraios the construction of the Athens-Peiraeus Railway brought to light and then obliterated a modest outdoor sanctuary of the People (*Demos*) and the Graces (*Charites*) (Plan, 3). A large marble altar which was found in place now stands in the National Museum; it bears a dedication of the year 197/96 B.C. to Aphrodite Leader of the People and to the Graces. From other inscriptions it is known that the goddess Roma was also worshipped in this sanctuary.*

From literary references we know that the sanctuary of the Salaminian hero Eurysakes, son of Ajax, was on Kolonos Agoraios. At this sanctuary gathered workmen waiting to be hired. Several inscriptions which stood in the sanctuary have come to light southwest of the Temple of Hephaistos, but no structural remains have yet been found.*

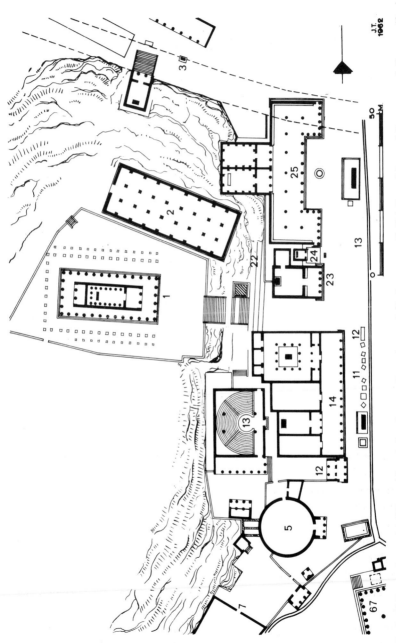

18. Buildings along the West side of the Agora. 2 = Arsenal (3rd century B.C.) 3 = Altar of Demos and Graces (2nd century B.C., now in National Museum).

4. Belvedere

Following the path southward from the east end of the Temple of Hephaistos we come to a modern belvedere on the brow of the hill. On the pedestal of the marble lectern is inscribed the name of Edward Capps (1866-1955) who as Chairman of the Managing Committee of the American School of Classical Studies was in large part responsible for the initiation of the Agora excavations.

On top of the lectern is a restored view of the Agora and environs as they appeared from this spot (Fig. **19**). Immediately in front of us at the foot of the hill lie the ruins of the principal administrative buildings of the ancient city. We continue down the path and recognize on our left the round floor of the Tholos.

5. Tholos* (Figs. **20-22**)

In the *Constitution of the Athenians* (43, 3) Aristotle writes:

> Those members of the Council (*Boule*) who are acting as chairmen (*prytaneis*) first eat together in the Tholos, receiving pay from the city; they next arrange the meetings of the Council and the Assembly.

Other sources, which dwell not so much on function as on shape, make possible the identification of this round building as the Tholos, erected about 465 B.C. to replace an earlier structure.

Remains of the first period of the Tholos proper comprise only a few wall blocks of poros at the west (two courses), north and southeast. The rest of the outer wall has been restored in dry masonry to the level of its latest floor in order to help conserve the building. In its original form the Tholos had no porch. Its floor was of hard-packed clay and lay at a level 45 centimeters (1-1/2 feet) below the present floor. There were six interior columns, the stumps of three of which are visible in the western half of the building; they are of poros and unfluted. Roof tiles belonging to this period were recovered. In the time of Augustus the porch was added, and soon afterwards a pavement of marble chips was put in, still visible at a number of points.

The tholos underwent an extensive remodeling, probably in the 2nd century A.D. The inner columns were cut down and the building was

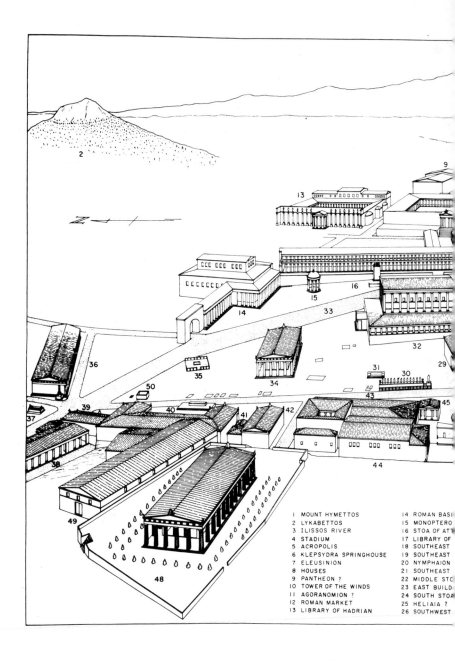

1 MOUNT HYMETTOS	14 ROMAN BASI
2 LYKABETTOS	15 MONOPTERO
3 ILISSOS RIVER	16 STOA OF ATT
4 STADIUM	17 LIBRARY OF
5 ACROPOLIS	18 SOUTHEAST
6 KLEPSYDRA SPRINGHOUSE	19 SOUTHEAST
7 ELEUSINION	20 NYMPHAION
8 HOUSES	21 SOUTHEAST
9 PANTHEON ?	22 MIDDLE STO
10 TOWER OF THE WINDS	23 EAST BUILD
11 AGORANOMION ?	24 SOUTH STOA
12 ROMAN MARKET	25 HELIAIA ?
13 LIBRARY OF HADRIAN	26 SOUTHWEST

ATHENIAN
AGORA
A.D. 150

27 TRIANGULAR SHRINE	40 STOA OF ZEUS ELEUTHERIOS
28 CIVIC OFFICES	41 TEMPLE OF ZEUS PHRATRIOS
29 SOUTHWEST TEMPLE	AND ATHENA PHRATRIA
30 EPONYMOUS HEROES	42 TEMPLE OF APOLLO PATROOS
31 ALTAR OF ZEUS AGORAIOS ?	43 METROON
32 ODEION	44 BOULEUTERION
33 PANATHENAIC WAY	45 PROPYLON TO BOULEUTERION
34 TEMPLE OF ARES	46 THOLOS
35 ALTAR OF THE 12 GODS	47 STRATEGEION ?
36 POIKILE STOA	48 HEPHAISTEION
37 ALTAR	49 ARSENAL ?
38 ROMAN STOAS	50 CROSS-ROAD SANCTUARY
39 ROYAL STOA	

W. B. DINSMOOR, JR.
1980

19. *Restored perspective view of the Agora and environs, from the west in
ca. A.D. 150.*

49

20. Aerial view of the tholos/bouleuterion complex.
Compare the plan, fig. 20A.

domed. The floor was paved with marble slabs bedded in mortar and
the walls were revetted with marble. Subsequently the wall was
strengthened by a ring of concrete; this may have been necessitated
by damage done in the Herulian sack. The building was finally
abandoned about 400 A.D., presumably a consequence of the
widespread destruction of that time. In the earlier periods of the
Tholos a small room was attached to its north side; only a few blocks,
belonging to various periods, are preserved. This was probably the
kitchen. To the southeast of the Tholos, but within its precinct, are
the massive foundations for a fountain fed by a pressure water pipe.
Incorporated into the foundations are earlier wall blocks of the
Tholos, presumably removed after the damage in 86 B.C.

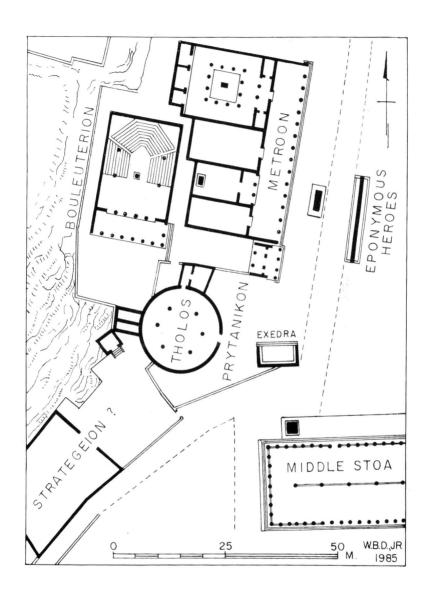

BOULEUTERION

METROON

EPONYMOUS HEROES

PRYTANIKON

THOLOS

EXEDRA

STRATEGEION ?

MIDDLE STOA

0   25   50   W.B.D.,JR.
                                  M.   1985

20a. Plan of the administrative buildings along the west side, as seen in the photograph fig. 20.

21. Model of the Tholos, showing one possible restoration of the roof of diamond-shaped tiles, supported within on six columns.

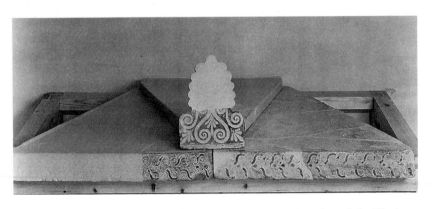

22. Painted eaves tiles and decorative antefix from the edge of the Tholos roof (ca. 465 B.C.).

52

It was in the Tholos that the Athenian government had its headquarters. Here a number of the chairmen slept at night so that there were always responsible officials on hand. A set of standard weights and measures was kept here (examples are in the Museum, p. 242). The building was the heart of the city administration and the seat of various cults connected with civic life. A marble inscription of about 200 A.D. found beside the building records the dedication of certain plants to the Phosphoroi, minor goddesses known to have been worshipped in the Tholos. Problems of interpretation remain as to how to roof the Tholos with the unusual diamond-shaped tiles recovered as well as how to restore accommodations for 50 or so diners in the building.

The predecessor of the Tholos, Building F (Fig. **23**), was destroyed by the Persians in 480/79 B.C. Built in the mid-6th century B.C., it is made up of a colonnaded court surrounded by rooms of various shapes and sizes and looks in plan like a large-scale house. Originally it may have served the Peisistratids as a palace; following their expulsion it was presumably used as an official dining hall as was its

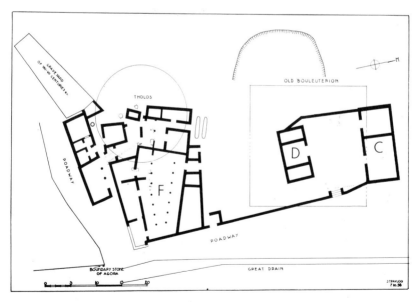

23. *Early buildings along the west side: Building F, mid-6th century B.C.; Building C, early 6th century B.C.*

successor, the Tholos. At the northwest corner of the archaic building was a long broiling pit, clearly designed to meet the needs of a large company. The rubble stonework foundations have been largely covered over again to assure their preservation; their tops project above the ground to the south of the Tholos.

6. Early Cemetery South of the Tholos* (Fig. 23)

At a still deeper level to the south of the Tholos was encountered a family burial plot containing 22 graves of the 8th, 7th and early 6th centuries B.C. The offerings from one of the more richly furnished graves are exhibited in the Museum (p. 228). The area of the old graveyard was not built over in later times; it was enclosed and appears to have been regarded as a sacred place. In the early Roman period the enclosure was adorned with a columnar gateway set in its south side, an arrangement commonly found in the sanctuaries of heroes (*heroa*). The four-columned porch was put together of Doric elements reused from some earlier building. To make room for its erection the course of the Great Drain was diverted over a length of some 30 meters. On the steep hill slope at the northwest corner of the enclosure are the foundation beddings for a small rectangular structure, perhaps a shrine, approached by a short flight of steps. To the left of the ancient steps and to the right of the modern is a marble base for some dedication.

7, 8. Administrative Buildings South of the Tholos*

Since the Tholos was the pivot about which the administration of the city-state revolved, facilities for various departments of the administration were naturally placed nearby. The principal buildings serving this purpose were the meeting place of the Council and the record office; these stood to the north of the Tholos. But other more modest buildings which have come to light to the south and southwest of the Tholos may be recognized as the offices of other administrative bodies. Such buildings were called by the Athenians *archeia*, i.e. the headquarters of various administrative boards (*archai*).
One such building (Plan, 7) stood to the southwest of the Tholos from which it was separated by the sacred area above the ancient

54

cemetery. This area may indeed have served as a forecourt to the building. The structure itself was set in a deep cutting in the slope of the hill. The trapezoidal plan comprised a central courtyard bordered by seven or eight rooms; a cistern with two mouths lay beneath the court. The construction dates from soon after the middle of the 5th century B.C., but beneath the floors of the period have been noted foundations of an earlier structure, while the plan of the 5th century building has been confused by various concrete foundations of Roman date.

The size and the prominent position of this building, as also the great effort involved in leveling the site, indicate that we have to do with an important public establishment. A likely candidate is the Strategeion, the headquarters of the ten generals (*strategoi*). An inscription of the 3rd century B.C. which had stood in front of the Strategeion was found a few meters to the east of the present building, and other inscriptions relating to the strategoi have come to light around the southwest corner of the Agora. In the Strategeion the military commanders transacted their business, dined and sacrificed in common. They are known to have made dedications to a hero Strategos who may have been the tutelary divinity of the shrine to the southwest of the Tholos.

To the south of the Tholos, in the triangular space between the Great Drain and the west end of the Middle Stoa, are the scanty remains of a crowded group of small buildings dating chiefly from the 5th and 4th centuries B.C. (Plan, 8).* Their plans are more distinct in the drawing than on the ground. Three buildings may be distinguished; they stood on the north, west and south sides of a courtyard with a well near its middle. The southern building comprised a single row of three rooms; the western consisted of eight rooms in two rows; the northern had one small and one large room which shared a colonnade facing on the court.

The plans of these buildings are less suitable to houses than to shops or offices. Their proximity to the Agora, and more specifically to the Tholos and Bouleuterion, suggests that they too were part of the public offices (*archeia*). Here, for instance, may have been accommodated the public auctioneers (*poletai*) who had to do among other duties with the sale of confiscated properties and with the leasing of the state-owned silver mines at Laureion. A number of inscriptions recording such leases have been found around the southwest corner of the Agora. From a well of the late 5th century B.C. at the northern tip of the triangular area was recovered a *klepsydra* or water clock of the type used for measuring speeches in the law courts (Museum, p. 244), while a number of bronze ballots used by members of the jury in recording their votes have also come to light within the triangular area. Such a concentration of material, rare within the excavated area, suggests that some law court had met in the area or had stored its equipment in one of the buildings.

9. House of Simon the Cobbler (Figs. 24, 25)

The remains found in the north part of the triangular area (Fig. 24) on the other hand, are of a more private nature. The excavations

24. *Ruins of the house of Simon the Cobbler, 5th century B.C., set up against an Agora boundary stone (center foreground).*

revealed the foundations of a couple of rooms facing onto a courtyard in which was a well and a cesspool. In levels of the second half of the 5th century B.C. were found many large-headed iron hob-nails of the sort used in the soles of heavy boots, as well as a group of bone eyelets for laces (Fig. 25). They were numerous enough to suggest the existence of a shoemaker's shop. The base of a drinking cup found in the same context bears the name of its owner, Simon (Museum, p. 241). This may well have been the shoemaker of that name whose shop near the Agora is known to have been frequented by Sokrates:

> *"Simon, an Athenian, a shoemaker. When Sokrates came to his workshop and discoursed, he used to make notes of what he remembered, whence these dialogues were called 'The Shoemaker's'."*
>
> (Dio. Laert. II, 13.122; see also Xenophon, *Mem.* IV, 2.1 and Plutarch, *Moral.*776b.)

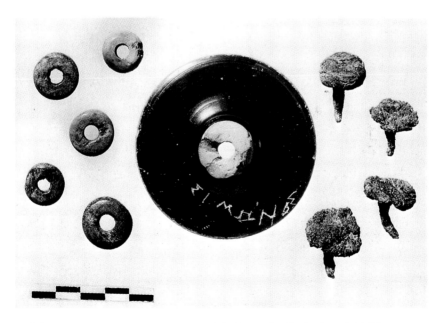

25. *Bone eyelets, iron hobnails, and the base of a black-glazed drinking cup inscribed with the name of Simon.*

All the buildings in the triangular area were demolished in the middle of the 2nd century B.C. to make way for the west end of the Middle Stoa. Their walls were stripped down to ground level, and the foundations were overlaid by the gravelled surface of a roadway that carried around the west end of the Stoa, replacing an earlier north-to-south road that was overlaid by the Stoa. Toward the southwest corner of the area, and convenient to the entrance to the Agora, a small public latrine was now built beside the West Branch of the Great Drain. There are remnants of the deep plastered channels and of the characteristic flooring made from the chips of roof tile.

10. Boundary Stones of the Agora (Fig. 26)

While in this area we may pause over two small monuments of singular interest for the topography of the Agora. These are rectangular posts of Parian marble each inscribed in Attic lettering of

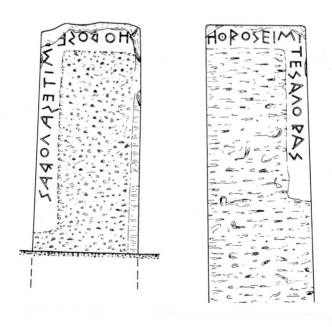

26. *Agora boundary stones, ca. 500 B.C.: left, under the west end of the Middle Stoa; right, southeast of the Tholos.*

about 500 B.C.: "I am the boundary of the Agora." One of these posts stands at the angle of a wall of the home of Simon the cobbler about 20 meters to the east of the Tholos; the other may be seen inside the west end of the Middle Stoa, again rising beside an early wall. In each case the marker has been placed in relation to a contemporary entrance to the Agora, and it is to be assumed that the other entrances to the square were similarly marked to emphasize the distinction between the Agora square proper and the many sacred and official precincts that bordered the open space. This formality was necessary because the Agora itself was a precinct from which certain types of criminals were barred by law and within which no private citizen was allowed to build.

Further evidence of the sacred nature of the Agora is to be seen at a higher level to the east of the first boundary stone. Here is the stump of a marble pedestal which supported a holy water basin (*perirrhanterion*) used for purification rites on entry into the Agora: "so the lawmaker keeps outside the perirrhanteria of the Agora the man who avoids military service, or plays the coward, or deserts..." (Aeschines III, 176). Two other such basins have been found in the excavations; although not found *in situ*, they probably come from other entrances to the square (Museum, p. 191). The difference in level between the boundary stone to the east of the Tholos and the adjacent perirrhanterion illustrates the depth of accumulation between the 5th century before Christ and the 1st century of our era.

11. The Great Drain and Its Branches* (Fig. 27)

Standing beside the first of the two boundary stones of the Agora we look north into the main channel of the Great Drain.

The drainage of the Agora area together with the adjacent hill slopes was assured by a simple but effective system of stone-lined cloacae. The channels were covered with loosely jointed stone slabs, the tops of which were flush with the gravelled surface of the square. Although these great drains received a certain amount of sewage from nearby houses and shops, their primary function was to handle the torrents of surface water that descended into the square at times of heavy rain. It was the neglect of this drainage system in late antiquity that led to the silting of the area.

27. *Great Drain, late 6th/early 5th century B.C.*

In the early years of the 5th century a drainage channel was constructed on the west side of the area, presumably as part of a program to improve the setting for the first substantial civic buildings to be erected in the Agora, i.e. the Heliaia (Plan, **68**) and the Old Bouleuterion (Plan, **14**). Starting with a funnel-shaped open mouth at a point about 20 meters to the east of the (later) Tholos, the new drain followed a very regular course almost due north to issue from the square through its northwest corner. Bearing westward at this point it joined a still larger cloaca, probably the canalized form of the Eridanos brook, to continue northwestward under the Panathenaic Way and eventually to pass through the city wall alongside the Sacred Gate.

The original construction of the drain may best be studied to the east of the Metroon. Here the channel measures one meter in both width and depth. The walls are of hard breccia beautifully jointed in polygonal style; the floor is paved with limestone. Most of the original cover slabs of soft yellowish limestone have been replaced through the ages with miscellaneous material including gravestones, inscribed stelai, even statues. Farther north, opposite the Stoa of Zeus and the Royal Stoa, the channel becomes much deeper and is built of soft poros in ashlar masonry; this represents a rebuilding in the 4th century B.C.

At the turn of the 5th-to-4th century the single line of drain was supplemented by two feeders, one coming from the southeast, the other from the southwest, to join the original channel in a Y-shaped formation at a point opposite the Tholos. The eastern branch had its beginnings, like the archaic drain, high in the gully between the Acropolis and Areopagus. Thence it descended on a northwesterly course, probably following an earlier line of the Panathenaic Way, to a point beneath the east end of the (later) Middle Stoa (Plan, **67**). Here it bent sharply westward to join the main stem. The western branch drained the valley between the Areopagus and Pnyx and entered the Agora on a northeasterly course in the bottom of the valley between the Areopagus and Kolonos Agoraios. Both branches in their lower parts were comparable in dimensions with the main channel; they were built of soft poros in regular masonry.

The whole of this ancient drainage system, having been cleared and reconditioned by the excavators, again functions perfectly and keeps the entire area dry.

We now resume our examination of the administrative buildings, moving on to those that stood north of the Tholos.

12. Gateway to the New Bouleuterion

Access to the New Bouleuterion (Plan, **13**), the meeting place of the Council, was through a roofed gateway (*propylon*) of the Ionic order (Plan, **12**), the foundations of which are to be seen just south of the Metroon (Plan, **14**). This gateway, along with the passage that led back and the porch at the south end of the New Bouleuterion, all appear to be of the second half of the 4th century B.C. In front of the Propylon are traces of a drinking fountain.

13. New Bouleuterion* (Figs. **28, 20, 20A**)

The New Bouleuterion (Council House) occupied a terrace cut back into the hillside northwest of the Tholos. It was built at the end of the 5th century B.C. apparently to take the function of its eastern neighbor, the Old Bouleuterion. It was in the Bouleuterion that members of the Council of 500 (*Boule*) held the meetings in which they did committee work and prepared legislation for the Assembly. The Council, made up of 50 citizens from each of the ten tribes, was chosen by allotment each year, and these tribal groups of 50 served in succession as group chairmen (*prytaneis*) of the Council.

The outline of the New Bouleuterion may be seen in the cuttings for its foundation walls, some blocks of which remain. To the south of

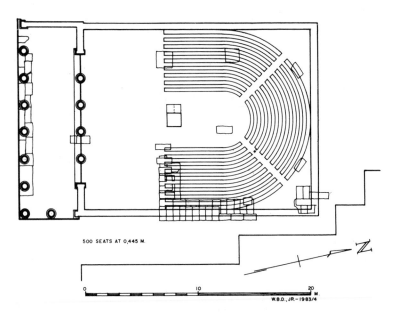

500 SEATS AT 0,445 M.

W.B.D., JR.–1983/4

28. Restoration of the New Bouleuterion showing relationship to existing foundation, late 5th B.C. The auditorium seems to have faced south, though the restoration of the seating, curved or rectilinear, is uncertain.

the building the hillside has also been cut back and faced with retaining walls to the south and west to form a forecourt or open square in front of the building. It seems clear that the auditorium faced south though little evidence for the original seating arrangements survives. The condition of the dressed bedrock within the area suggests, however, that in the beginning the seats were of wood and supported on wooden beams. A number of curved marble floor slabs found within the building and now lying along its west side indicate that at some later date curved seating of stone was installed.

Two large bottle-shaped cisterns, cut in the rock just west of the building, gathered rain water from its roof. They are joined by a tunnel with a cistern to the southwest of the Tholos which probably took its water from the roof of that building. This capacious reservoir was no doubt intended primarily to meet the housekeeping needs of the Tholos.

14. Metroon and Old Bouleuterion (Figs. **20, 20A, 29**)

The *Metroon*, built in the second half of the 2nd century B.C., consists of four rooms of various sizes sharing a colonnade that faces eastward toward the square. Three steps of Hymettian marble and an Ionic column base of Pentelic marble are preserved toward the south end of the colonnade. In the line of the north wall a pair of orthostates remain in position; elsewhere only the foundations are preserved.

The building accommodated both the sanctuary of the Mother of the Gods (*Meter Theon*), from which it took its name, and the state archives. The second room from the south, which has the plan of a small temple, was probably the actual sanctuary of the goddess. If so, the heavy foundation in front of the building opposite this room might well have held the altar. The first and third rooms from the south presumably contained the actual state documents, written on papyrus and parchment. The large northern room had two storeys around a central court with an altar at its middle. The function of this room is unknown, though it may have served as the reading room. Alternatively, the open court covers the early temple of the Mother and it may well have housed her cult.

The mosaic pavement in the third room from the south does not

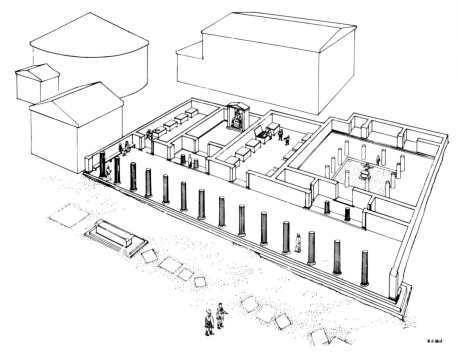

29. *The Metroon in its second phase, mid-2nd century B.C.*

belong to the original building but dates from a partial reconstruction in the early 5th century A.D. It lies at a much lower level than the original floor of the building. In the same late period the northern room was rearranged in the form of a basilica. The purpose of the building in this late period is obscure, though a sculpted plaque with palm tree and menorah found in the area suggests the possible use of the room as a synagogue.

The area inside the Metroon has been excavated to bedrock, which lies in some places as much as three meters below the top of the front foundation (now partially refilled). Remains of several earlier buildings have come to light.

Old Bouleuterion: Directly behind and partly underneath the foundation for the southern part of the Hellenistic colonnade is a massive foundation of Acropolis limestone. At the north this foundation turns west at right angles and runs under the Hellenistic wall. The earlier building was square, 20 meters on a side, and dates from early in the 5th century B.C. (Fig. **3**). It has been identified as the Old Bouleuterion, perhaps built soon after the reforms of Kleisthenes to accommodate the newly formed Council of 500. In addition to serving as a council house the building sheltered the famous statue of the Mother of the Gods, a work attributed by some ancient sources to Pheidias, by others, with more probability, to his favorite pupil, Agorakritos. A miniature copy of the Roman period is shown in the Museum (Fig. **30**). Here too were stored various documents of public interest written on papyrus or parchment or whitened wooden tablets, and occasionally on marble. Toward the end of the 5th century, with the growing complexity of administration, a more systematic procedure was introduced into the keeping of public records, and something like archives in the modern sense of the word began to take shape. It may indeed have been the accompanying need for more space that led to the construction of the New Bouleuterion. We may assume that the meetings of the Council from now on took place in the new building while the old continued to be used as a sanctuary and as a repository of records.

30. Miniature copy of the statue of the Mother of the God, the original of which stood in the Metroon.

65

Contemporary with the Old Bouleuterion, and oriented in relation to it, was a small archaic temple presumably of the *Mother of the Gods,* some foundations of which may still be seen in the north room of the Metroon (Fig. **3**). This temple seems to have been destroyed by the Persians in 480/79 B.C. and as such was never rebuilt. But the name and function of the Metroon indicate that worship of the Mother continued in the area.

In the colonnade in front of the northern room of the Metroon is a foundation belonging to a smaller and still earlier building (Building C). Within the northern room itself are other walls of the same building (Fig. **23**); this earlier structure dates from the early 6th century B.C., i.e. from the time of Solon, and may have served as a sort of *Primitive Bouleuterion.* This building is too small to have been an assembly hall, but had rather an administrative function; the Council of this early period will have met in the open air perhaps in the area between this building and the predecessor of the Tholos (p. 53).

These structures, together with those already noted in the Tholos area, are the earliest public buildings that have been found in Athens; from the time of Solon the Agora and the seat of government were apparently established in this area.

15. Monument Bases near the Metroon

In front of the Metroon and around its northeast corner is a thickset row of monument bases, an indication of the prominence of this area. None of the individual monuments has been identified. The excavation showed that some of the bases had probably been stripped after the Roman sack of 86 B.C.

16. Statue of Hadrian* (Fig. 31)

Near the northeast corner of the Metroon has been set up a statue of the Emperor Hadrian (117-138 A.D.). It was found in the early years of the excavation lying in the Great Drain a little to the east; the torso in fact had been reused in late antiquity as a cover slab for the drain. Despite the absence of a head, the identification as Hadrian is certain because of the decoration on the corselet: Athena, flanked by her

66

31. Statue of the
Emperor Hadrian
(117-138 A.D.) with
cuirass showing
Athena and Wolf of
Rome.

symbols, the owl and the serpent, and crowned by two Winged
Victories, stands upon the wolf which is suckling Romulus and
Remus. The sentiment of "captive taking the captor captive" is
peculiarly suitable to the Philhellene Hadrian. This is perhaps the
statue of Hadrian which Pausanias saw near the Stoa of Zeus (I, 3.2).

Crossing the Great Drain behind Hadrian, and noting its well-preserved masonry, we turn south to visit several lesser monuments.

17. Monument of Quintus Trebellius Rufus *

To the east of the Great Drain has been set up a large marble statue base reassembled from many fragments found in this area. The principal inscription on the face of the pedestal records a vote of thanks to Quintus Trebellius Rufus, a benefactor of the Athenians, who came from the city of Toulouse in Narbonese Gaul; included in the honors are the wife and son of Trebellius Rufus. Lower on the face of the stone are two letters addressed to the Athenian councils and people. That on the left, very fragmentary, was written by the governing body of the province of Narbonese Gaul. In the letter on the right the local magistrates and senate of Toulouse thank the Athenians for the honors which Athens has bestowed on their compatriot. The date is towards the end of the 1st century A.D., but the nature of Trebellius Rufus' benefactions is unknown.

Near the pedestal of Trebellius Rufus are several bedding blocks for bronze stelai triangular in section.* These may be the stelai on which were engraved the lists of ephebes, the young men undergoing military training. Aristotle (*Ath. Pol.* 53, 4) speaks of such a stele "in front of the Bouleuterion, beside the Eponymoi."

18. Altar of Zeus Agoraios (?)* (Fig. 32)

A little to the east of the Trebellius Rufus monument are the remains of a large altar of Pentelic marble. From the style of the workmanship it can be dated to the late 4th century B.C. The presence of letters on the ends of the blocks, however, in a style current in the first centuries before and after Christ, can only mean that the altar was dismantled at the time and re-erected in its present position. The letters were inscribed by masons so that the blocks could be correctly reassembled. A cutting for a monument of similar size has been found on the Pnyx, and it may well be that the altar originally stood there. It was moved at a time when the Pnyx had been replaced by the Theatre of Dionysos as a meeting place for the Assembly. The divinity to whom the altar was dedicated may have been Zeus

32. *Altar of Zeus Agoraios (?), 4th century B.C., moved into the Agora in Roman times.*

Agoraios, the inspirer of oratory. This attribution best explains a scholiast's comment that "Zeus Agoraios is established in the Agora and in the Assembly Place." The great scale of the altar is easily appreciated in the existing step blocks, where one block provides two steps, and in the high orthostate with delicate moldings which formed part of the altar proper.

The oak and laurel flanking the altar were planted in 1954 by King Paul and Queen Frederika to inaugurate the program of landscaping.

19. The Peribolos of the Eponymous Heroes (Figs. 33, 34)

In front of the Metroon-Bouleuterion complex and to the east of the Great Drain are the remains of a long pedestal enclosed by a fence. From the reference in Pausanias (I, 5) we know that the pedestal supported statues of the ten legendary heroes of Attica who became the patrons of the ten groups (or tribes) into which Kleisthenes, in 508 B.C., divided the population of Attica for administrative and

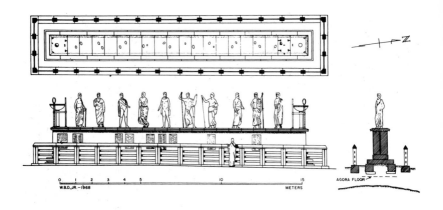

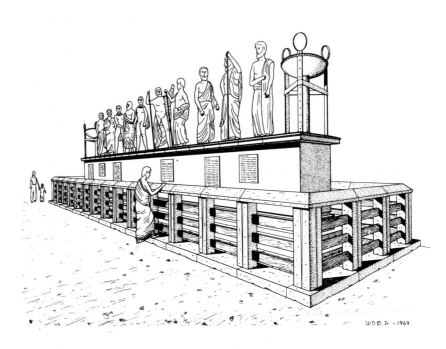

33, 34. Restored drawings of the monument of the Eponymous heroes, 2nd half 4th century B.C., before addition of new tribal heroes.

political purposes. The original heroes, as named by Pausanias, were Hippothoon, Antiochos, Ajax, Leos, Erechtheus, Aigeus, Oineus, Akamas, Kekrops and Pandion. In 307/6 B.C. the number was increased by the addition of Antigonos and Demetrios, Kings of Macedon, who, however, were dropped from the list a century later when Athens and Macedon became embroiled in war. Ptolemy III Euergetes, King of Egypt, was added in 224/3 B.C.; Attalos I, King of Pergamon, in 200 B.C.; Hadrian, Emperor of Rome, about 125 A.D.

In addition to this honorary function the monument served a practical purpose as the official notice board of the city. Here, for instance, were posted drafts of proposed new laws for consideration by the citizens, lists of men called up for military service and notices of impending lawsuits.

Enough remains to indicate the design of the monument. The high continuous pedestal was crowned by a marble course of which two blocks have survived. In the top of one are cuttings for the feet of a slightly more than life-size bronze statue. The other block, from one end of the pedestal, carried a large bronze tripod. The marble course projected far enough to protect the notices which, as we know from the ancient authors, were written on whitened wooden boards and hung on the face of the pedestal. The fence consisted of stone posts and crowning member with wooden rails; in a reconstruction of the Roman period the stone was replaced by white marble on the east side.

The monument of the Eponymous Heroes is mentioned already by Aristophanes in the *Peace* of 421 B.C. But the architectural style and the ceramic evidence indicate for the existing monument a date after 350 B.C., nor is there any trace of an earlier structure on this site. The original monument must have stood elsewhere, perhaps on a foundation that has come to light under the west end of the Middle Stoa.

A close study of the surviving blocks has revealed the ingenious ways in which provision was made for the fluctuating number of statues. The final accession, that of Hadrian, required a southward extension of pedestal and fence. Much old material was employed by the thrifty Athenians, including an inscribed base of the year 50 B.C., which may still be seen at the southeast corner of the enlarged enclosure.

Few other monuments illustrate so vividly the actual mechanics of Athenian civic administration, and no other demonstrates so clearly the relations between Athens and her powerful neighbors in the Hellenistic period.

20. Southwest Temple* (Fig. 35)

At some time after the construction of the Odeion (Plan, **41**), but before the erection of the Civic Offices (Plan, **21**), the angle between the Odeion and Middle Stoa was occupied by a newly founded sanctuary. The temple consisted of a cella with a porch facing west. Masonry has survived only at the southwest corner, consisting of heavy conglomerate blocks above a packing of broken stone set in crumbly lime mortar. Elsewhere the plan has been recovered only from beddings. The superstructure was built of reused material from a classical Doric building which originally stood at Thorikos, in

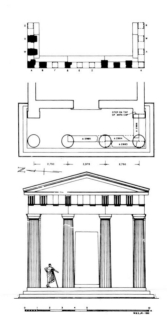

35. Restored drawing of reused Doric architecture in the Southwest temple, Early Roman.

southeastern Attica. After the destruction of the Southwest Temple the pieces were used again in the late Roman fortification wall (Plan, **49**, Fig. **92**).

21. Civic Offices*

The modest complex of buildings at the foot of the terrace of the Middle Stoa and to the west of the Odeion dates from the 2nd century A.D.

The principal building comprised three rooms diminishing in size from east to west in such a way as to interfere as little as possible with traffic through the southwest entrance to the Agora; a still smaller fourth room at the west end of the building was demolished in the interest of freer circulation.

The large east room had a northern porch. At the east and west sides of the room a low bench built of clay with plastered top and front stood against the wall. In the middle of the room was found a large marble tripod base which had been salvaged from elsewhere (Museum, p. 198). The holy water basin (*perirrhanterion*) mentioned above (p. 59) stood in the angle between the third and (now missing) fourth room from the east; only a marble stump remains. A miniature washroom filled the corresponding angle between the second and third rooms from the east. In the angle between the first and second rooms from the east stand a pair of marble slabs which were found nearby and have been set up on their original pedestal. These slabs have representations of roof tiles carved on their faces; they undoubtedly served as official standards (Fig. **36**). This provision for the control of commerce is reminiscent of the weights and measures maintained in the Tholos and suggests that the building was designed to provide additional space for the public offices originally accommodated in the Tholos and Metroon. Its public character is further illustrated by the beddings for stelai in front of the second room from the east.

Between the Civic Offices and the Odeion are the remains of a small colonnade with a compartment at its east end corresponding to the east room of the Civic Offices. Nothing remains but the conglomerate foundations; their high level indicates that the builders of the stoa adjusted their ground level to the Southwest Temple.

36. Tile Standard;
marble model for
terracotta rooftiles.
Found in the Civic
Offices.

22. Benches on Kolonos Agoraios* (Fig. 37)

On the lower slope of the hill are a few blocks of soft, gray poros, the remains of four rows of simple benches. Dating from the second half of the 5th century B.C., they clearly served as a meeting place for one of the law courts or governing bodies of Athens. Such a meeting place, known as the "synedrion," is known to have been in the vicinity.

23. Temple of Apollo Patroos* (Fig. 38)

A small Ionic temple, tetrastyle in antis, is identified by Pausanias as the Temple of Apollo Patroos, who was worshipped by the Athenians as Apollo the Father because of the legend which made him the father of Ion, founder of the Ionian race of which the Athenians were

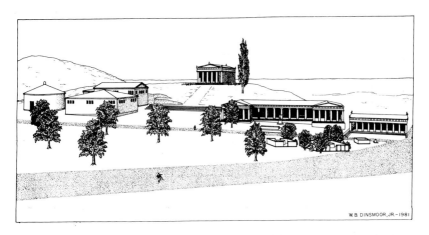

37. *Buildings along the West side of the Agora in the 5th century B.C. From left to right: tholos, old Bouleuterion, new Bouleuterion, Hephaisteion, Stoa of Zeus Eleutherios, Royal Stoa.*

a part. In this capacity Apollo was one of the patron deities of the state organization, especially in connection with the brotherhoods (*phratries*); children of Athenian citizens were formally presented to fellow members of the brotherhood and to Apollo Patroos.

According to Pausanias (I, 3.4), the cult statue was by Euphranor, a leading Athenian artist of the 4th century B.C. Euphranor's work has been recognized in a colossal statue found near the temple by the Greek Archaeological Society in their excavations of 1907; it now stands in the Stoa of Attalos (Museum, p. 193, Fig. **39**). Other statues of Apollo by Leochares and Kalamis which are mentioned by Pausanias may have stood in the porch of the temple on a pedestal formed by a curious thickening of the front walls.

Opening off the north side of the main room, or cella, of the temple is a smaller room, certainly contemporary; this was presumably an *adyton* or inner sanctuary, a familiar feature in temples of Apollo. The temple seen by Pausanias dates from the third quarter of the 4th century B.C. Beneath the floor level of its cella are slight remains of an earlier building, possibly a temple. An arc of its curved west wall and a small square base of poros remain, but have been covered over.

75

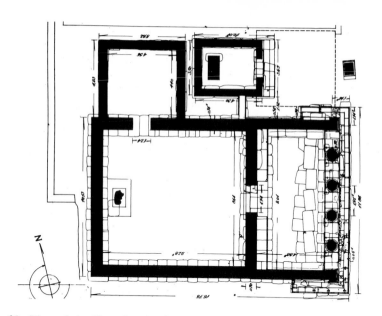

38. Plan of the Temple of Apollo Patroos, 2nd half 4th century B.C.

39. Apollo Patroos (?) perhaps by Euphranor, 2nd half 4th century B.C.

In a casting pit a few feet to the south of the temple (no longer visible) was found a mold for the casting of a bronze statue of Apollo, now in the Museum (p. 235). Statue and temple date from the middle of the 6th century B.C. This early sanctuary was undoubtedly destroyed by the Persians in 480/79 B.C.

24. Temple of Zeus Phratrios and Athena Phratria* (Fig. 38)

Immediately to the north of the Temple of Apollo are the conglomerate and limestone remains of a smaller temple, dated to the middle of the 4th century B.C. It has such intimate relations with the slightly later Temple of Apollo Patroos to the south that the divinities worshipped here should be Zeus Phratrios and Athena Phratria. As the principal deities of the ancestral religious brotherhoods, or phratries, membership in which was almost a prerequisite of Athenian citizenship, these divinities were closely associated with Apollo Patroos. The altar inscribed to Zeus Phratrios and Athena Phratria, now set up on the base in front, was found on the east side of the excavations. Nothing remains of the superstructure of the little temple which in its original form was only a cella. The massive foundation to the east, largely made of conglomerate blocks, was for a porch added about the middle of the 2nd century B.C., during the great Hellenistic building activity in the Agora.

25. Stoa of Zeus Eleutherios* (Fig. 37)

To the north of the Temple of Apollo are the remains of the Stoa of Zeus, a colonnade the two ends of which were bent forward and treated like temple facades; the northern end has been largely cut away by the Athens-Peiraeus Railway. The distinctive plan of the building was adapted for use in several other Greek cities (Thasos, Megalopolis, Kalauria, Delos). The building dates from the last third of the 5th century B.C. Zeus was honored here as the god of freedom and deliverance. The Stoa was also a popular promenade and place of rendezvous; Sokrates is said by both Xenophon and Plato to have met his friends in this stoa for conversation or just to sit or stroll. Of the Stoa itself the poros foundations remain over much of the west side and south end. At the south end also are some step blocks of

Hymettian marble. The line of the east front has been fixed from a few surviving blocks and the foundation trench; it has been filled out with modern masonry. Inside the foundations for the west and south walls is a lighter bedding for a continuous bench or couch. Down the middle of the building are square poros foundations for interior columns. The outer Doric order is represented on the ground by several fragmentary column drums and cornice blocks of white marble; of the inner Ionic order only very small fragments were found. On the front foundations of the Stoa there is also a battered fragment from the poros frieze course, the back of which is lightly stippled; this is a surface treatment that extended over the whole interior face of the wall. A retaining wall of squared blocks protected the back of the building against the steep hillside.

In front of the south wing of the Stoa the excavators came on one almost complete and one more fragmentary marble figure of Victory (*Nike*), now in the Museum (p. 214). These must have been akroteria from the outer angles of the wing facades. The use of figural akroteria on a stoa is exceptional and is perhaps to be explained by the fact that the Stoa of Zeus was a sacred as well as a civic building. Pausanias (I, 3.3-4) records wall paintings by Euphranor: the Twelve Gods, a group of Theseus, Democracy and the People, and the Battle of Mantinea (362 B.C.); but of these nothing remains.

Most of the many dedications associated with the Stoa had some significance for the delivery of the city or the preservation of its freedom. Chief among them was a statue of Zeus Eleutherios, i.e. Zeus of Freedom, mentioned by Pausanias as being in front of the Stoa; it stood presumably on the round pedestal of which traces were found on the axis of the building. A statue of the Emperor Hadrian seen by Pausanias in front of the Stoa is probably to be identified with the one noted above, p. 66. Shields of warriors who had died fighting bravely in defence of Athens were hung in the Stoa; according to Pausanias, a number of these were carried off by the soldiers of Sulla after the sack of Athens in 86 B.C.

In early Roman times the hillside was cut back behind the Stoa to make way for a two-roomed Annex. Each of the two chambers had its own vestibule approached through the back wall of the Stoa; the rooms were paved with marble, and in the southern was a long statue base. The temple-like aspect of the arrangement was completed by the construction of a large altar in front of the Stoa, now exactly overlaid by a marble pile. (Compare the scheme of the cult place in the Metroon, p. 63.) We may perhaps recognize in the Annex the seat of an imperial cult in which successive emperors were worshipped in close association with Zeus Eleutherios; both Augustus and Hadrian in fact bore the epithet "Eleutherios."

Beneath the Stoa were found remains (no longer visible) of a small archaic structure (6th century B.C.) surrounding a rectangular base appropriate for a statue. To the east are slight traces of what appears to have been the altar. Since the Stoa was certainly sacred to Zeus, its predecessor may have been a shrine of the same divinity. The earlier establishment was destroyed by the Persians in 480/79 B.C. From that time until work began on the Stoa the area was occupied by various industrial establishments such as ironworks and potteries.

26. Royal Stoa (=Stoa Basileios)* (Figs. 40-42, 56)

The northernmost building on the west side of the Agora has come to light in the new excavations beyond the railway. Since that area is not yet (1989) open to the public we may view it by climbing the stairs behind the Stoa of Zeus and looking down from the railway bridge or from the belvedere to the north of the bridge.

"First on the right," remarked Pausanias (I, 3.1) as he entered the Agora, "is the so-called Royal Stoa (*Stoa Basileios*) in which the Royal Archon (*Archon Basileus*) sits during his year of office." After long years of uncertainty the point where Pausanias entered the square was established by the excavations of 1970, and the Royal Stoa appeared in precisely the place indicated in his account. It stood near the west end of the narrow area excavated between the railway and the modern Hadrian Street to the north.

The Royal Archon was one of the three principal magistrates of Athens. As the heir to the actual king of earlier days he had inherited many administrative responsibilities pertaining both to religion and to legal matters: superintendence of the Mysteries, of the festival of Dionysos called the Epilenaia, of the torch races, of many ancestral sacrifices, of lawsuits involving homicide and impiety. It was for this reason that Sokrates was required to appear before the Royal Archon in the Stoa when accused of impiety by Meletos in 399 B.C.

40. Remains of the Royal Stoa, seen from the south.

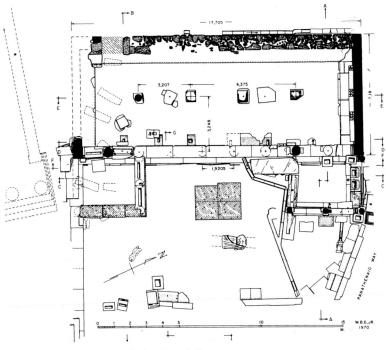

41. Actual state plan of the Royal Stoa.

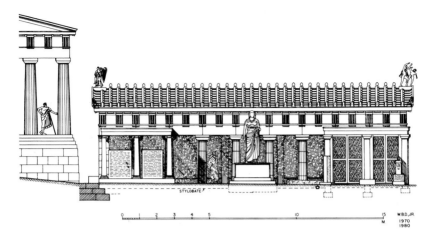

42. *Restored elevation of the Royal Stoa, seen from the east, ca. 300 B.C.*

From numerous references in the ancient authors we learn much else about the uses of the Stoa. On the walls of the building and on stelai in front of it were written up the ancestral laws of Athens associated with the names of Drako and Solon and revised at the end of the 5th century B.C. On a stone in front of the building the archons stood each year to take their oath of office, swearing above all to preserve the laws.

In the light of its importance and fame the Royal Stoa proves to be surprisingly small in scale and modest in design. The plan is a rectangle measuring overall about 7.50×17.70 meters. Solid walls closed the west, north and south sides. Along its front stood eight Doric columns above two steps; its interior had four columns of the same order, all of poros. The north wall is preserved to a height of three courses of fine ashlar masonry of poros; the south wall, which had been largely destroyed by the railway in 1891, has been partially restored by the excavators. At the foot of the wall on all three sides, but best preserved at the north, is the stone underpinning for a continuous platform about 0.85 m. wide and 0.56 m. high. Three rough poros blocks at the north end formed part of the core of this platform. Behind the stylobate are various bedding blocks; a series of

81

three blocks regularly spaced behind the midpoints of the three southernmost intercolumnar spaces held wooden posts perhaps for the support of a light barrier to provide some degree of privacy for meetings. The Council of the Areopagus when meeting in the Royal Stoa is reported to have protected itself from intrusion by means of a rope barrier. Of the superstructure little has been found: a couple of Doric capitals, fragments of frieze, cornice and roof tiles and, most interesting, some small pieces of the terracotta sculptural groups which Pausanias saw on the roof of the Stoa: Theseus throwing Skiron into the sea and Hemera carrying off Kephalos.

The area in front of the building was bordered to north and south by banks of stone steps that extended out from the two ends of the facade. At the south three steps remain, at the north, two; their outer ends have not yet been found. These steps permitted the area in front of the Stoa to be kept level despite the sloping terrain. Thrones for distinguished guests also existed. Two pairs of such, made of poros, may be seen where they were reused in front of the north end of the Stoa; fragments of a later series, of marble, were also found.

The style of the architecture, combined with the evidence from stratification, points to a date for the Stoa in the neighborhood of 500 B.C. On the other hand, the reuse of much old material in the foundations (Fig. 43) would be more explicable if the building had been erected after the Persian sack of 480/79 B.C. There is no clear trace of an earlier building on the site of the Stoa. A family burial plot of the Submycenaean period (11th century B.C.) has come to light beneath the south end of the building.

Small columnar wings were later erected against the facade of the Stoa, each with three columns in its front. Between the columns of the south wing are sockets for the reception of large marble stelai which in this position would have been sheltered from the rain yet easily read from either side. Here perhaps were displayed some of the stelai bearing sections of the ancient laws as revised at the end of the 5th century. Several fragments of such have been found in the Agora excavations, and a nearly complete stele discovered in 1843, inscribed with two sections of Drako's Law on Homicide, was to be set up, according to its own text, "in front of the Royal Stoa." Technical indications on the surviving masonry at the northwest corner of the building suggest that there may have been a marble

43. Front steps of the Royal Stoa, showing reused column shafts in the foundations (now reburied). View from the NE.

facing on the back wall designed to receive the main part of the law code.

The stone (*lithos*) on which magistrates stood to take their oath of office has come to light immediately in front of the Stoa, close by the north wing (Fig. **44**). It is a massive block of limestone measuring 0.95 m. wide, 2.95 m. long and 0.40 m. high, roughly trimmed on the sides, worn smooth on top by centuries of use.

On the axis of the Stoa and between its two wings is the conglomerate foundation for the pedestal of a large statue. The marble torso was found nearby and is now exhibited in the Stoa of Attalos (p. 209). Dating from the second half of the 4th century B.C., the figure presumably represents the goddess Themis, the personification of law and the protectress of oaths. It was by her side, and with the law codes clearly visible to left and right, that the archons swore to preserve the laws of the city.

44. *The Lithos, or oath-stone, in front of the Royal Stoa, seen from the southeast. The terracotta drain in the foreground dates to the 4th century B.C.; the north wall of the stoa may be seen in the background.*

In front of the Stoa at its north end are several rectangular sockets, some of them cut in marble blocks, others sunk into the reused thrones. In these sockets stood schematic representations of the god Hermes, commonly referred to as Herms. A concentration of such Herms is reported by the lexicographer Harpokration in relation to the Painted Stoa and the Royal Stoa, some erected by private individuals, others by magistrates. The excavations in front of the Royal Stoa have in fact yielded parts of about a score of Herms ranging in date from the late 5th century B.C. into the 3rd century A.D. The inscriptions when preserved record dedications by citizens who had served as Royal Archons, additional evidence for the identification of the Royal Stoa.

The inscription on the face of the marble Herm base that stands *in situ* in front of the northernmost column position of the Stoa records the names of the poets and producers of the comedy and tragedy that had won the prizes in the year of the dedicator's term as Royal Archon, a year near the beginning of the 4th century B.C. (Fig. **45**). Since at least one of the producers was not a citizen but a resident alien, these plays were undoubtedly performed at the festival called the Epilenaia.

From a well to the south of the Royal Stoa and from a pit to the west of the building have been recovered great quantities of pottery of the 2nd and 3rd quarters of the 5th century B.C. Both cooking vessels and tableware are represented. Many of the bases bear the ligature ⟨Ξ⟩ , i.e. *demosion*=state property. From this we may infer the existence somewhere nearby of an official mess (*syssition*) such as is known to have existed in the Tholos (p. 47) and the prytaneion. The little building was remarkable not only for the variety of purposes which it served but also for its long life. Damaged severely

45. *Herm base inscribed with the name of the King Archon, Onesippos, recording winning playwrights and producers in the theatrical contests ca. 405-380 B.C. Found in place on the steps of the Royal Stoa.*

by fire early in its existence (note the traces on the north wall and the stylobate), the Stoa was rebuilt and enlarged by the addition of the wings, and these in turn underwent many alterations. The debris found above the floor indicates a date of about 400 A.D. for the final destruction and abandonment of the Stoa.

27. Crossroads Enclosure* (Figs. 46-48, 56)

Conspicuous in front of the Royal Stoa is the deep channel of the Great Drain, which is here about to issue from the Agora and join the still larger cloaca that flows beneath the modern Hadrian Street. Also visible are the stone surface gutters of both the western street and the Panathenaic Way, dating to the late 2nd century B.C.

A small shrine in the form of a square enclosure stood opposite the south wing of the Royal Stoa. The enclosing wall consists of upright slabs of poros once capped by a crowning member. An original doorway in the north wall was subsequently closed because of the rising ground level. The enclosure dates from the latter part of the 5th century B.C. It was clearly erected around a bold outcropping of the native rock which is still visible within the enclosure and which had presumably been a sacred place from earlier times. A mass of votive offerings that began in the closing decades of the 5th century (small vases, lamps, loomweights, knuckle bones, jewelry) suggests the worship of youthful female divinities.

The rising ground level gradually obscured the shrine so that by the 2nd century of our era when Pausanias passed this way, only the much worn top of the parapet projected, and this failed to attract his attention.

Just to the north of the enclosure opens the mouth of a well with a massive poros curb. It came into use at about the time that the enclosure was built, i.e. the late 5th century B.C. The well may indeed belong to the shrine since it was used through the 4th and 3rd centuries B.C. as a dumping place for many more votive offerings. Its clearance also yielded part of the archives of the Athenian cavalry corps of the 4th and 3rd centuries B.C., including many lead tablets, each inscribed with the official description and evaluation of a cavalry mount (Museum, p. 239, Fig. 145).

46. Aerial view of the Crossroads Enclosure, 5th century B.C., west road and great drain at the top, Panathenaic Way at the right. Lines of the two roads given by the stone gutters, with the Crossroads shrine and well within the angle.

47. Crossroads Enclosure, with votive pottery as found.

28. Late Roman Round Building* (Fig. 9)

Above the enclosure were found the remains of a round building of the 5th century after Christ; its southern half had been exposed already by the railway builders in 1891. Its diameter (18 m.) was close to that of the classical Tholos, and the presence of buttresses suggests that this building also, like the Tholos in its later life, was domed. Little survived but the rough lower foundations of concrete and a capacious drain which led out from near the center of the floor; this was all removed in 1974. The building had a short existence in antiquity; its ruins supported a wall of the later 5th or 6th century, perhaps for an aqueduct to supply a water mill (p. 145). The purpose of the round building is still obscure.

48. *Restored perspective of NW corner of the Agora showing Crossroads Enclosure (foreground), Royal Stoa (left), Panathenaic Way (center), Altar of Aphrodite (top, center) and Stoa Poikile (top right).*

Statues of Harmodios and Aristogeiton*
The Orchestra in the Agora*

The assassins of the tyrant Hipparchos in 514 B.C. were Harmodios and Aristogeiton. Although they had been motivated chiefly by a personal grudge, the dramatic circumstances of their deed and of their own subsequent deaths hastened their heroization as the liberators of Athens from despotic rule. Some time after the expulsion of the tyrant's family in 510 B.C. the two men were honored with bronze statues made by Antenor, one of the leading sculptors of the day. These were carried off by the Persians in 480/79 B.C., but they were soon replaced with a new group made by Kritios and Nesiotes in 477/6 B.C. The first group was sent back from Persia by Alexander the Great or one of his successors, and from then on both groups stood together in a conspicuous part of the Agora. They were the first of many honorary statues to be placed in the Agora.

89

The only part of the original monument found thus far is a small fragment of the base for one of the groups which retains part of the epigram (Museum, p. 238). This marble came to light a little to the southeast of the Temple of Ares (Plan, **38**), but since the context was of Turkish or modern date, the provenance cannot be trusted for the precise location of the monument. Pausanias (I, 8.5) recorded the groups not far from the statues that stood around the Temple of Ares. The current excavations may eventually bring to light the base of the monument, but more probably it was swept away without having been recorded by the builders of the railway in 1891.

According to the lexicographer Timaios, the Tyrannicides stood on the Orchestra. Of the Orchestra another lexicographer, Photios, writes: "The name was first used of the orchestra in the Agora, then of the semicircle at the bottom of the theater, where the choruses sang and danced." From an intriguing reference in Plato's *Apology* (26d-e) we learn that books could be bought at the Orchestra in the time of Sokrates. A clue to the location of the Orchestra within the Agora is given by other testimonia. In the Agora was a famous bronze statue of the Theban poet Pindar. It had been erected by the Athenians in appreciation of a flattering dithyramb which he had composed in their honor. This statue was variously located by the ancient authors: in the vicinity of the Temple of Ares (Pausanias), in front of the Royal Stoa (Pseudo-Aeschines). The site was chosen, perhaps, with reference to the place where Pindar's dithyramb had been performed by a cyclical chorus, and this place was undoubtedly the Orchestra. These indications would appear to locate the Orchestra in the northern part of the Agora.

Herms in the Agora* (Figs. **49, 50**)

Since repeated reference must be made to "the Herms" in discussing the monuments that stood around the northwest corner of the Agora, we may pause a moment to consider the meaning of the term. In this context "Herm" means a representation of the god Hermes in which the most vital parts, i.e. head and genitals, are rendered naturalistically while the trunk and arms are given only a schematic, angular shape. This form of representation was particularly suited to the god Hermes in the discharge of one of his many functions, the guar-

49. Herm head from the Crossroads Enclosure, 5th century B.C.

50. Herm head from the Stoa behind the Royal Stoa, 2nd century A.D., buried at the end of the 4th century A.D.

dianship of thoroughfares and entrances. It is not surprising, therefore, that Herms were set up around the northwest corner of the Agora, near the principal entrance to the square. According to the passage in Harpokration noted above (p. 84) these Herms extended from the Royal Stoa and the Painted Stoa. Many of those beside the Royal Stoa have now been found, and another group may be expected to come to light near the Painted Stoa which stood on the other side of the Panathenaic Way. We hear of a third stoa in this area within which Herms were erected in such numbers that the building came to be called the Stoa of the Herms. A reference in the orator Antiphon shows it to have been standing already by about 425 B.C. A clue to a more precise location of the building was provided by the discovery of an inscription of 282/1 B.C. reused in a wall of the early Roman period some 60 meters to the northwest of the Royal Stoa; according to its own text the stele was to be set up "in the Stoa of the Herms."

The cluster of Herms at the northwest corner of the Agora must have been one of the most distinctive features of the place. "The Herms" are repeatedly given as a point of reference: for the setting up of inscriptions, for the location of a barbershop, for defining the haunts of Sokrates and of the cavalry officers, as a starting point of an equestrian exercise.

Because of their prominence as well as their proximity to the House of Poulytion the Herms of the Agora were undoubtedly among the prime targets of the Herm-Choppers (*Hermokopidai*) who threw the city into a state of frenzy in 415 B.C. by mutilating the Herms on the eve of the departure of the Sicilian Expedition (Thucydides 6.27). The damage done on that night is illustrated by the replacement of the nose on a Herm found in the Agora, and by the discovery of the head of a Herm broken from its shaft and thrown into the crossroads enclosure toward the end of the 5th century B.C. (Fig. **49**).

Distinct from "the Herms," but probably not far from them stood the Hermes of the Agora, a much admired bronze statue of the god. It is said to have been near a gate which undoubtedly marked an entrance to the Agora, and close also to the Painted Stoa.

29. Approach to the Agora from the Dipylon Gate* (Fig. 51)

From our vantage point on the railway bridge above the Stoa of Zeus and the Royal Stoa we may contemplate the approach to the Agora that was followed by most visitors and notably by our indispensable guide, Pausanias, in the middle of the 2nd century A.D.
Having come up from the Peiraeus, Pausanias entered the city of Athens through the principal gate, the Dipylon. Immediately within the gate he noted the Pompeion, the building for the marshaling of the Panathenaic procession, the ruins of which have been fully explored by Greek and German archaeologists. Then followed a sanctuary of Demeter which may be the source of a statue base signed by Praxiteles and found in 1936 at the north foot of Kolonos Agoraios (Museum, p. 194).
Pausanias makes particular mention of the stoas which bordered the road from the Dipylon Gate to the Agora (I, 2.4-5). In front of them, he tells us, stood bronze statues of famous men and women. Behind them he found various shrines, a gymnasium of Hermes and a sanctuary of Dionysos which had been installed in the house of Poulytion. This house was notorious as the place in which Alkibiades and his boon companions on a summer night in 415 B.C. had parodied the Mysteries of Demeter and had then gone forth to mutilate the Herms.
The line of the main street followed by Pausanias, together with something of the colonnades that bordered it, has now been explored in its upper course where it approached the Agora. It was clearly an interesting and impressive example of the type of colonnaded street so much in vogue in Greek cities in the Roman imperial period. The roadway proper, with a graveled surface, was 20 meters in width, while the stoas were each about 6.50 meters wide.
Of particular interest is the southernmost of the colonnades, a two-aisled stoa. With the aid of a plan (Fig. 51), the ruins of its eastern end can be distinguished below us. A solid median wall divided the building into two aisles of which the northern faced onto the main street, the southern onto a lesser, parallel street that passed close by the north foot of Kolonos and gave access to the Sanctuary of Demos and the Graces. The southern colonnade was all of poros with simple Doric columns standing on a single step. The northern

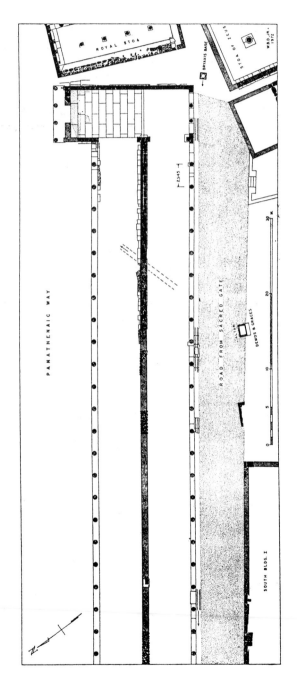

51. *Stoa northwest of the Agora, facing the Panathenaic Way and the Sacred Way.*

colonnade was apparently intended to be similar, but in its final form its columns stood on three steps, the lowest of poros, the two upper of marble, thus providing room for many spectators to view the passing scene. None of the columns of the northern colonnade has yet been found. The greater number of steps in the northern aisle meant that its floor level was appreciably higher than that of the south aisle. Communication between the main street and the lesser street to the south, as also with the south aisle of the stoa, was provided by a roofed passageway incorporated into the plan of the east end of the building.

The construction of the stoa probably began in the early 2nd century B.C., but it seems to have continued over a long period with many changes, among which may be noted the partial walling up of the colonnade of the south aisle and the conversion of part of the building into closed shops. Destroyed in the Herulian sack of 267 A.D., the stoa was subsequently rebuilt, only to suffer again in the troubles at the end of the 4th century. Once more the building was restored; it continued in use into the 580's.

30. Late Roman Building (Fig. 9)

Descending again into the main excavation we make our way eastward toward the Altar of the Twelve Gods. In doing so we pass through the conspicuous concrete foundations of a large rectangular structure, dating from the beginning of the 5th century A.D. A series of rooms on the north, south and west faced onto a central court through a continuous porch. The entrance was undoubtedly from the east. The building is closely contemporary with the Late Roman Complex (Plan, 41) to the south, and the two may have been connected, but no clue has yet been found to the specific function of the northern building.

Beneath the Late Roman Building were found remains of at least a dozen monument bases of various sizes and dates. Some of these may well have carried statues mentioned by Pausanias (I, 8.3-5) when describing this area.

31. Sanctuary of the Twelve Gods* (Figs. 52, 53)

Thucydides (VI, 55.1) tells us that Peisistratos, the son of Hippias and grandson of the more famous Peisistratos, during his archonship (522/1 B.C.) set up in the Agora an altar to the Twelve Gods. The sanctuary, which consisted of a fenced area or *peribolos* with an altar at the center, has been identified by an inscription on a marble statue base found in place against the southwest wall of the enclosure. The inscription reads: "Leagros, son of Glaukon, dedicated (the statue) to the Twelve Gods."

Only the southwestern part of the peribolos is visible, the rest being under the railway to the north. Digging conducted within the railway right-of-way has established the plan. Its location in the open part of the Agora close by the Panathenaic Way made the sanctuary a popular place of asylum; the altar was also considered the heart of Athens, the central milestone from which distances to outside places were measured. The sanctuary was destroyed by the Persians in 480/79 B.C. and rebuilt toward the end of the 5th century B.C., with additional repairs made in the 4th century. As preserved, the monument has a low sill with cuttings and dowel holes for the

52. Corner of the peribolos of the Altar of the 12 Gods, with the Leagros base and other monuments in foreground. Most of the rest of the monument lies hidden under the Athens - Peiraeus railway. View from the west. 6th-4th centuries B.C.

53. *Restored view of the Altar of the 12 Gods.*

attachment of a low stone fence which surrounded the altar, now missing in the railway cut.

To one's right upon approaching the western entrance to the enclosure is a poros base with a round cutting in its top. This probably held a holy water basin (*perirrhanterion*). A little farther to the west is a stone water basin set to its full depth in the ground. It drew water through a branch of the stone water channel that bordered the west side of the Agora carrying off the overflow from the Southwest Fountain House. The water was needed, no doubt, in connection with sacrifices in the Sanctuary of the Twelve Gods, perhaps also for watering the trees or shrubs that are attested by planting holes around the shrine. Plato recommended that the overflow from the public fountains should be used for watering the precincts of the gods (*Laws* 761c; *Kritias* 117b).

To the south of the Sanctuary of the Twelve Gods are the remains of a ground altar (*eschara*) of the late 6th century B.C. This type of altar is usually associated with a hero.

97

32-34. Northeast Side of the Agora (Fig. 54)

The new excavations to the north of the railway are not yet open to the public (1989). Scholars desiring access may request the key from the guard at the North Gate. From the bridge over the railway just inside the gate one gains a general view of the area.

Having completed our survey of the west side of the ancient square, we turn to the north side. Since 1969 the excavations to the north of the railway have been directed toward determining the general line of the north edge of the Agora and distinguishing the various buildings that closed this side of the square in its successive periods.

One of the most important results of the recent exploration is the clarification of the road system in this part of Athens. It is now apparent that the trunk road coming up from the main gate of the city, the Dipylon, forked into three branches at the northwest corner of the Agora. The middle branch continued on a southeasterly course diagonally across the square toward the Acropolis; since this was the route followed by the procession in the national festival of the Panathenaia, it was sometimes called the Panathenaic Way. A second branch led almost due south to serve the public buildings on the west side of the Agora. A third branch diverged toward the east.

The eastern half of the north side was sufficiently cleared by 1972 to permit a sketch of its history. The earliest phases are represented by a Mycenaean chamber tomb, short lengths of retaining wall that may be as early as the 8th century B.C., and pockets of debris from the Persian destruction of 480/79 B.C. Only in the post-Persian rebuilding does the edge of the square become clearly defined with the erection of a pair of modest buildings comprising rows of one- or two-roomed shops facing south across the square. These appear to have suffered in the Roman sack of 86 B.C. In the first century A.D. a large public building was built, of which there has been exposed only a deep southward-facing porch of the Ionic order (Plan, **32**). Its massive foundations of miscellaneous reused material, salvaged no doubt from buildings destroyed in 86 B.C., overlie the slight remains of the old shop buildings and are clearly visible from the railway bridge.

Farther to the east one can make out areas of marble flooring. These belong to a large Basilica erected in the middle of the 2nd century

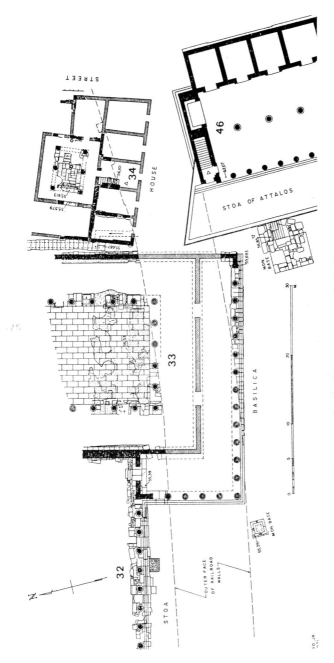

54. Stoa (1st B.C./A.D.), Basilica (2nd A.D.) and Roman house along E. half of North side.

99

A.D. with its major axis north-to-south (Plan, **33**). The Ionic porch of the older building to the west was now extended around the south end of the Basilica in an L-shaped scheme. The consequence of this bold intrusion for the realignment of thoroughfares in this part of Athens and the spatial relation between the new Basilica and the Library of Hadrian to the east can be elucidated only by future exploration.

As yet only the south end of the Basilica has been exposed, but the plan appears to be normal for this type of building. Within a closed rectangle a marble-floored central nave some 15 meters wide was surrounded by a corridor six meters in width. In addition to the marble flooring, many fragments of marble wall revetment and sculpted piers came to light in the excavation. The newly found Basilica is an impressive example of the more closed type of building which in the Roman imperial period came to supplement the old open stoa as a place for public intercourse.

To the east of the Basilica are the remains of a substantial house of the Roman period, two storeys in height and with a colonnaded court (Plan, **34**). The plan appears to have included a row of five one-room shops facing south onto the cul-de-sac that remained to the north of the Stoa of Attalos.

Following the Herulian sack of 267 A.D., the area was refurbished in the early 5th century A.D. A pair of parallel foundations bordered the south side of the ancient road in the eastern part of the area. Some of their rough masonry has been left above the floor of the Basilica. These lend themselves to restoration as a colonnade; a corresponding portico is probably to be restored on the north side of the road.

Prominent in the excavated area to the west of the North Gate is a large round altar made of white marble above a two-stepped base of blue marble (Fig. **55**). The drum is encircled by a Doric frieze, the four metopes of which were each filled with an ox skull (*boukranion*). The style suggests an early Hellenistic date, but the altar must have been moved from elsewhere in late antiquity since in its present location it has no proper foundation; it also intrudes on the Panathenaic Way.

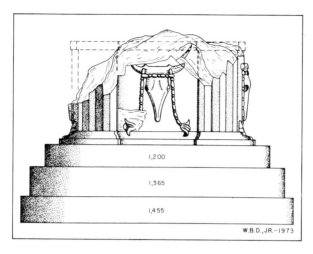

55. Hellenistic altar with boukranion.

35. Stoa Poikile (Painted Stoa) (Figs. 56-59)

The most recent excavations (1980-) lie beyond the present fenced area of the archaeological zone, along the north side of Hadrian Street. They can be reached by leaving the site through the North Gate (the railway bridge) and turning left (west). They appear on the right some 50-75 meters down the road.

The long stepped foundations visible in the east part of the area are the end of a long stoa, most of which still (1990) lies hidden under modern houses further east. Though only a fraction of the building has been exposed, enough has been recovered to restore it as a Doric stoa facing south, with an interior of Ionic columns. Most of the building was made of different limestones, though the Ionic capitals were of marble. The structure is well designed, carefully built, and one of the more lavish secular buildings in Athens. The step blocks, for instance, were all cut to the same length, with the joints fastened by means of iron double-T clamps leaded in. According to the pottery associated with its construction, the building should be dated to the period 475-450 B.C. Of all the stoas of Athens it holds the

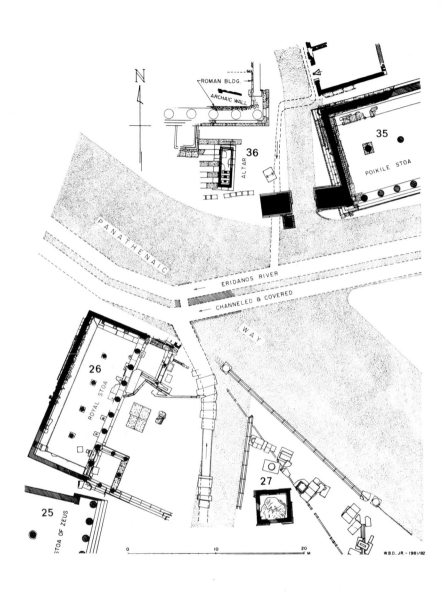

Inside figure labels:

N

ROMAN BLDG.

ARCHAIC WALL

35

36

ALTAR

POIKILE STOA

PANATHENAIC

ERIDANOS RIVER

CHANNELED & COVERED

WAY

26

ROYAL STOA

27

25

STOA OF ZEUS

0   10   20
M

W.B.D., J.R - 1981/82

56. Plan of the Northwest Corner of the Agora, showing the recent excavations at the top, from left to right: Altar of Aphrodite (6th/5th centuries B.C.), two piers for a gateway (late 4th century B.C.), foundations of the Stoa Poikile (ca. 470-460 B.C.). Royal Stoa and Crossroads Enclosure at bottom (south).

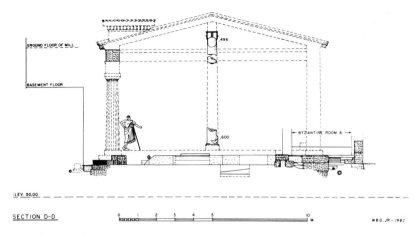

GROUND FLOOR OF MILL
BASEMENT FLOOR

.496

.600

BYZANTINE ROOM 6

LEV. 50,00

SECTION D-D

0   1   2   3   4   5   10 M.

W.B.D. JR - 1982

57. *Restored cross-section of the Painted Stoa, showing Doric columns outside, Ionic within.*

58. *Detail of the steps at the west end of the Painted Stoa, ca. 470/460 B.C.*

103

59. *Restored perspective of the west end of the Stoa Poikile.*

preferred location, along the north side of the Agora square, looking right up the Panathenaic Way to the Acropolis. It has the southern exposure recommended for stoas in order to take advantage of the warmth of the low winter sun while presenting its back wall to the cold north wind. Pausanias saw the Painted Stoa as he made his way along the north side of the square, and this new stoa thus corresponds to what we know about the Painted Stoa in terms of size, date and location; the identification of the remains as those of the Painted Stoa therefore seems probable.

The building was first known as the *Peisianaktios*, after the man responsible for its construction, Peisianax, who may have been the brother-in-law of Kimon. Soon after its construction, however, it was decorated with a series of large paintings, and the building became known by the popular name *Poikile* (Painted), which appears as its official name in inscriptions by the 4th century B.C.

The paintings were done on large wooden panels (*sanides*) by the outstanding artists of Greece: Polygnotos, Mikon and Panainos. The works are referred to time and again by ancient authors and are described in some detail by Pausanias, who saw them still in place after 600 years. They depicted scenes of Athenian military exploits, both mythological and historical: the Athenians against the Amazons, the Greeks at Troy, the Athenians defeating the Spartans at Argive Oinoe and — by far the most famous — the Athenian victory over the Persians at Marathon. Pausanias' description is as follows:

> The last part of the painting consists of those who fought at Marathon. The Boeotians of Plataia and the Attic contingent are coming to grips with the barbarians; at this point the action is evenly balanced between both sides. In the inner part of the fight the barbarians are fleeing and pushing one another into the marsh; at the extreme end of the painting are the Phoenician ships and the Greeks killing the barbarians who are tumbling into them. In this picture are also shown Marathon, the hero after whom the plain is named, Theseus, represented as coming up from the earth, Athena and Herakles — the Marathonians, according to their own account, were the first to recognize Herakles as a god. Of the combatants, the most conspicuous in the picture is Kallimachos, who was chosen by the Athenians to be polemarch, and of the generals, Miltiades.

After they were seen by Pausanias in the 2nd century A.D., the paintings were all removed, apparently at the time of the bishop Synesios, who wrote ca. 400 A.D.:

> May the ship's captain who brought me here perish miserably. Present day Athens possesses nothing venerable except the illustrious names of places. When the sacrifice of a victim has been completed, the skin is left as a token of the animal that once existed; in the same way now that philosophy has departed hence, all that is left for us is to walk around and wonder at the Academy and the Lyceum, and, by Zeus, the Poikile Stoa after which the philosophy of Chrysippos is named, now no longer many coloured; the proconsul took away the sanides to which Polygnotos of Thasos committed his art.

In addition to these illustrations of Athenian exploits, the Stoa housed more tangible reminders of her military triumphs, which were seen by Pausanias:

> In the Poikile are deposited bronze shields. On some is an inscription saying that they were taken from the Skionaians and their auxiliaries; others, smeared with pitch to protect them from the ravages of time and rust, are said to be the shields of

the Lakedaimonians who were captured at the island of Sphakteria.

The battle of Sphakteria at Pylos in 425/4 B.C. was one of the great Athenian triumphs of the Peloponnesian War; 292 Spartans were captured alive, and their armor apparently remained on public display for close to 600 years. One of the captured shields from the battle has been found in the excavations (Figs. **60, 61**). It is round, measuring about one meter in diameter, with a relief border decorated with a guilloche pattern. The bronze is badly corroded and damaged so that the original weight cannot be determined; presumably there was an inner lining of leather, now missing. The shield was found in a cistern that was filled up in the 3rd century B.C., and it cannot therefore have been seen by Pausanias, although it is certainly one of the same series. This is known because of the punched inscription across the front: "The Athenians from the Lakedaimonians from Pylos."

As well as displaying paintings and captured arms, the Stoa was used for a wide variety of other functions. Unlike most of the other stoas in the Agora, it was not built for any specific purpose or activity or for the use of a single group of officials. Rather, it seems to have served the needs of the populace at large, providing shelter and a place to meet just off the Agora square. To be sure, it was used on

60. Bronze shield taken by the Athenians from the Spartans at Pylos (425 B.C.) and displayed as a trophy on the Painted Stoa.

61. Drawing showing punched inscription and guilloche pattern of Pylos shield.

occasion for official functions. A proclamation summoning those qualified to attend the Eleusinian mysteries was made from the stoa every year, and it was used for legal proceedings as well. Demosthenes mentions an arbitration held here, and inscriptions of the 4th century B.C. refer to full courts of 501 jurors using the building. In addition to its official purposes the stoa was also used informally by a mixed throng of people. This is clear from the abundant references in the written sources to the frequent use of the stoa by those whose trade depended on a crowd: sword-swallowers, jugglers, beggars, parasites and fishmongers. Among those who came regularly were the philosophers, who could expect to find a ready audience in this convenient meeting place. There are references to cynicism and other unspecified philosophies being taught in the Stoa, but one branch of Western philosophy is particularly associated with the Painted Stoa. It was founded by the philosopher Zeno, who came from Kition on Cyprus in the years around 300 B.C. He preferred the Painted Stoa and met here so regularly with his followers that they took their name from this particular stoa which served as their classroom. Diogenes Laertius, writing in the 3rd century A.D., gives the clearest account:

He used to discourse in the Poikile Stoa, which was also called Peisianaktios, and derived the name Poikile from the painting of Polygnotos... Henceforth people came hither to hear him, and for this reason they were called Stoics.

The stoa, filled with crowds from the Agora and frequented by philosophers, fits well the picture of the kind of liberal and elegant resorts that Kimon is said to have built for the city, a popular *lesche* where Athenians came together to discourse, argue and learn.

Running along the back wall of the Stoa was found an aqueduct of large terracotta pipes, carrying water in a westerly direction (Fig. **62**). The same line has been found further west by Greek and German archaeologists, heading toward the Academy, which Kimon is said to have beautified by planting trees and providing water. Given its date, direction and association with the stoa, this pipeline is probably the aqueduct which watered the Academy.

62. Terracotta pipeline (right) behind the Painted Stoa, taking water westward, toward the Academy, ca. 470/460 B.C.

Behind the stoa are two courses of fine ashlar blocks. These make up the south wall of a row of western-facing square rooms which opened onto the road which ran northwest along the west end of the Painted Stoa. They are probably small shops or industrial establishments dating to the classical period.

Resting on the steps of the Painted Stoa are the foundations of a pier measuring 2.70 by 3.30 meters. Some 2.50 meters to the west are similar foundations, not so well preserved and today carrying a much later Ionic column base (Fig. **56**). Together these two piers originally supported a monumental gate which spanned the narrow street leading off to the northwest. The gate was seen by Pausanias, who describes it just before his account of the Painted Stoa and says that it carried a trophy celebrating an Athenian victory over the Macedonians in 303/2 B.C. None of the superstructure has been recognized and the form of the gate is uncertain.

36. Altar and Sanctuary of Aphrodite Ourania (Figs. **56, 63-64**)

Just west of the foundations of the gate may be seen the remains of an altar. A platform of hard purplish limestone is preserved, measuring 5.10 by 2.40 meters. On top stood the altar itself, although now only its southern half survives. The core of the altar was made up of soft, yellowish, poros limestone blocks set on edge ca. 0.30 m. apart, around which were set orthostates of white marble from one of the Cycladic islands, probably Paros or Naxos. The orthostates are carved with a handsome molding at the base. The crowning course is missing, though two pedimental end pieces decorated with floral motifs were found nearby and are probably from the altar. Pottery found up against and inside the base suggests that the altar should be dated to ca. 500 B.C., as does the use of marble from the islands rather than the local quarries on Mount Pentele, which first began to be exploited extensively around 490 B.C.

Its identification as an altar is certain from the form of the monument as well as from the ashes and bones of the sacrifices found inside the core, mostly pigs, sheep and goats, with an occasional bird. The identification as an altar of Aphrodite seems likely. Pausanias describes a sanctuary of Aphrodite Ourania (Heavenly Aphrodite) at about this spot after he passes the Hephaisteion and makes his way to

63. Altar of Aphrodite, ca. 500 B.C., seen from the south.

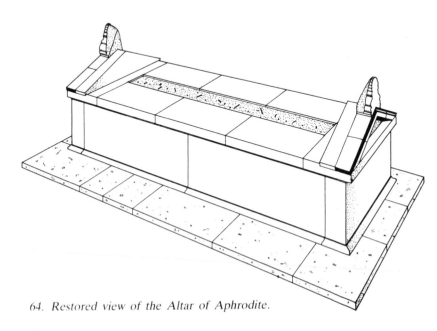

64. Restored view of the Altar of Aphrodite.

110

the Painted Stoa along the north side of the square: "Nearby is a shrine of Aphrodite Ourania... The statue still extant in my time is of Parian marble and is the work of Pheidias." Two fragments of a marble relief found in the area clearly depict Aphrodite and add their weight to the identification. At present we are uncertain as to the limits of the sanctuary. Originally, it may have been a simple open-air shrine with the altar standing alone, though Pausanias' account of a statue carved by the master sculptor Pheidias suggests a temple as well.

Approaching the altar from the east are some foundations of rubble and concrete. They date to the 5th century A.D. and originally supported a colonnade which ran along the north side of the Panathenaic Way in late Roman times, when the level of the street was much higher.

Behind (north of) the altar are more foundations set at a higher level. They seem to be the foundations for a small prostyle temple of the Roman period which overlooked the area of the altar from the north. Excavation along the north side is proceeding to both east and west of the area described here (1990) in order to fully expose both the Painted Stoa and the Sanctuary of Aphrodite.

37. The Panathenaic Way* (Fig. 65)

Before returning to the main area of the excavations we may pause a moment to look up toward the Acropolis along the line of the broad graveled road, the Panathenaic Way. Following as it did a natural course for traffic from the principal city gate toward the upper and central parts of the city, the road was in constant use at all times. But it took its name and special character from its role as the route of the procession or great parade of the national festival of Athens, the Panathenaia.

The Parthenon frieze gives a splendid impression of the event with emphasis on some of its more glamorous aspects: the cavalry, the racing chariots, sacrificial cows and sheep, young men and girls bearing equipment to be used at the sacrifice. On the frieze the spectators of the procession are the heroes of Attica and the gods of Olympos. In actual fact the procession was watched by the citizens of Athens and their guests, for whose convenience on this occasion

65. *Panathenaic Way, just west of the northern entrance to the Agora, showing the starting line blocks (late 5th century B.C.) and cuttings to support wooden bleachers* (ikria).

special wooden grandstands, or *ikria*, were erected in the Agora. Within the Agora proper, the graveled surface on which one walks today is identical with that of antiquity. For the steep stretch between the southeast corner of the square and the upper limits of the Eleusinion (Plan, **56**) heavy stone paving was eventually laid, but this was done only in the 2nd century A.D.

The retention of a graveled surface within the square was probably dictated by other uses of the roadway in connection with the national festival. The normal Greek word for the Panathenaic Way, *dromos*, implies a race course, and there is reason to believe that track events originally took place here. A row of square stone bases socketed to hold temporary wooden posts in the line of the Panathenaic Way and to the east of the Altar of the Twelve Gods represents in all probability the starting point for such races (Folding Plan) (Fig. **65**). The installation dates from the second half of the 5th century B.C., at which time, long before the construction of the South Square, a straight-away of the required length (600 Greek feet) would have fit into the open square. A race course has also come to light in the middle of the Agora of ancient Argos.

Equestrian exercises also took place on the Panathenaic Way and the cavalry actually trained there:

> Go forth Manes, to the Agora, to the Herms, the place frequented by the phylarchs, and to their handsome pupils, whom Pheidon trains in mounting and dismounting.
>
> (Mnesimachos, in *Athen.* IX, 402)

In a remarkable example of a correlation between literary and archaeological evidence, the name of the trainer Pheidon appears on 30 stamped clay discs found in the crossroads well alongside the Panathenaic Way (Fig. **66**; Museum, p. 239).

The most spectacular cavalry contest, a sham battle (*anthippasia*) which formed part of the Panathenaic Festival, was held outside the city in the Hippodrome. It is worth noting, however, that parts of several monuments commemorating victories in cavalry displays have come to light in the Agora. One is a base of the 4th century B.C. sculpted by Bryaxis, now in the National Museum; this was found in 1891 *in situ* just behind the Royal Stoa. Another is a relief with riders found in 1971 near the same place (Museum, p. 205; Fig. **132**). Furthermore, the *apobates race*, in which a passenger in armor leapt

66. *Clay tokens stamped with the name of Pheidon, the hipparch in Lemnos, who was responsible for training cavalry recruits in the Agora, 4th century B.C.*

on and off a swiftly moving chariot, continued to take place in the Agora, as we know from inscriptions, at least as late as the 2nd century B.C.; according to Athenian tradition this daring event was the oldest in the roster of the Panathenaic games. The sculpted base of a victory monument for this contest has been found below the Eleusinion (Museum, p. 208).

With the construction of the Panathenaic Stadium outside the city walls in the third quarter of the 4th century B.C. most of the athletic events were undoubtedly transferred from the Agora to that better appointed setting.

The festival and the procession continued into late antiquity. Himerios, who lived and taught in Athens in the 4th century A.D., gives a vivid vignette of the Panathenaic ship that carried Athena's new robe (*peplos*) to the Acropolis and of "the Dromos which, descending from above, straight and smooth, divides the stoas extending along it on either side, in which Athenians and the others buy and sell" (*Orat.* III, 12).

Descending again into the main excavation we turn right.

38, 39. The Temple and Altar of Ares* (Fig. 67)

The large rectangular area now covered with crushed stone between the Altar of the Twelve Gods (Plan, **31**) and the Odeion (Plan, **41**) represents the solid foundation podium of the Temple of Ares, identified as such by Pausanias (I, 8.4). Ares, god of war, was one of the first divinities worshipped in Athens and was associated with Theseus' defeat of the Amazons. The temple is dated to the third quarter of the 5th century B.C.; a close study of the fragments from the marble superstructure which came to light around the foundations has shown that it was almost a twin of the Temple of Hephaistos on the hill above and was possibly designed by the same architect. The blocks of the temple foundations are best seen at its east end, while some of the architectural marbles are arranged at the west end of the building. They include step and wall blocks, column drums, triglyph blocks and a restored cornice block. These stones bear carefully cut mason's marks which indicated the exact position of each within the building. East of the temple and on its axis is the

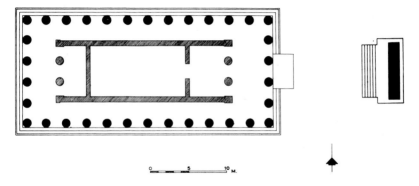

67. *Restored plan of the Doric temple of Ares, 5th century B.C., moved into the Agora in Roman times.*

foundation of a large marble altar, undoubtedly connected with the temple.

The central akroterion from the apex of the east front of the temple (now in the National Museum) portrays a youthful female figure without wings. A number of lovely figures in relief (Museum, p. 206) were also found in the vicinity of the temple, chiefly toward its east end. A statue of Athena, possibly the one seen by Pausanias in the temple, came to light south of the building (Museum, p. 206).

Fragments of a delicately carved marble sima from the Temple of Poseidon at Sounion have been found in the environs of the Ares Temple. The sima was presumably salvaged for reuse on the Ares Temple in its new location.

The style of the surviving architectural fragments fixes the date of the original construction of the temple in the 430's B.C.; the altar was added about a century later. The letter forms of the mason's marks, however, are of the Augustan period, as is also the latest pottery found beneath the temple foundations. The conclusion is inescapable that the temple, together with its altar, was transplanted toward the end of the 1st century B.C. Where the building originally stood has been much debated. Temple and altar were probably moved on the order of the Emperor Augustus, whose adopted son Gaius Caesar is honored in an inscription as "the New Ares."

40. Sacred Repository by the Panathenaic Way* (Figs. 68-69)

Between the Altar of Ares and the Panathenaic Way we look down into a modern stone-lined pit at an underground repository consisting of a stone wellcurb resting on and surrounded by large reused blocks of poros. This little cylindrical chamber was originally closed by means of a stopper cut from an old Doric capital and secured by iron clamps (now in the Museum storerooms). When the installation was first made, the top of the stopper was buried to a depth of 0.55 m. (about two feet). Although the pit had been rifled in antiquity, enough of the contents remained to suggest its purpose. The material was evidently of a votive nature, comprising such things as figurines of horses, chariot groups, rectangular plaques for suspension and shields, all made of terracotta and all appropriate to the worship of

68. Sacred Repository by the Panathenaic Way, 5th century B.C.

69. *Small finds from the Sacred Repository.*

heroes. The offerings had been made in the 7th and 6th centuries B.C.; they were gathered up and buried in the 5th century. It appears probable that the objects had first been dedicated to the heroic dead in one of the many early tombs in the area; the tomb or sanctuary may have been disturbed accidentally in the 5th century, after which the old offerings were piously reburied in the stone container.

117

41. Palace (?)* and Odeion of Agrippa* (Figs. 9, 70-75)

These two large structures, situated south of the Temple of Ares, are closely interrelated. The earlier of the two, the Odeion or Concert Hall, itself preserves the evidence of two periods of construction, but it is in large part overlaid by the later Palace with which we may begin.

At the north rise four massive pedestals belonging to the Palace. On the north face of the westernmost pier is a set of plans of the building. Made of reused material, the pedestals now support three colossal figures (Fig. 70); of a fourth figure, numerous fragments, including

70. *Giant from Phase II of the Odeion, mid-2nd century A.D., reused as the facade of the "Palace", 5th century A.D.*

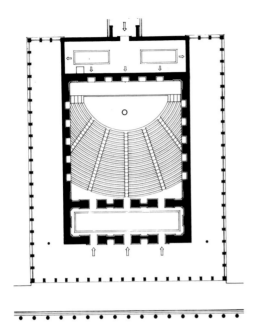

71. Plan of the Odeion,
Phase I,
late 1st century B.C.

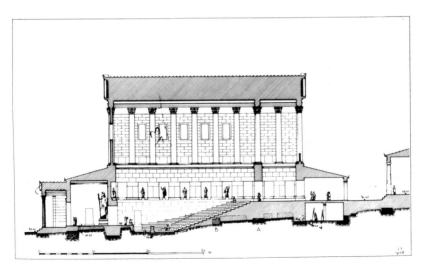

72. Cross-section of the Odeion, Phase I.

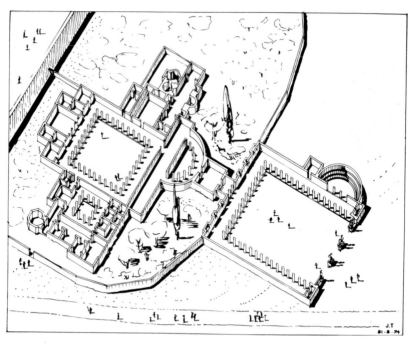

73. Perspective view of the "Palace", early 5th century A.D.,
seen from the NE. The giants are at the lower right.

the head, have been found (Museum, p. 197). Originally there were
six figures, two on each of the middle piers and one in each lateral
position. These statues, conspicuous among the monuments of the
Agora, were investigated by the Greek Archaeological Society in the
19th century, when the structure became known as the "Stoa of the
Giants"; the two fallen westernmost figures were re-erected at the
same time. Only one of the figures, the easternmost, is actually a
Giant in the Greek sense of the term, with his legs ending in serpents'
tails; the other two are Tritons, their human bodies ending in fishes'
tails. On the front of the marble base of each figure is carved in relief
an olive tree with a serpent twined around the trunk.

The figures in their present position belong to the monumental
facade of a very large building complex constructed soon after 400

120

74. *Model of the Odeion, Phase I, seen from the NW, late 1st century B.C.*

75. *North facade of the Odeion, mid-2nd century A.D.,
with addition of giants and titans.*

A.D.; it covered the ruins of the Odeion and much ground beside, as far south as South Stoa II. This structure has the characteristic features of a large public residence or palace, with numerous rooms, bathing facilities, courts and gardens. It may have served as the seat of a governor or the like. The complex was abandoned in the 6th century A.D.

Beyond the Giants and Tritons lay a great rectangular courtyard whose walls, built of rough stone and cement, may be traced above the remains of the Odeion. Further south is a rectangular lobby and a semicircular corridor leading to a second large courtyard which was flanked on the west by a bathing establishment and on the east by a complex of rooms grouped around a third court. These can best be seen on the way through the East Building and Middle Stoa (p. 176 ff.). The basement storey of the eastern range of rooms in this southeastern complex is comparatively well preserved and illustrates the characteristic combination of brick and rubble stone masonry of the period. Some of the architectural members from the upper rooms of this part of the building are of fine workmanship and suggest that we have here a suite of some importance, perhaps connected with administration. From the southeast and southwest corners of the great courtyard spring long walls, presumably to enclose gardens.

The Odeion, which had originally occupied the site of the main courtyard of the Palace, was built about 15 B.C. on the axis of the Agora in the area which until then had been part of the open square. It was the gift of M. Vipsanius Agrippa, the minister and son-in-law of the Emperor Augustus, and was thus also known as the "theatre in the Kerameikos called the Agrippeion." In the original plan the main entrance for spectators was at the south, from the terrace of the Middle Stoa, while the north facade had only a small portico which gave access to the scene building (Figs. **72, 74**).

The orchestra of the Odeion, which is slightly less than a semicircle, is paved with slabs of varicolored marble. At the east, one marble seat of the lowest row is preserved and traces of other rows were found. The auditorium, with a seating capacity of about one thousand, had a span of 25 meters and was originally roofed without interior supports; this is one of the boldest ventures in roofing known from the ancient world. The stage, which was decorated with an ornamental front composed of alternating marble slabs and Herms

(Museum, p. 197), and the scene building have been walled around with modern masonry to conserve them.

To east, west and south the auditorium was bordered by a two-storeyed portico, the lower storey being a simple basement, the upper an outward-facing balcony from which citizens might look down upon the square. In the southern part may be distinguished the walls and some column stumps of the lower storey. Various architectural members belonging to the building have been discovered: a large Corinthian capital from the building was found in 1891 during excavations for the Athens-Peiraeus Railway along the north edge of the Agora; it now stands on the terrace of the Middle Stoa to the south of the Odeion.

The Odeion was seriously damaged around the middle of the 2nd century A.D. when the roof of the auditorium collapsed. It was rebuilt almost immediately, but a cross-wall was inserted which reduced the seating capacity by about one half. The north facade was completely remodeled at this time. The small porch was removed and the scene building was turned into a portico. The Giants and Tritons, originally three of each, were set up as supports for the architrave of the portico, and other sculptural ornament was added (Fig. **70**). The torsos of the Tritons were copied from the Poseidon of the Parthenon west pediment; the Giant follows the type of the Hephaistos of the east pediment. Two draped seated figures, probably portraits of philosophers, which formed part of the sculptural ornament, have been set up to mark the line of the Odeion facade at this time. This rebuilding may be dated to shortly after the visit of Pausanias, who apparently saw the building in its first form, that of a normal odeion. References in Philostratos indicate that in its later form the building was used as a lecture hall.

The Odeion was destroyed by fire in 267 A.D. Most of the blocks were carried off to the east a few years later to be reused in the Post-Herulian Wall, but some bulky pieces not useful as building material were left behind. About 400 A.D., by which time the Athenians had again ventured out beyond the narrow confines of the Post-Herulian fortification, the Palace was constructed in this area. The colossal figures, salvaged from the debris of the Odeion, were moved a short distance to the north of their original positions and were re-erected to adorn the new facade.

123

42. Monument Bases East of the Odeion

The triangular area to the east of the Odeion is thickly strewn with foundations for monuments both large and small. Those toward the south were obviously placed in relation to the terrace wall of the Middle Stoa. A closely set series of small bases must have been aligned with the Panathenaic Way in its final course. The three large bases toward the northern apex of the triangle appear to have taken their alignment from an earlier course of the same road before it was moved eastward by the construction of the Middle Stoa. One of these large bases, the second from the north, is of particular interest since it has the form of a tomb: the joints of the masonry are pointed on the exterior to keep water out, and the roof of the chamber was supported on stone beams. This was conceivably the tomb of some distinguished person who was given the rare honor of burial beneath the Agora.

The many inscribed bases for individual statues which have been set up on either side of the Panathenaic Way in this area were recovered by the 19th century excavators from the Post-Herulian Wall at the south end of the Stoa of Attalos. Many of the statues probably stood originally alongside the road between the classical and the Roman Agora (p. 135). Dating from the 2nd and 3rd centuries A.D., they record honors paid to individuals by the Athenian state.

The stone water channel bordering the road in this area was laid in the 2nd century B.C., and the present surface of the roadway was formed at that time.

43. Monopteros* (Fig. 76)

West of the Stoa of Attalos in its northern part is a circular building some eight meters in diameter dating from the middle of the 2nd century A.D. Three of its decorated cornice blocks survive, along with many fragments from its column shafts of mottled green marble. The ring of eight columns supported a brick dome, one of the eariest known in Greece. There was no wall, hence our building was a "monopteros." This small, colorful building may have sheltered the statue of some divinity.

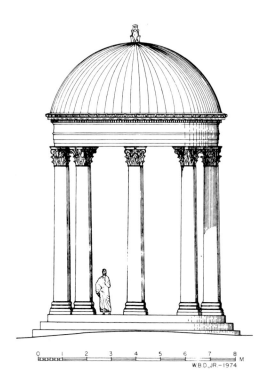

76. Monopteros,
2nd century A.D.,
restored view.

44. Early Buildings beneath the Stoa of Attalos* (Figs. 77-79)

Deep beneath the north half of the Stoa of Attalos and extending both to east and west of the Stoa are the foundations of a series of public buildings, most of which have been identified as law courts. The identification is based on the discovery among their ruins of various bronze articles known to have been used in the courts, notably a group of six ballots which still lay on the floor in one of the rooms (Fig. 78; Museum, p. 245).

The earliest structures of the series, dating from the late 5th and 4th centuries, consisted of unroofed enclosures in which presumably the large juries assembled (Fig. 77). In the late 4th century B.C. this old complex made way for a single large building, the Square Peristyle, a cloister-like structure with colonnades on all four sides of a central

125

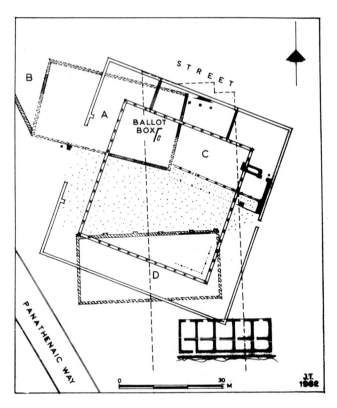

77. *Plan of early buildings (lawcourts?) under
the north end of the Stoa of Attalos.*

court (Fig. **79**). This building was never finished, but it was carried to
the point at which much of it could be used, and it did in fact continue
in use until demolished to make way for the Stoa of Attalos in the 2nd
century B.C. The courts presumably met in the deep porches.
These buildings have for the most part been reburied for their better
protection, but parts have been kept accessible in the basement of the
Stoa of Attalos; for admission apply at the Museum Office.
A small structure comprising five pairs of rooms on an east to west
line stood for a few years between the demolition of the Square
Peristyle and the start of work on the Stoa of Attalos; its foundations
underlie the central part of the Stoa. The plan of the building is

78. "Ballot box" as found, with ballets in situ, under the Stoa of Attalos, ca. 400 B.C.

appropriate for shops. Quantities of cooking vessels found in the rear corridor indicated that there were also eating facilities.*
Numerous tombs of the Mycenaean and Protogeometric periods came to light in front of and under the Stoa of Attalos; these have been reburied. One of the Protogeometric graves from this area is exhibited in the Museum (p. 226).

45. Bema and Donor's Monument*

Almost on the axis of the Stoa of Attalos and in front of its terrace wall are two large rectangular foundations. The western has been

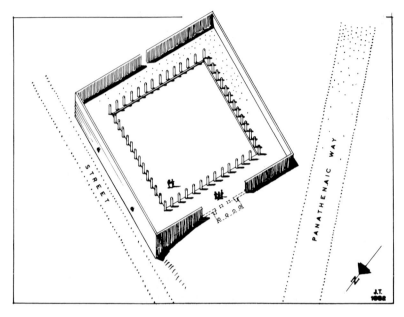

79. *Square peristyle under the Stoa of Attalos, ca. 300 B.C.*

identified as a *bema*, or speaker's platform, on the evidence of
Athenaeus who relates that

> *(Athenion), mounting the Bema which had been built for the*
> *Roman generals in front of the Stoa of Attalos and standing*
> *upon it, looked at the crowd gathered all around. Then lifting*
> *his eyes, he said, "Men of Athens..."*

This scene took place in 88 B.C., so that construction of the Bema
must be dated between that time and the erection of the Stoa of
Attalos ca. 150 B.C. Steps led up to the top of the platform at its

80. Stoa of Attalos, mid-2nd century B.C., reconstruction (1953-1956).

129

northwest and southwest corners. The concentration of monument bases along the Panathenaic Way opposite the Bema indicates that this was another of the most frequented parts of the Agora.

The second monument, set close against the terrace wall of the Stoa, is contemporary with that building; it presumably honored the donor, Attalos II. More than one hundred blocks of its superstructure have been recovered from the Post-Herulian Wall; they have been stacked along the Panathenaic Way to the west of the base. It was a tall pedestal mostly of Hymettian marble, almost identical with the "Monument of Agrippa" at the entrance to the Acropolis. On top of it stood a life-size four-horse chariot group of bronze at about the level of the second storey of the Stoa. Many years later, as an inscription from the monument records, the Athenian people rededicated the monument to the Emperor Tiberius just as they rededicated the similar Hellenistic monument in front of the Propylaia to Agrippa. This type of monument seems to have been popular. Similar chariot groups probably stood on the base now built into the tower close by the Library of Pantainos (Plan, **48**), and on the foundations still visible at the northeast corner of the Odeion (Plan, **41**).

To both north and south of the Donor's Monument is an almost continuous row of bases for other sculpted groups which once enlivened the terrace wall of the Stoa.

46. Stoa of Attalos* (Figs. **80-84**)

We continue south toward the entrance to the Stoa of Attalos. Let us pause a moment in front of the dedicatory inscription which has been set up at the foot of the Stoa terrace wall. Carved in large letters, once painted red, the inscription occupied a prominent place on the architrave above the lower storey of columns. Although fragmentary, it gives us the name of the donor: "King Attalos, son of King Attalos and of Queen Apollonis," i.e. Attalos II, King of Pergamon 159-138 B.C. Like the scions of several other royal families of the Mediterranean world in the Hellenistic period, Attalos had studied in the schools of Athens as a young man; upon ascending the throne he made this splendid gift to the city of his alma mater.

On our left as we turn in from the Panathenaic Way to enter the Stoa

81. South end of Stoa of Attalos, before reconstruction.

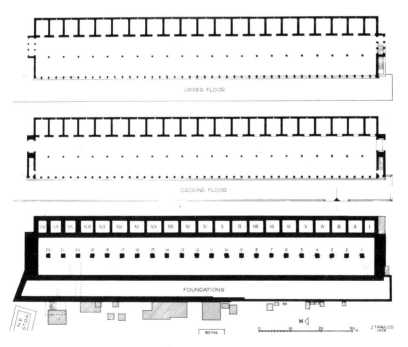

UPPER FLOOR

GROUND FLOOR

FOUNDATIONS

BEMA

N

J. TRAVLOS
1958

82. Plans of the Stoa of Attalos.

83. Cut-away model of the Stoa of Attalos, showing interior arrangment.

84. Interior of the ground floor of the the Stoa of Attalos, looking north.

stands a massive pillar of Pentelic marble, 2.51 m. high, triangular in cross section. It once supported a bronze tripod. According to the inscription on the side of the base (*I.G.* II^2, 3114) the monument commemorated a victory in choral singing won by the tribe Kekropis in a year toward the end of the first century A.D. It was paid for by a joint subscription on the part of both the sponsors (*choregoi*) and the participants. The monument speaks: "I distribute glory to the contributors in proportion to my debt to each." The base was found by the excavators of the last century standing in the southeast corner of the Stoa of Attalos.

After undergoing various slight alterations in the course of four centuries the Stoa shared in the destruction of 267 A.D.; note the effects of fire on the inner face of the south end wall. A few years later it was incorporated in the Post-Herulian Wall, at which time the facade and all the columns were dismantled to be used in strengthening the rear part of the building. The back rooms continued in use into Turkish times. The excavation of the building, having been carried out at intervals through the 19th century by the Greek Archaeological Society, was completed by the American School. In the years 1953 to 1956 the Stoa was rebuilt primarily to serve as the Agora Museum (see below, p. 191).

The building is an excellent example of the fully developed type of stoa. On each of its two storeys a two-aisled colonnade was backed by a row of 21 rooms which served chiefly as shops. A broad terrace ran the whole length of the building, supported on a retaining wall which, as we have seen, provided a backdrop for a close-set row of sculpted monuments.

The chief function of the Stoa was to provide a sheltered promenade for informal intercourse, which must also have assured its success as a shopping center. The shops were no doubt rented by the state to individual merchants so that the building would have served as a source of revenue as well as an ornament to the city. Note the adaptation of the Doric order for a stoa, a building designed for use by numerous people, unlike a temple. The columns are more widely spaced for easy access, and the lower third of each exterior column is left unfluted so as to prevent damage by people and goods passing in and out of the colonnade.

Enough of the walls and architectural members survived to make possible a detailed and certain restoration. Specimens of the various ancient members have been incorporated in the reconstruction, especially toward the south end of the building near the entrance. The restoration has been carried out in the same materials as the original: marble for the facade, columns and interior trim, limestone for the walls and terracotta tiles for the roof. The upper floor and the roof are now supported on beams of reinforced concrete enclosed in wooden shells which reproduce exactly the spacing and dimensions of the original beams of solid wood.

The building depended for effect on its overall proportions, on the pleasing differences in scale between the lower and upper orders, on the interesting play of light and shade and on the richness of its materials. Monotony was mitigated in various ways, notably by the employment of four different types of column capital: Doric outside below, richly carved and elongated Ionic outside above, canonical Ionic inside below and an adaptation of the Egyptian palm capital inside above.

Access to the upper floor was provided by an outside stairway set against either end of the building. The southern stairway was removed, however, around 100 A.D. to permit the widening of a street; it was replaced by an inside staircase set in the southernmost shop. This later arrangement has been reproduced in the reconstruction. Observe the evidence for the line of the original stairway on the outer face of the south wall of the Stoa. The space beneath the original staircase at each end of the building was utilized as an exedra or alcove around three sides of which ran a marble bench. The mouth of the alcove was arched: the first known example of a visible arch in an Athenian building.

The design of the wooden doors has been recovered from cuttings in the marble jambs and thresholds and from the analogy of surviving ancient tomb doors made of marble in imitation of wood. Observe the cuttings for shelving in the ancient parts of the walls of the southernmost two shops. In the south wall of the second shop are sockets for the ends of joists that supported a mezzanine floor inserted in the Roman period.

At the south end of the Stoa Terrace a small fountain has been installed in the place of a much larger fountain contemporary with the Stoa. The restored fountain and its benches form, as indicated by the inscribed stele set beside them, a memorial to Theodore Leslie Shear, Field Director of the Agora Excavations from their inception in 1931 until his death in 1945.

Photographs and drawings to illustrate the restoration of the Stoa are exhibited in the second room from the south on the ground floor. A model of the north end of the building stands on the upper floor toward the north end.

47. Street to the Roman Market Place* (Figs. 85, 86, 90)

We leave the Stoa through a doorway at its southwest corner and ascend a few modern steps to a small square. When the Library of Pantainos (Plan, 48) was built (around 100 A.D.) the staircase at the south end of the Stoa and the exedra beneath were pulled down to make room for the realignment of the street running eastward from the Panathenaic Way to the Market of Caesar and Augustus, the Roman Agora. This street was not designed for wheeled traffic since it started with a flight of steps which led up to the paved level space between the Stoa and the Library of Pantainos. At the eastern end of this paved area stood an archway of which the threshold block and the lower parts of the piers remain. The archway was embellished with a small fountain, the water for which flowed through a bronze pipe set in the west face of the southern pier. The little square itself was paved with marble, and at the time of its formation the south end of the Stoa of Attalos was revetted with marble. A large monument stood at the southwest corner of the square facing the Panathenaic Way. The substantial foundations of this base are partly obscured by a tower of the Post-Herulian fortification.

Starting from the arch at the southeast corner of the Stoa of Attalos, a marble-paved street headed directly toward the main entrance to the Market of Caesar and Augustus, the so-called Gate of Athena. A little short of that gateway, however, this east-west street was interrupted by a road descending from the south. Crossing this road one mounted a monumental stairway to reach the higher ground in front of the Gate of Athena (Fig. 88).

The main east-west street, about 10 meters in width, was bordered on the south by an Ionic colonnade of the Library of Pantainos, of which the stylobate and some column bases remain in place (Fig. 90). A

85. Stoa along
the street leading
to the Roman
market place, ca.
100 A.D.,
looking East.

marble gutter in front of the steps carried off rain water. The colonnade served as a common facade for twelve rooms that varied a good deal in size and shape. Most of the rooms were undoubtedly shops, but several have unusual features that imply other uses. The fifth from the west was particularly outstanding. Its floor and walls were revetted with marble; a long pedestal rose against its back wall; the column bases in the colonnade in front of the room were distinguished by square plinths. Reused at a late period in the front wall of the room is a base with an inscription recording the dedication of a statue of the Emperor Trajan (98-117 A.D.) by Herodes, father of the more familiar Herodes Atticus and chief priest of the cult of the Emperor. The room perhaps served as a shrine for the imperial cult.

86. Restored view of the street leading to the Roman market.

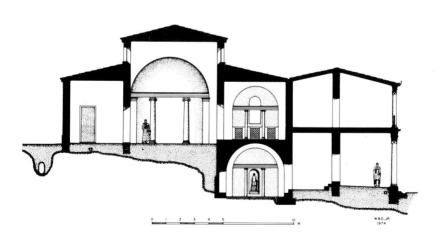

87. Cross-section of the Late Roman Building, incorporating the earlier Street Stoa, 5th century A.D.

Fortune has preserved the epistyle from the colonnade in front of the fourth room. An inscription on its face tells us that the People built and paid for the *plateia*, i.e. the broad street, out of their own revenues. The stoa on the south side of the street is to be dated around 100 A.D.; its construction is closely interlocked with that of the Library of Pantainos (Plan, **48**).

Deep beneath the remains of the stoa of Roman date lie the foundations of several earlier buildings dating from the end of the 5th and from the 4th centuries B.C. The plan of one, comprising a double row of rooms such as are commonly found in shop buildings, suggests the commercial use of this part of the city already in the classical period. The contents of a well abandoned in the early 4th century B.C. attest the existence of eating and drinking establishments as well as of local industries such as the working of bone and horn and the making of terracotta figurines.

The colonnade and related rooms suffered in the sack of 267 A.D., but extensive rebuilding took place in the early 5th century (Figs. **87-89**). From this period dates the suite of three prominent and well-preserved rooms behind the line of the old colonnade. One entered the series of communicating rooms through a doorway in the north wall of the middle room. The western room, with a marble floor, marble wall trim and wall niches for statues, was evidently the principal chamber. No clue has been found to the use of the rooms. At a higher level to the south are the remains of a large house-like building which once extended over the suite of semi-basement rooms. One can distinguish a colonnaded courtyard and a large apsidal room. The old colonnade bordering the street was at least partly restored in this period, with the addition of a second storey, as shown by the discovery of many members of a small upper Ionic order with cuttings for a parapet.

The subsequent history of the area is well documented by stratified deposits running down into the 8th century. This contrasts with the history of the region of the old Agora proper, which lay outside the Post-Herulian Wall; there one finds little evidence of habitation after the barbarian inroads of the 580's.

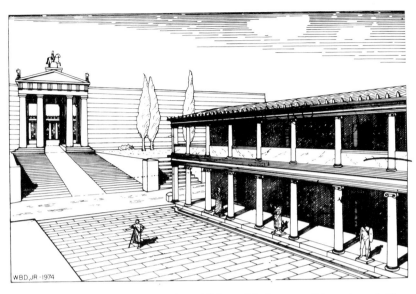

88. Elevation of Street Stoa with addition of 2nd storey, 5th century A.D.

89. Suite of basement rooms, early 5th century A.D.

139

48. Library of Pantainos* (Figs. **90, 91, 96**)

The next building to the south of the Stoa of Attalos was the Library of Pantainos. Little remains of earlier buildings on the site, but from the number of wine jars, drinking cups and cooking vessels found in wells one may infer the existence here, as in the area to the east, of taverna-like establishments as early as the 5th century B.C. The Library was almost completely demolished by the builders of the Post-Herulian Wall, which follows the line of the western colonnade of the Library at this point. The most important of the blocks incorporated into the fortification wall is the inscribed lintel of the main doorway of the Library (in the east face of the Wall, near the center). The inscription tells us that a certain Titus Flavius Pantainos, his son and his daughter, gave "the outer colonnades, the peristyle, the library with its books and all the furnishings at their own expense." The inscription may be dated close to the year 100 A.D. A second inscription found in the area contains regulations for the use of the Library (Museum, p. 238, Fig. **91**):

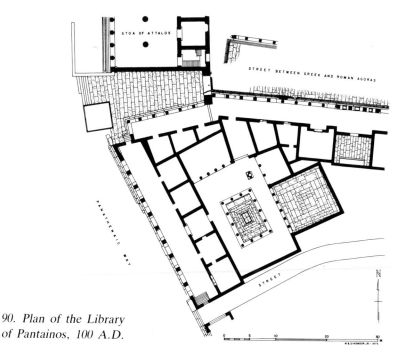

90. Plan of the Library of Pantainos, 100 A.D.

91. Library Rules,
ca. 100 A.D.

No book is to be taken out since we have sworn an oath. (The library) is open from the first until the sixth hour.

The main element of the building was a large square room at the extreme east end, its floor and walls once revetted with marble. Its walls are preserved only a little above floor level, but they were probably thick enough to have contained the cupboards in which the book rolls of papyrus and parchment would have been stored. This room faced westward through a row of columns onto a colonnaded courtyard: a pleasant place to stroll, to read or to reflect. This peristyle was bordered on north and west by rooms which probably had no connection with the Library as such, unless to add to its revenues by rental. Thus the suite of two rooms at the south end of the western range was certainly used as a sculptor's studio. The excavators came upon quantities of marble chips, emery for the polishing of marble and several pieces of sculpture.

The "outer colonnades" of the dedicatory inscription are readily recognized in the Ionic stoas which faced westward onto the Panathenaic Way and northward toward the Stoa of Attalos and along the east-west street. These more visible parts of the building were

141

executed in worked marble of very respectable quality, in striking contrast to the shabby rubble masonry of the inner walls.

An ancient library was commonly adorned with appropriate sculpture. It is tempting, therefore, to associate with the Library of Pantainos the personifications of the Iliad and Odyssey which were found nearby and which now stand in the Stoa of Attalos (Museum, p. 195); but no appropriate pedestal has yet been found within the building.

49. Post-Herulian Wall* (Fig. 92)

Having traversed the Library of Pantainos from north to south we turn west across the line of the Post-Herulian Wall. After the Herulian raid in 267 A.D., the Athenians, seeing that the Roman armies were no longer able to protect the frontiers and that they themselves were unable to defend the long circuit of their ancient walls, built a new and much shorter inner circuit. To hasten the work they used blocks from buildings that had been destroyed or badly damaged in the barbarian raid.

Starting at the so-called Beule Gate, near the present entrance to the Acropolis, this wall follows the line of the Panathenaic Way down the hill, past the Eleusinion and the Library of Pantainos, to the Stoa of Attalos. In this stretch there were three gates, each set in the line of an earlier street. The shops of the Stoa were left standing, and their front wall, some 12 meters or 39 feet high, was reinforced along its west face by means of a supplementary wall built of blocks drawn both from the Stoa itself and from other buildings in the Agora. In the Stoa of Attalos area there were three towers, a huge one at the north, a smaller one near the middle built from blocks of the Donor's Monument and Bema, and a third at the south. All three have now been demolished. The tower at the south end of the Stoa was one of a pair flanking a gateway and was built almost entirely of inscribed monuments from the Agora. It was later converted into a chapel of the Panagia Pyrgiotissa (Our Lady of the Tower) and was demolished about 1860. The tower at the south side of the gate still stands.

From the north end of the Stoa of Attalos the fortification wall turned east (a section of it is visible behind the Stoa) and continued to the Library of Hadrian which it incorporated as it had the Stoa of

92. *Late Roman fortification wall (ca. 280 A.D.), built of reused material
after the destruction of the Herulians in 267 A.D.
Note Doric column drums at left, from SW Temple (fig. 35).*

Attalos. Beyond the Library of Hadrian it ran east for about two
hundred meters, then turned south and may have joined the Acropolis circuit again, though no further trace has been found.
This wall has been known to archaeologists for many years. Opinions
as to its date have ranged from the mid-3rd century A.D. (i.e.
Valerian) to the 15th century (Frankish). Actually, as the current
excavations have shown, construction was begun after the disaster of
267 A.D. and was still in progress at least as late as 280 A.D. Various
wealthy Athenians of the period were made responsible for the
different sections. An inscription found near the east gate (*I.G.* II^2,
5199) gives the credit for its building to Claudius Illyrius. Another
(*I.G.* II^2, 5200), found by the gate at the south end of the Stoa of
Attalos, has been translated by Christopher Wordsworth:

143

Nor Cyclopean hand with labour strong
This pile did raise, nor Amphionian song.

The wall shows evidence of repairs (hence the various dates suggested for its construction) and seems to have remained in use until Turkish times. The best preserved stretch of the fortification now visible is that just south of the Stoa of Attalos where there are two towers and the curtain between them. The wall, with an average thickness of about 3-1/2 meters, had well-built outer and inner faces enclosing a more loosely packed core. It consisted entirely of reused materials: architecture, sculpture and inscriptions. Note a pair of Ionic columns of white marble extracted from the wall in 1959 and now laid in front of it; a third column of the same series has been set up in the Museum (p. 215). The most characteristic is a series of Doric columns just slightly smaller than those of the Temple of Hephaistos. A bottom and top drum and a capital from one of these columns have been assembled at the northeast corner of the Southeast Temple; other drums remain in the wall. Style and quality of workmanship point to a date in the latter part of the 5th century B.C. These columns have been shown to derive from a building at Thorikos on the east coast of Attica; they were presumably removed and brought to Peiraeus by sea in the 1st century A.D. when Thorikos was already desolate, and reused in the Southwest Temple (p. 72; Fig. 35).

50. Late Roman Water Mill and Oil Mill* (Fig. **93**)

A little to the west of the Post-Herulian Wall are the remains of a water channel built of rubble masonry. One can follow this channel northward for about thirty meters to its present end near a slot-like structure about five meters long and four meters deep. In the west wall of this pit is an arched aperture which opens into an adjoining room. These are the remains of a water mill. The channel carried the water necessary to turn the wheel which revolved in the slot or race. The axle of the wheel was housed in the socket and passed through the opening in order to turn the millstones which then ground the flour in the neighboring room. The wheel was of the "overshot" variety, as the heavy lime deposit north of the axle line makes clear. The mill mechanism seems very close to that described by Vitruvius

93. *Perspective drawing of the water mill, 5th/6th century A.D.*

(X, 4-5), even though the Agora mill is some centuries later. Several of the disc-like millstones, much worn, were found in the room, together with hundreds of small bronze coins which had fallen through cracks in its wooden floor. The mill was in operation from soon after 450 to about 580 A.D., and is one of the earliest water mills in Europe of which we have detailed knowledge. This was only one in a chain of three mills turned in succession by the same water. The water came down from the south in an aqueduct. First it turned a mill of which the wheel pit was sunk through the porch of the Southeast Temple (Plan, **52**). Continuing northward the water next operated the well-preserved mill that we have just visited. From here the water was conveyed in a northwesterly direction in a channel at first underground and then supported on arches to supply the third

145

mill which was totally destroyed by the construction of the railway in 1891.

On the other side of the Panathenaic Way from the water mill are the remains of a contemporary mill for making olive oil. Two elements have survived. A massive drum of volcanic stone formed the lower part of a grinding machine in which the olives were reduced to pulp. Nearby lies a marble block on which the bags of pulp were piled and then subjected to pressure, no doubt by means of a beam anchored at one end; the oil flowed into a channel surrounding the top of the block and thence into a container.

51. Southeast Stoa* (Figs. 94-96)

South of the Library of Pantainos, and separated from it by a narrow street, stood another public building that faced on the Panathenaic Way. At present only the front of the building is accessible: a continuous deep porch of the Ionic order. Excavations made in 1965 in the garden of the large 19th century house to the east (believed to have belonged to the Colettis family which gave Greece an early Prime Minister, 1844-1847) revealed the plan of the rear part: a simple row of eleven one-roomed shops. The outer face of the Post-Herulian Wall rests directly on the stylobate of the earlier building, but one can easily recognize tumbled parts of all the elements of the facade: the square plinths and round bases on which the columns stood, the smooth shafts and the capitals of the Ionic columns, the epistyle and cornice. Coming from the Panathenaic Way one normally entered the porch of the building near its midpoint where the level of the floor coincided with the level of the sloping street. In this prominent part the stylobate is of marble rather than of poros, which is used in the rest of the stylobate. Because of the sloping terrain the part of the colonnade to the south of the entrance rested at a level several feet above that of the northern part. Stairs in the middle and at both ends of the porch enabled one to traverse its full length and to continue down into the corresponding porch of the Library of Pantainos. The building dates from the middle of the 2nd century A.D.

If the light is right one may distinguish the graffiti on the shaft of a column of the Southeast Stoa that stands upright in the area of its porch: the profiles of human faces, hunting scenes, Herms, sundials.

146

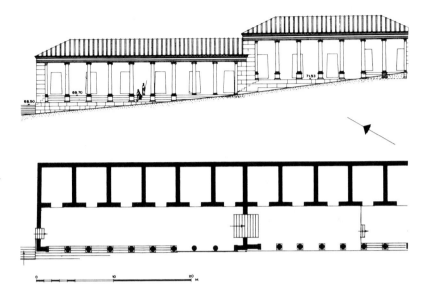

94. *Plan and elevation of the Southeast Stoa, 2nd century A.D.*

52. Southeast Temple* (Figs. 96, 97)

The paving of the Panathenaic Way, dating from the 2nd century A.D., is especially well preserved in front of the Southeast Stoa; note the deep wheel ruts. On the west side of the street opposite the Southeast Stoa are the slight remains of a temple of the early Roman period. The plan comprised a cella and a north porch of eight columns looking down the Panathenaic Way. Near the middle of the cella is a mass of rough masonry that formed the core of a large statue base. Scattered bedding blocks attest to a floor of marble stabs in the front part of the cella. The side and back walls of the cella were of rubble masonry once covered with stucco. The foundations for the porch, on the other hand, were massively built of reused squared blocks.

95. Graffiti and doodles on a column of the Southeast Stoa.

Certain elements from the superstructure of the porch have been recognized among the reused material in the adjacent part of the Post-Herulian Wall. These include Ionic columns of a temple of Athena of the 5th century B.C. which originally stood at Cape Sounion.

148

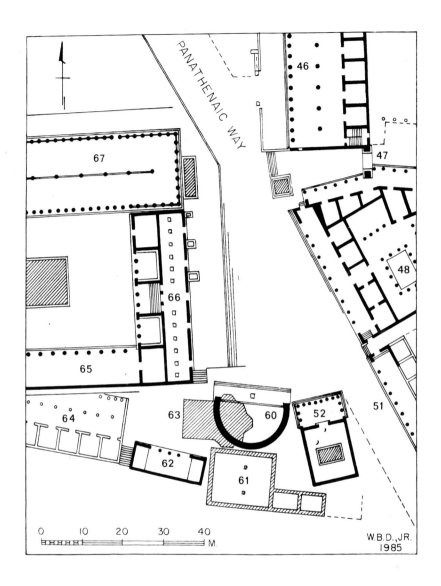

96. Southeast corner of the Agora.
46. Stoa of Attalos; 47. Street to Roman Market; 48. Library of Pantainos;
51. Southeast Stoa; 52. Southeast Temple; 60. Nymphaion; 61. Mint; 62.
Southeast Fountainhouse; 63. Church of Holy Apostles; 64. South Stoa I;
65. South Stoa II; 66. East Building; 67. Middle Stoa.

149

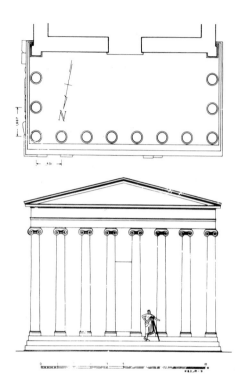

97. Restoration of Ionic architectural elements from Temple of Athena at Sounion (5th century B.C.) reused in the Southeast Temple in the Agora, late 1st century A.D.

Within the cella of the temple the excavators came upon three fragments of a colossal marble statue, a heavily draped standing female figure which undoubtedly stood on the great pedestal. The two larger fragments are now sheltered by a roof to the south of the temple. The stance and drapery style are close to those of the Caryatids of the Erechtheion though the scale is twice as great. The Agora statue may be recognized as an original work of the late 5th century B.C.

Long after the temple was destroyed and its stonework plundered by the builders of the Post-Herulian Wall, the wheel pit of a water mill was set deep down in the area of its porch. This was the uppermost in the chain of three water mills, the best preserved of which we have just encountered.

53-55. Agora to Eleusinion

The Eleusinion and the various monuments on the north slope of the Areopagus are outside the fenced enclosure of the Agora Excavations and may be visited free of charge. The visit, however, is recommended only to specialists.

The Panathenaic Way continues upward with a gentle slope to issue from the southeast corner of the Agora. Just beyond this point the Way is crossed by the road that skirted the south side of the Agora and led into the eastern parts of the city. This roadway was respected by the builders of the Post-Herulian Wall, who left a gateway on its line. At the south side of the gate, and close against the face of the fortification wall, are the remains of a small fenced sanctuary (Plan, **53**) sacred no doubt to some divinity of the crossroads such as Hekate.*

The deep wheel ruts which mark the Panathenaic Way as it leaves the Agora practically cease at the road intersection: most wheeled traffic evidently turned to east or west on the crossroad. South of the crossroad the paved Way continues at a steeper gradient.

In the southeast angle between the Panathenaic Way and the east-west street are slight remains of what appears to have been another modest sanctuary (Plan, **54**). The enclosure wall, of conglomerate, dates from the Hellenistic period. One round and several rectangular monument bases have come to light within the enclosure. The whole area has been very much disturbed, and no clue has been found for the identification of the cult. In the Roman period, presumably after the cult had been abandoned, a row of rooms, four large and one small, was inserted into the west side of the area; only the concrete foundations remain. These are most probably shops.

To the west the Panathenaic Way is bordered by the remains of an aqueduct (Plan, **55**). The massive concrete piers must have supported arches of stone masonry on which would have rested the water channel at a level sufficiently high to assure an effective head of water at the ornamental fountain house (*nymphaion*) inside the southeast corner of the Agora (Plan, **60**). The upward course of the aqueduct may be followed to a square settling basin and thence eastward beneath the Panathenaic Way on a line parallel to the back wall of the stoa that closed the south side of the Eleusinion (Plan, **56**); in this stretch the water was carried in an underground channel vaulted in brick. The source of the water was presumably the Hadrianic water system completed in 140 A.D. The stonework of the aqueduct bordering the Panathenaic Way was stripped away to be reused in the Post-Herulian Wall in the late 3rd century. In the 5th century this section of the aqueduct was rebuilt in a crude style to supply the needs of the new establishments which had now arisen in the Agora; some of the underpinning of this later period may be seen above the concrete piers of the earlier.

56. Eleusinion* (Fig. 98)

The sanctuary called the Eleusinion was an Athenian branch of the great shrine of Demeter and Kore at Eleusis to which the initiated made their pilgrimage each year along the Sacred Way. It was ranked with the Parthenon and the Theseion among the most venerable sanctuaries of Athens. Each year, on the day following the celebration of the Mysteries, the Council of 500 held a session in the Eleusinion. The spacious sanctuary was protected by a strong wall; for this reason it was one of the few places apart from the Acropolis not to be occupied by refugees in the early years of the Peloponnesian War (Thucydides II, 17.1).

After long speculation the site of the sanctuary has been fixed by excavations to a location at the east side of the Panathenaic Way on the north slope of the Acropolis, about halfway between the Stoa of Attalos and the Propylaia. Various discoveries combine with the evidence of Pausanias and other literary sources to make the identification certain. Inscribed dedications to the Eleusinian deities have been found on the site, as well as deposits of ritual vases particularly sacred to Demeter and Kore; these had been dedicated to the goddesses and later were carefully buried by the priests when room had to be made in the shrine for more. From this area have come to light many pieces of the stelai recording the sale of property confiscated from Alkibiades and others accused of mutilating the Herms and parodying the Eleusinian Mysteries; the stelai are known to have stood in the Eleusinion. The eastern limit of the sanctuary has not yet been excavated.

Near the middle of the excavated area is a rectangular building with

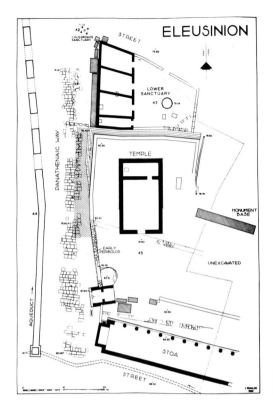

98. *Restored plan of the Eleusinion, as excavated.*

one large room and behind it a smaller chamber, presumably an *adyton* or inner sanctum. The entrance to the main room was probably through its south end. Because of the steeply sloping site the north end of the building was supported on a massive foundation of Kara limestone very carefully worked. During construction the plan was altered and the building was extended eastward. The style of the masonry and the evidence from stratification point to a date near the beginning of the 5th century B.C.

The south end of this building disturbed the north wall of an "Early Peribolos" dating from about the middle of the 6th century B.C. The best preserved part of this early enclosure is a length of massive wall of Acropolis limestone along its west side. No trace of a temple has come to light which could be associated with this early period of the sanctuary, but a sprinkling of primitive terracotta figurines and miniature vases found in the area may have been votive offerings. In the latter part of the 5th century B.C. a long narrow pedestal was erected to the east of the temple. It conceivably supported the series of ten or more marble stelai on which was recorded the sale of the property of those who profaned the Mysteries of Demeter in 415 B.C. In the second half of the 4th century B.C. a marble gateway was built at the southwest corner of the sanctuary to take the place of an earlier entrance. Inside the entrance are a number of monument bases now stripped to their lowest foundations. Probably also in the 4th century the retaining walls to the north and west of the temple were thickened, and steps were constructed outside the enclosure wall from which spectators might watch the passing processions.

In the early Roman period the sanctuary was extended southward to admit a colonnade that faced northward across the open area. The foundations for its columns and much of its back wall remain, as does the bedding for a wall that delimited a terrace in front of the building. An east-west roadway bordering the south side of the Eleusinion separated the main sanctuary from a less well-defined area on a ledge in the rising hillside. Toward the southeast corner of this area are the ill-preserved remains of a small round structure of early Roman date made of reused blocks. The discovery of four small poros altars in the vicinity of the round structure suggests that we have to do with a sanctuary, perhaps one related to the Eleusinion proper (the altars are now on the terrace of the Stoa of Attalos); several of the deposits of ritual vases noted above were found within the limits of this area.

Pausanias, after describing a fountain house called the Ennea-krounos, continued (I, 14.1):

> There are two temples above the fountain house; one belongs to Demeter and Kore; in the other, that of Triptolemos, there is a statue of him.

After a digression on Triptolemos, Pausanias refers to "the sanctuary at Athens called the Eleusinion" and then again mentions the temple in which was the statue of Triptolemos. He was prevented by a dream, he tells us, from revealing more about the Eleusinion. This dream has not only deprived us of an account of the sanctuary but has also left uncertain the relationship between the two temples and the Eleusinion. It seems likely that the excavated temple is that of

Triptolemos, and that the main buildings of the Eleusinion still lie buried farther to the east.

57-59. The North Slope of the Areopagus

Those who have made their way up as far as the Eleusinion, and who have sturdy shoes, may wish to explore the north slope of the Areopagus. The excavation of this vast area has yielded little of interest for the classical period, but it has added much to some of the earliest and again to some of the latest chapters in the history of Athens.

Through the Mycenaean, Protogeometric and Geometric periods (14th - 8th centuries B.C.) the hillside was used as a burial ground. Particularly noteworthy were the large Mycenaean chamber tomb* of about 1400 B.C. opened in 1939 on the northeast shoulder of the Areopagus, and the richly furnished grave of a woman of the 9th century B.C. found in 1967 at the north foot of the hill. The crumbly nature of the rock has made it necessary to refill all the tombs, but the principal groups of grave furnishings are exhibited in the Museum (pp. 223 ff.).

From the 6th century B.C. onward habitation is attested. Throughout later antiquity, the hillside was a thickly settled residential area served by a main road that ran westward from the Eleusinion following the contours of the hillside. The long continuity of habitation has tended to obliterate the remains of earlier periods, but house plans of the 6th-5th centuries B.C. have been recovered in a block near the middle of the lower slope. The individual houses were modest both in scale and furnishings: two to eight rooms grouped informally around a small courtyard without porches.

More conspicuous and more readily intelligible are the remains of several large houses of late antiquity that can be reached easily by leaving the Panathenaic Way and proceeding westward from the Eleusinion. We pass on the right the exiguous remains of a number of shabby houses, some of which were occupied by marble workers in the 2nd and 3rd centuries A.D. Then we look down onto the foundations of a large house, the central element in which was a room with a semicircular apse toward the south (Plan, 57). To east and west were courtyards, that to the east having a complete peristyle

155

with a well in the middle of the court; rooms of various sizes, some twenty in all, were grouped around the courtyards. Farther to the west and lower down is another house of comparable plan. These were perhaps the residences of successful teachers (sophists) of the 4th and 5th centuries A.D., some of whom are reported to have provided lodgings in their own houses for their favorite pupils and to have done their teaching at home in well-appointed lecture rooms. On the other side of the road, and above the first house with the apsidal room are the recently uncovered remains of another extensive residence (Plan, **58**; Figs. **99-101**).* Already in the 4th century B.C. the site had been occupied by a substantial house, but the remains which one now sees belong chiefly to the 4th and 5th centuries A.D. This house also boasted two courtyards, and it had besides a bathing area with hot and cold rooms. The visitor to the site will be chiefly interested, however, in a curious apartment opening off the south side of the main colonnaded courtyard of the house (Fig. **102**). Descending by a flight of steps flanked by columns one entered an apsidal room that once glowed with the rich colors of a mosaic floor and marble-revetted walls. The mosaic, in an elaborate geometric design, is confined to a broad Pi-shaped border in the rectangular part of the room. The apse, toward the east, was covered with a half dome, and in its floor was a semicircular stepped basin. Water was supplied by a natural spring farther to the east, the flow from which had been exploited by the property owners in various ways for centuries before. The room was probably a triclinium, a cool retreat for summer dining with couches placed on the mosaic. We should have expected the panel within the mosaic borders to have been occupied by a mythological scene likewise done in mosaic, and this was probably the original arrangement. The panel is now filled with *opus sectile* of coarse workmanship in which the central motif is a cross executed in deep red stone (Fig. **103**).

It may be that the cross is symbolic and an indication that the owners of the house were now Christian. Conversion, or a change of ownership from pagan to Christian, is attested at the same time by the treatment accorded a rich collection of sculpture which had previously adorned the house. A number of pieces, including a head of Nike, a statue of Herakles, a bust of Helios, a bust of the Emperor Antoninus Pius and three private portrait busts, were deposited in

156

99. Restored plan of the Omega House, on the slopes of the Areopagos, 4th century A.D.

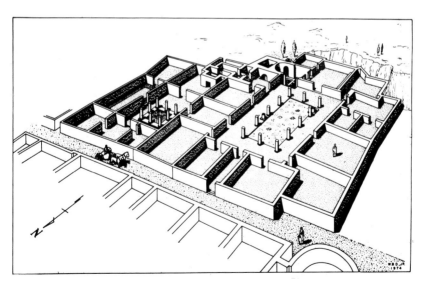

100. Partially restored perspective of the Omega house, from the NW. 4th-6th centuries A.D.

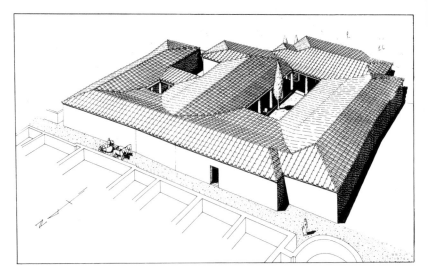

101. Fully restored perspective of the Omega house.

102. Pool and arched niches of the Omega house, from the West.

158

two wells, which were then closed, while on a votive relief which remained above ground the heads of the pagan divinities were deliberately mutilated (Museum, p. 201). All this happened in the early years of the 6th century A.D., whereas the house itself was not destroyed until the Slavic invasion of the 580's.

To the student of classical Athens the Areopagus means above all the meeting place of the Council of the Areopagus, the most venerable governing body and court of law in the city. That body certainly had its own council house (*bouleuterion*) somewhere on the hill, but its exact site has not yet been recognized. At times the Council held its meetings elsewhere, for instance in the Royal Stoa (Plan, **26**). Thus we do not know with certainty where St. Paul stood when he was summoned before the Council to expound his faith. Local tradition,

103. Mosaic floor of the Omega house, 4th century A.D., central panel reset in 6th century A.D.

nevertheless, has always associated the Apostle with the hilltop. This is demonstrated above all by the establishment here of the Church of St. Dionysios, a member of the Council of the Areopagus who was Paul's most famous convert.*

To reach the Church of St. Dionysios we return to the Panathenaic Way and proceed upward almost to the saddle, then turn right among the pine trees (Fig. **104**). The ruins of the small basilica occupy a ledge at the foot of a vertical cliff (Plan, **59**). To the west and north of the church are the remains of the Archbishop's Palace which was connected with St. Dionysios through much of the 16th and 17th centuries. The present church dates from the middle of the 16th century, but the presence of a number of graves of the 6th-7th centuries suggests the existence of a much earlier church on the site.

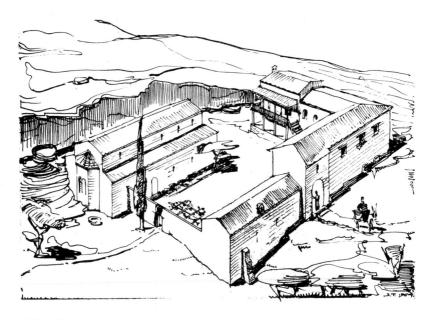

104. Church of St. Dionysios on the slopes of the Areopagos, 16th century A.D.

60. Nymphaion* (Figs. 96, 105)

Returning to the Agora proper, let us look at the series of buildings that closed its south side.

Partly beneath the Church of the Holy Apostles and partly exposed to the east are remains of a northward-facing, semicircular fountain house of the type commonly known as *nymphaia* from their resemblance to the cave sanctuaries of the Nymphs. Its most conspicuous remains are the heavy concrete foundations for the floor of a semicircular water basin and traces of three continuous steps and a parapet across the front. Water was brought in from the southeast in

105. *Nymphaion at the southwest corner of the Agora, 2nd century A.D. (Tentative restoration by S. Walker and N. Sunter.)*

a high-level aqueduct (Plan, **55**). The great thickness of the outer wall suggests that its face was broken by niches for sculptures. Fragments of appropriate sculpture have been found nearby, among them a torso of the "Venus Genetrix" type in which a water pitcher has been substituted for the apple in the left hand of the Goddess (Museum, p. 206). Pieces of marble revetment and carved architectural ornament attest to the rich adornment commonly found in nymphaia of the Roman period. In plan the building recalls the Exedra of Herodes at Olympia and the 2nd century A.D. remodeling of the Fountain of Peirene at Corinth, both works of Herodes Atticus. The Athenian building, which drew its water from the aqueduct completed in 140 A.D., also dates from about the middle of the 2nd century.

61. The Athenian Mint* (Figs. **96, 106-107**)

To the south of the Church of the Holy Apostles, and in part overlaid by both the Church and the Nymphaion, are the remains of a large building from the end of the 5th century B.C. Rooms of various shapes and sizes were grouped along a large courtyard beneath which flowed the East Branch of the Great Drain.

The identification of the building is not yet certain, though various pieces of evidence have suggested the Mint (*Argyrokopeion*): the discovery on the floor of the building of numerous blanks for the making of bronze coins, the existence in the building of water basins and furnaces, the discovery nearby of a 5th century B.C. inscription relating to minting and one of the 4th century B.C. recording the names of supervisors of the Mint. This combination of clues makes the identification probable. Recent excavations (1977) recovered more evidence for the minting of bronze coins in the 3rd and 2nd centuries B.C., but no evidence has come to light for the minting of silver. The building went out of use in the 1st century B.C., at a time when Athens ceased minting bronze coins.

62. Southeast Fountain House* (Figs. **96, 108-109**)

To the west of the Mint, and separated from it by a narrow alley, are the remains of a fountain house built in the last quarter of the 6th century B.C. The building was a long rectangle in plan with its entry

106. Balloon photograph of the area of the Mint, partially covered by the Church of the Holy Apostles.

107. Restored plan of the remains of the mint, ca. 400 B.C.

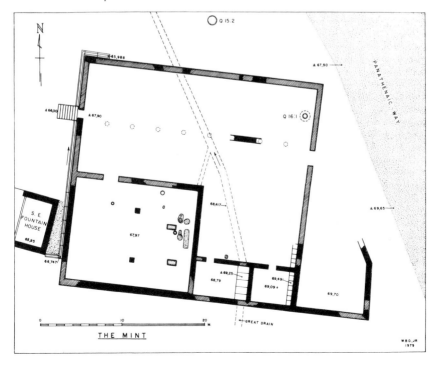

THE MINT

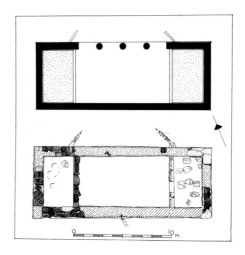

108. Actual state and restored plans of the Southeast Fountain House, 2nd half 6th century B.C.

from the north. At either end was a shallow basin once floored with thin marble slabs. The walls of the building, at least in their lower parts, were constructed of carefully jointed Kara limestone; a Z-shaped clamp remains in place near the northeast corner. Water was delivered to a point at the middle of the back wall by a terracotta pipeline which entered the region of the Agora from the east, running beneath the ancient street. We may suppose that the water was conveyed in channels within the thickness of the wall to supply a series of spouts, doubtless in the shape of animal heads. From these ever-flowing spouts the girls of nearby households would have filled their water jugs, one of the most popular subjects among Athenian vase painters of the late archaic period. The overflow from the basins was carried off in a northeasterly direction, by means of an underground terracotta pipeline, to be used elsewhere.

This fountain house stood midway between the Odeion of Agrippa and the Eleusinion, i.e. at the point where Pausanias in his account of the Agora (I, 14.1) mentioned the Enneakrounos, the nine-spouted

109. Juncture of overflow pipes from the basins of the Southeast Fountain House, 2nd half 6th century B.C.

fountain house erected by the tyrant Peisistratos or by his sons. Frequent references in the ancient authors leave no doubt that the Enneakrounos was the most famous fountain house in Athens; because of its great antiquity its water continued to be used for sacred purposes, e.g. for bathing before marriage. The large and elaborate fountain house had been preceded, according to the authors, by a simple spring with a visible source known as *Kalirrhoe*, i.e. the Fairflowing. While Pausanias believed this fountain house to be the Nine-Spouted one, Thucydides and other authors place the Enneakrounos and Kalirrhoe spring south of the Acropolis in the bed of the Ilissos River. Our fountain house must be one of the archaic fountains of Athens which by Pausanias' time was apparently shown as the famous Peisistratid fountain.

63. Church of the Holy Apostles* (Figs. 96, 110-111)

The Church of the Holy Apostles, dating from about 1000 A.D., is the only monument now standing of the many buildings that covered the Agora in mediaeval times. After undergoing repeated alterations and enlargements through the centuries, the church was restored to its original form in the years 1954-1957 with the aid of a grant from the Samuel H. Kress Foundation of New York.

The plan of the church is a unique variant of the cross-in-square with apses at the ends of the four arms of the cross, the western apse being enclosed by a low narthex. Four columns help to support the dome. The outer walls are decorated with "kufic" ornament (Arabic writing developed in the city of Kufa) in brickwork. The altar, the altar screen and the marble floor have been restored on the evidence of original fragments. The few wall paintings that have survived in the main body of the church date from the 17th century. On the walls of the narthex have been placed some contemporary paintings removed from the Chapel of St. Spyridon, which formerly stood above the Library of Pantainos (Plan, 48). Here too, in the left corridor, are a few fragments of painting from the Church of St. George in the Temple of Hephaistos (Plan, 1). The richly carved marble slab in the north end of the narthex is the front of a sarcophagus for which an alcove had been thrust out here early in the history of the church. (*See the plans on the wall at the south end of the narthex.*)

On shelves to the south of the Southeast Fountain House and on nearby walls have been assembled the more characteristic carved marbles of the early Christian and Byzantine periods found in the course of the Agora excavations. The great majority must come from buildings which stood elsewhere in Athens.

64. South Stoa I* (Figs. 96, 112-116)

The remains of this building can best be viewed by ascending the stairway southwest of the Church of the Holy Apostles to the ancient street that bounded the south side of the Agora. Test trenches cut

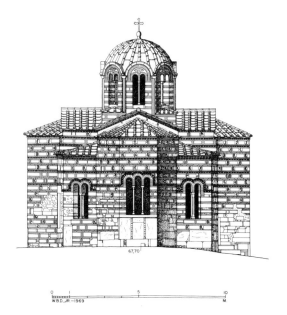

110. *Church of the Holy Apostles, ca. 1000 A.D., east elevation.*

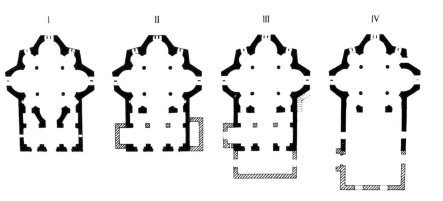

111. *Church of the Holy Apostles, showing successive additions.*

167

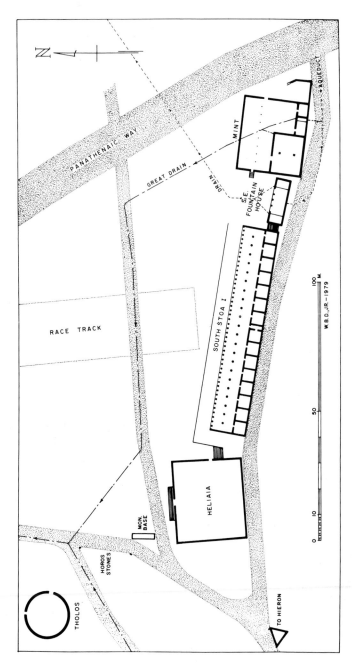

112. *South side of the Agora in the late 5th century B.C.*

through the stratified road have shown that this had been an important thoroughfare at least since the Bronze Age. Its course determined the placing of all the early public buildings on the south side of the Agora. The road surface has been restored to the level of the 5th and 4th centuries B.C.

South Stoa I was bisected diagonally and the west half was destroyed by the building of South Stoa II. Enough survives, however, to permit the recovery of the design with fair assurance. The earlier building dates from the late 5th century B.C., and for two and a half centuries it dominated much of the Agora by virtue of its size and elevated site. The plan comprised a row of 15 rooms which shared a two-aisled colonnade, and in front of that a terrace which compensated for the terrain's downward slope toward north and west. The interior walls were of sundried brick (Fig. **113**) above socles of soft

113. Mudbrick wall of South Stoa I, as found, 430-420 B.C.

114. Aerial view of the east end of South Stoa I, with dining rooms, ca. 430-420 B.C.

poros; the rear wall, now rebuilt, was entirely of stone since it served also as a retaining wall to support the roadway. The colonnade was also of poros; several stylobate blocks and a fragmentary Doric capital (now in storage) survive.

The rooms are closely uniform in size, and they are alike in having the front door set slightly off-center. The middle room is exceptional in that it was approached not directly from the porch like the other rooms but through a narrow anteroom to the east. This is an arrangement reminiscent of the dining suites in contemporary houses at Olynthos. The fifth room from the east in our building was floored in a way characteristic of dining rooms of the classical period: a slightly raised border surfaced with pebble-studded cement encircled the room to support the wooden dining couches (Fig. **115**). The eccentricity in the placing of the doorway is also an indication of dining rooms: it permitted the most economical distribution of dining couches of standard size. The rooms of South Stoa I would each have accommodated seven couches. In several cases a slight accumulation of ash in the middle of the room indicated the use of fire, probably in braziers, for heating or cooking. In a couple of the rooms benches of plastered clay had been built against the walls.

For the use of the building the most explicit clue is provided by an inscription of 221/20 B.C. found in the third room from the east. The text records the handing over of a set of official weights and measures by the Commissioners of Weights and Measures (*Metronomoi*) to their successors of the following year. The names of the five commissioners and of their two secretaries are recorded. It appears probable that these commissioners had their headquarters in the building. There would have been room for a number of the other administrative boards of similar size which constituted the Athenian civil service. We would assume therefore that these rooms too would

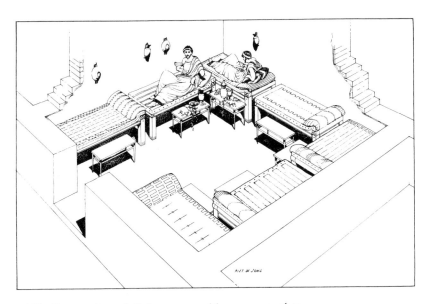

115. *Restoration of dining room with seven couches.*

have been referred to by the Athenians as *archeia*; whether the building had any other name we do not know. In addition to providing office space the stoa would also have offered dining accommodation in which the officials could take their midday meals in common. Note that the dining room accommodated seven men, just the members attested for the board of Metronomoi including secretaries.

65-70. South Square (Fig. 117)

We now turn to the examination of a complex of buildings which bordered the south side of the main square of the Agora and which for want of an ancient name we may designate as the South Square. This lesser square took shape in the course of the second and third quarters of the 2nd century B.C. through the construction of the Middle Stoa, the East Building and South Stoa II in that sequence. The new construction evidently took cognizance of an older building of the 6th century B.C., believed to be the Heliaia, which was in fact organically incorporated into the South Square at its southwest corner. The function of these buildings is problematic; law courts, sanctuary, gymnasium, and commercial agora have all been proposed.

Near the middle of the South Square are the slight remains, consisting of a few scattered foundation stones, of two buildings; both of these, to judge from their plans, were temples. The eastern building was clearly peripteral with columns on all four sides; the western had a broad cella with a porch only on its east end. Both date from the Hellenistic period, probably the late 2nd century B.C., and both appear to have suffered in the Roman sack of 86 B.C. In the general rehabilitation of the South Square in the 2nd century after Christ the western temple was rebuilt and its porch floored with marble. We have as yet no clue to the divinity worshipped in either temple.

For convenience in viewing the remains of the various buildings we will proceed in an order the reverse of the sequence of their construction. We begin therefore with South Stoa II, and to see it to better advantage we go back down the steps toward the front of the Church and then down a second flight.

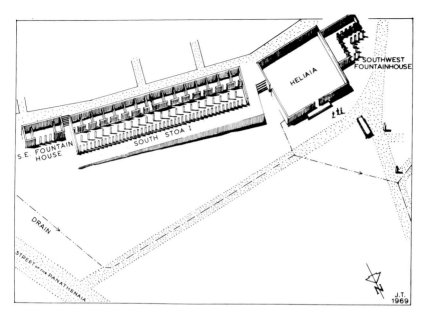

116. South side of the Agora, ca. 300 B.C.

65. South Stoa II* (Figs. **96, 117-119**)

South Stoa II was a simple one-aisled colonnade comprising thirty columns of the Doric order supported on two steps. Setting marks for two of the columns are preserved at the east end of the Stoa. All the elements of the facade are represented by very small fragments found in front of the building (now in storage). The original rear wall was of large, regular limestone blocks with a backing of conglomerate. Near the middle of the back wall was an arched niche for a fountain. The water came from a great stone aqueduct beneath the street to the south of the Stoa; it poured into a basin formed by a parapet across the front of the niche (Fig. **119**).

The facade of the Stoa was of reused material taken from the Square Peristyle at the northeast corner of the Agora (Plan, **44**) when that building was demolished to make way for the Stoa of Attalos; this applies to steps, columns and entablature. The evidence for reuse is

173

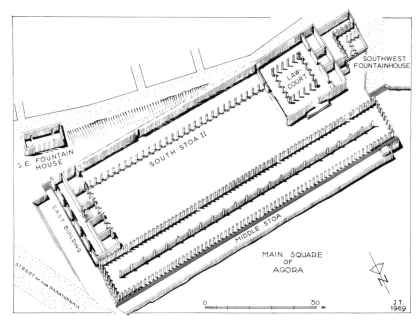

117. South Square after Hellenistic additions, ca. 140 B.C.

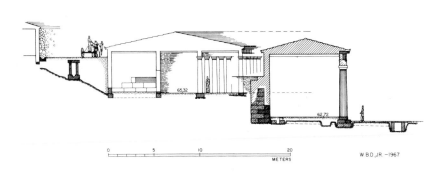

118. Cross-section, showing relationship (left to right) of south street, aqueduct, South Stoa I and South Stoa II.

174

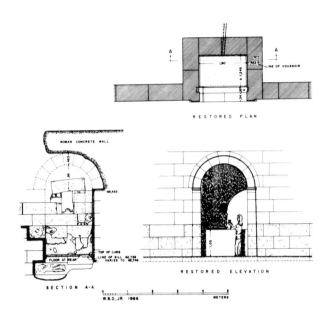

RESTORED PLAN

ROMAN CONCRETE WALL

TOP OF CURB
LINE OF SILL 68,726
VARIES TO 68,746

FLOOR AT REAR

SECTION A-A

RESTORED ELEVATION

W.B.D.,JR. 1966

METERS

119. Fountain in back wall of South Stoa II, 2nd century B.C.

especially clear in the case of the steps; on their tops are numerous traces of superimposed blocks in places where such blocks could not have existed in the present building. Elsewhere on the tops of the steps in the eastern part of the Stoa are incised a number of large letters of the Greek alphabet. These too date from the first period of the building, at which time there would appear to have been one letter between each pair of columns, presumably a system of numbering the bays of the colonnade.

On top of the back wall of the Stoa toward its east end have been placed two blocks from the entablature of the Square Peristyle: one from the triglyph and metope frieze, one from the cornice. These members had been reused elsewhere in the Agora; they are displayed here to illustrate the entablature which was employed, at second hand, in South Stoa II. They are cut from a distinctive kind of travertine, and the workmanship is worthy of the period when they were made; the specialist will perhaps recognize in another battered block displayed in the same place a frieze block from one of the four inner corners of the Square Peristyle.

South Stoa II suffered in the Roman sack of 86 B.C. and was subsequently dismantled. Industry intruded into the desolate area and flourished in the 1st and early part of the 2nd centuries A.D. Great quantities of slag from the smelting of iron, and chips from the working of marble were found in the excavation.

In the 2nd century A.D., probably in the time of Hadrian (117-138 A.D.), the industrialists were banished and the area was cleaned up. At this time the rear wall of the Stoa was rebuilt with a backing of concrete, of which a long section remains in the middle part of the building. There is, however, no reason to believe that the colonnade was ever rebuilt, and the reconstruction of the back wall was apparently to support an aqueduct.

66. East Building* (Figs. **96, 117**)

The east end of the South Stoa II was thrust against the front of a small, slightly earlier structure with a north-south orientation which we shall call the East Building. This earlier building was evidently designed to close the east end of the new square. It seems also to have served as the formal entrance to the square.

The building was approached by way of a broad terrace along the whole of its east front. A wide flight of steps led down to the terrace from the east, and a narrow stairway from the south. The front foundation of the building is too narrow to have supported a colonnade; it is to be restored rather with a wall broken by several, perhaps five, doorways. The interior was divided into two parts by a wall on its median line. The west half comprised five compartments, whereas the east was a single long hall.

The eastern room was floored with marble-chip mosaic in which were set a number of low marble bases about 0.90 m. (3 ft.) square. Four of these bases remain, and from the indications in the earth fill the series is to be restored as twelve in all, divided into two groups of six separated by an open interval on the axis of the building. In the top of each base are four shallow square sockets; perhaps the best explanation of these is that they served to retain in a fixed position some piece of wooden furniture with four legs, such as a table or chest.

One may observe in this room some interesting indications of the activities of the marble workers who occupied the area after the Roman sack of 86 B.C. Narrow grooves in the tops of the marble bedding blocks were made by saws cutting through large blocks of stone. Here and there in the floor are shallow depressions containing traces of the emery powder used in polishing marble. The rough tile work on the terrace also dates from this "industrial" period.

Of the five compartments in the west half of the building, the central one certainly contained a stairway by which one descended from the higher level on the east to the lower level of the South Square, the difference being about 1.70 meters. The next room to the south is to be restored, from indications in the foundations, as an exedra with two columns in its front and a marble bench around its other three sides. The southernmost room was provided with water which issued from spouts set in the face of the wall. The two northern rooms are too ruinous to permit restoration.

67. Middle Stoa* (Figs. 96, 117, 120-121)

We move on to the Middle Stoa, the earliest and largest unit in the building program of the 2nd century B.C. which resulted in the South Square. Let us start at the east end where the fabric of the building is best preserved.

With a length of some 147 meters and width of about 17.50 meters the Middle Stoa, in terms of ground plan, was much the largest building of the Agora. On all four sides it was enclosed by colonnades of unfluted Doric columns, 160 in all. The stumps of three of these columns still stand *in situ* above the canonical three steps at the east end of the Stoa; many more drums, recovered from the Post-Herulian Wall, have been set up around the building. The structure was divided longitudinally into two equal aisles by a row of 23 interior columns with intervening screen walls. These inner columns were presumably of the Ionic order, but nothing of this order has yet been recognized.

A close examination of the three column stumps at the east end of the Stoa will reveal traces of a thin parapet between the columns. Dowel holes in about one half of the surviving outer column drums indicate that similar parapets enclosed a considerable proportion of the total

120. Middle Stoa and South Square, seen from the upper floor of the Stoa of Attalos, 2nd century B.C.

periphery of the stoa; they were presumably confined to certain lengths at each end of the building. The parapets rose only about three quarters of the height of the columns, and were crowned with a nicely profiled capping course. The open space above admitted light and air.

The north facade of the Stoa was flanked by a terrace of generous width. Since the ground sloped gently down from east to west, this terrace through most of its length lay well above the floor level of the square and so commanded a splendid view across the Agora. Toward the west the terrace stopped short of the end of the building proper so as to minimize interference with the flow of traffic through the southwest entrance to the Agora. At the west end of the terrace are the foundations for a large monument, perhaps intended to honor some foreign monarch. In the early Roman period the monument was dismantled and the re-entrant angle at the corner of the building was filled with a stairway. The stoa terrace thus became an "expressway" across the width of the Agora, an arrangement that was

121. Doric entablature
of the Middle Stoa,
2nd century B.C.

especially convenient after the construction of the Odeion in the Augustan period.

The south flank of the Stoa was bordered by a marble gutter of which a little remains in place at the east end.

A long narrow monument base was set against the east end of the Stoa in the 2nd century A.D. This is a possible location for the sculpted group that included the Iliad and the Odyssey (Museum, p. 195). The two torsos came to light just to the east of the monument base; the inscribed plinth of the Iliad was found in a Byzantine well just to the west.

Apart from the columns, little of the superstructure of the Stoa has survived. Several of its epistylia, made of poros from Peiraeus, have been placed on the outer edge of the terrace near its east end; the backs of the blocks have suffered greatly from the fire that destroyed the building in 267 A.D. A few fragments of the frieze (in storage) indicated that the triglyphs were of fine-grained Aeginetan poros painted blue while the metopes were of white marble. The terracotta sima showed foliage in relief between the lions' heads, the whole richly painted (Fig. 121). Although the architectural forms are simple and the materials modest, the workmanship throughout is of a high order; evidently the project was supported by ample means. The construction of the main part of the Middle Stoa falls in the first half of the 2nd century B.C.

68. Heliaia (?)* (Figs. **112, 116**)

The large rectangular structure which was to constitute the south-western element in the South Square had for long before been prominent as an independent building. Erected in the 6th century B.C. on high ground at the south side of the square, it balanced the predecessor of the Tholos and the Old Bouleuterion on the west side. The site of the building is now sadly desolate. The best preserved part is the stepped foundation of the north wall. After examining this the visitor will do well to climb the modern stairs to the high road south of the building whence one can distinguish the outline of the foundations that have been filled out with modern masonry.

In its original form the building consisted of an enclosure open to the sky, approaching a square in plan and measuring internally about 26.50 × 31 meters. The enclosing wall was built of well-squared blocks of Aeginetan poros crowned by a double cornice. The exact height cannot be determined, but the thickness of the wall (0.48 m.) and the delicate treatment of the molding on the soffit of the cornice suggest that it was higher than a man's head. The principal entrance was in the middle of the north side; there was a lesser doorway in the east side. Because of the downward slope of the land three steps were set against the middle part of the north front, perhaps in connection with some more monumental treatment of the entrance. The clay floor inside the enclosure was made to slope gently toward the northeast corner from which point the surface water was carried off in a large stone drain.

In the course of its long existence the building underwent many alterations, of which only the principal can be noted here. Around the middle of the 2nd century B.C. a complete peristyle was inserted, and the building would seem to have been roofed with a lantern to provide light and air while assuring privacy. This building, along with its neighbors, suffered greatly in the Roman sack of 86 B.C. A number of stone catapult balls were found in its ruins. In the subsequent period of desolation this site, like that of the South Stoa and the East Building, was occupied by small industrial establishments: a potter's kiln and a marbleworking shop.

The building, given its large size, early date and location close to the Agora, has been tentatively identified as the Heliaia, the meeting place of the oldest and most important of the civil courts of Athens.

69. Water Clock* (Figs. 122, 123)

Against the north facade of the Heliaia, toward its northwest corner, are the clearly visible remains of a monumental water clock dating from about the end of the 4th century B.C. Water, drawn from the aqueduct which supplied the Southwest Fountain House, was made to fill a stone-lined vertical shaft, the bottom of which was sunk deep below ground level. The water was then allowed to escape through a very small aperture low down in the wall of the shaft. The falling water level, perhaps by means of a float, must have activated a pointer to indicate the passing hours. In the 3rd century B.C. the tank was modified to serve as a more sophisticated in-flow rather than out-flow clock. As a public timepiece the installation was well placed, close to one of the principal entrances to the Agora. It was dismantled in the 2nd century B.C., at the time the water clock in the Tower of the Winds was constructed several hundred meters to the east.

70. Southwest Fountain House* (Fig. 116)

To the west of the Heliaia are the foundations of a once splendid public facility which for want of an ancient name we may designate as

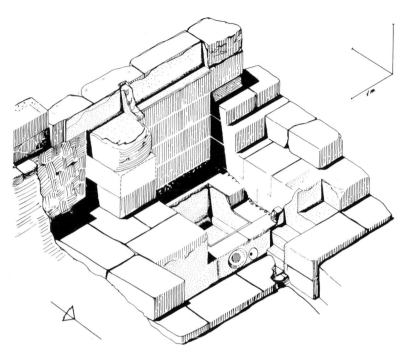

122. Drawing of remains of the waterclock (Klepsydra),
late 4th century B.C.

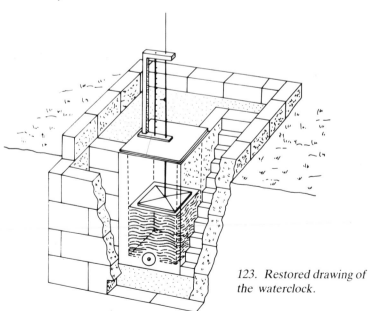

123. Restored drawing of
the waterclock.

the Southwest Fountain House. The building dates from the 4th century B.C., probably from the third quarter of the century. It underwent modifications in the later 4th and the 2nd centuries B.C., was destroyed in the sack of 86 B.C., was subsequently stripped to its lowest foundations and was never rebuilt.

The fountain house was well situated, for it made abundant fresh water readily available to those entering and leaving the Agora and also to the resident population in the densely inhabited area around the southwest corner of the public place. The building had to be set deep into the bedrock in order to conform with the level of the supply line, but this circumstance, no doubt, kept both the building and its water cool.

The water came from the east in a great stone aqueduct that underlay the street bordering the south side of the Agora. Bending north, the conduit passed between the Heliaia and the Fountain House to pour most of its water into the Fountain House, while reserving some for the needs of the Heliaia (Plan, **68**) and the Water Clock (Plan, **69**). It is worthwhile to peer through the iron grating at the southwest corner of the Heliaia in order to see a section of the ancient aqueduct. The channel was very solidly constructed of large slabs of soft poros laid horizontally for floor and roof, vertically for the walls. The water flowed in a small trench, semicircular in section, cut in the floor. The open channel above this, 0.45 m. wide and 1.20 m. high (1-1/2 × 4 ft.), was large enough to permit the passage of a workman engaged in cleaning or repairing.

The Fountain House itself was L-shaped. An inner row of columns divided the building into two parts: a basin and a porch. The front of the basin consisted of a parapet of hard poros set between the inner columns; over this the water was drawn. A small surviving fragment from the top of a parapet is deeply worn by the pitchers; it now lies on the foundation of the inner colonnade of the Fountain House. On the stylobate of the porch are traces of column bases 0.66 m. in diameter, but nothing remains either of the columns or of the entablature.

The Fountain House was soon enlarged by the construction of an annex at its southwest corner. Water was supplied by the westward extension of the great stone aqueduct. In the annex one could approach the wall from which the water issued and hold one's pitcher directly below the spout: a more satisfactory arrangement than dipping one's drinking water from a basin as in the main building. At a later date, probably in the 2nd century B.C., the southwest annex was abandoned in favor of a similar installation at the northeast corner of the original building.

71. Triangular Shrine* (Fig. 124)

Proceeding up the ancient road to the west of the Southwest Fountain House and under the branches of a wild pistachio tree we come to an important traffic intersection. From this point radiated roads going northeast to the Agora, southwest toward the Pnyx, west toward the Peiraeus Gate, east to the south borders of the Agora and southeast to the northern slope of the Areopagus. For the most part these ancient streets are narrow, irregular and roughly surfaced with gravel. Almost all of them are underlaid by drains and water channels that show countless repairs and adjustments. The most impressive is the road that bordered the south side of the Agora. Its well-kept gravel surface maintains a fairly uniform width of about six meters; along its south side ran a gutter to carry off the surface water from the higher ground above.

In the angle between the two roads coming from the east one will recognize the remains of a triangular enclosure once surrounded by a low wall of polygonally-jointed limestone masonry. Its sanctity is attested by an inscription on a marble post set against the face of the enclosure wall at the east end of the north side. The text reads "Of the Sanctuary" (*tou hierou*) in lettering of the latter part of the 5th century B.C. The ceramic evidence supports a date in this period for the construction of the triangular enclosure. A mass of rough masonry found at a lower level inside the enclosure in a context of the 7th century B.C. suggests that this had been a sacred spot much earlier.

Just to the west lie the remains of a house of the classical and Hellenistic periods where a sculptor, named Mikion, worked (Figs. **124, 125**).

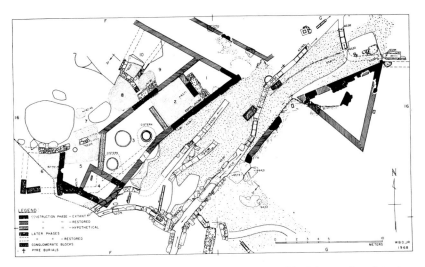

124. Plan of the Triangular shrine (5th century B.C.) right, and sculptor's house (5th-3rd century B.C.), left.

72. State Prison* (Fig. **126**)

About 60 meters to the southwest of the triangular shrine is a building of unusual plan which has been identified with some probability as the public prison of Athens (*desmoterion*). A long, narrow structure, it presented its north end to an important ancient street leading northwestward toward the Peiraeus Gate. Built in the mid-5th century B.C., the original foundations are recognizable from

125. Bone stylus inscribed with the name of the sculptor Mikion.

185

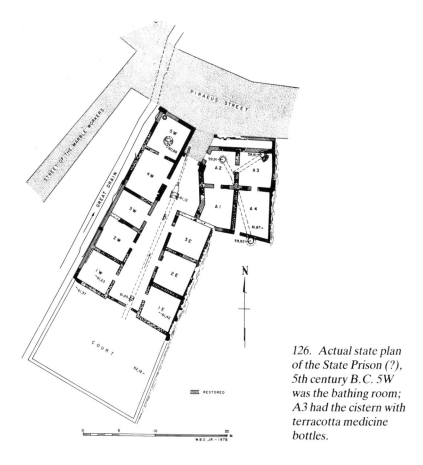

126. *Actual state plan of the State Prison (?), 5th century B.C. 5W was the bathing room; A3 had the cistern with terracotta medicine bottles.*

the prominent use of large blocks of cream-colored poros in the outer walls. The plan comprised two rows of square rooms, five in one, three in the other, separated and served by a corridor which led south to a large open courtyard. Incorporated in the northeast corner of the building is a semi-detached unit consisting of four rooms.

The state prison of Athens is best known from the casual references to it in Plato's *Phaedo*. This dialogue tells of the month which Sokrates spent in prison between his condemnation and his execution by the drinking of hemlock (399 B.C.). Our structure appears to satisfy the requirements, being close to a building that has good claim to be a law court (the Heliaia), adjacent to an important street and of appropriate date and size. In the northwestern room was found a large water jar and a basin set in the floor; such facilities might have served for the bath which Sokrates took before drinking the poison. In the ruins of the building were found thirteen small terracotta bottles of a type certainly used in antiquity for drugs and which perhaps in this case may have been intended to hold the powerful and carefully measured juice of the hemlock plant. It may not be entirely by chance that the ruins also yielded a small marble portrait of Sokrates (Museum, p. 242).

73. Bath at Northwest Foot of the Areopagus* (Fig. 127)

Prominent above and to the east of the State Prison are the extensive remains of a bathing establishment with a history that extended in some five major phases from the late 2nd century B.C. into the late 6th century A.D. Characteristic of its earliest phase was a round room in which some 20 stone bathtubs could have been placed radially against the enclosing wall; one of these tubs is now shown on the terrace of the Stoa of Attalos (p. 191). The irregularities of the terrain and the many vicissitudes suffered by the building resulted in a very informal plan in striking variance from that of the normal bath of the Roman period. The most readily recognizable element of the later phases is a large expanse of marble-chip floor at a high level; this belonged to the dressing room (*apodyterion*). To the south is a large cistern for the storage of water.

74. Residential-Industrial Area to West and South of the Areopagus*

The extensive excavations to the west of the Areopagus were begun with a view to finding a site for the Agora Museum. The wealth of ancient remains that came to light necessitated a change of plan and led to the reconstruction of the Stoa of Attalos to serve as a museum. The removal of vast quantities of silt, which reached a maximum depth of 12 meters, revealed a shallow valley between the Areopagus and the Hill of the Nymphs (now crowned by the National Observatory). This valley was drained by the west branch of the Great Drain. In addition to such public buildings as the Prison and the Bath, the area had been through most of antiquity a thickly settled residential-industrial district.

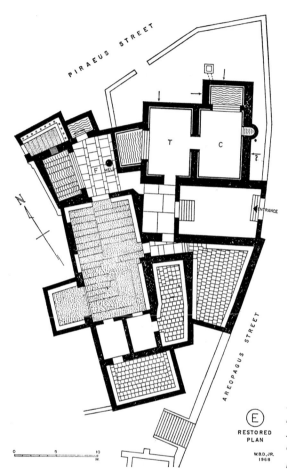

127. Plan of the Hellenistic/Roman bath, 2nd century B.C. - 4th century A.D. Last phase shown here.

In the bottom of the valley toward the southwest may be traced the foundations of several houses of the 5th and 4th centuries B.C. The typical plan comprised a number of rooms grouped around a courtyard with a well near its middle (Fig. **128**). Both construction and furnishings were modest: walls of rubble masonry, floors of clay, no mosaics, very few columns. These were presumably the dwellings of artisans who carried on their activities either within their own houses or in nearby shops of still more modest appearance (Fig. **129**).

HOUSES D·C V CENTURY PRE-DRAIN

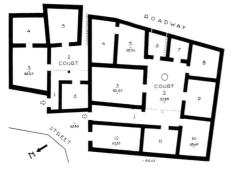

HOUSES D·C´ AFTER MID. IV CENTURY

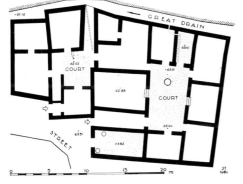

128. Plan of the two Greek houses in the residential area south of the State Prison, 5th and 4th century B.C.

Casting pits for the making of bronze statues have been found in the area, one of the 4th and one of the 2nd century B.C. (both have been refilled). Great quantities of marble chips attest to the carving of sculpture, especially in the 5th and 4th centuries B.C., while molds for the making of terracotta figurines of Hellenistic types show that coroplasts were also busy in the area.

In the Roman period the hill slopes both east and west of the valley were occupied by large dwelling houses. Their walls were painted in simple panelled schemes, and a few of the rooms were floored with mosaic. Most of these houses suffered in the Herulian sack of 267 A.D., but some were rebuilt to continue in use into the 6th century.

Here as elsewhere in the area of the Agora the earliest remains are burials. Two small chamber tombs of the Mycenaean period came to light near the bottom of the valley while a family cemetery comprising 48 burials ranging in date from the 8th through the 6th centuries B.C. has been explored on the west slope of the Areopagus.

To the south of the Areopagus, excavations in the 1890's by the German Archaeological Institute revealed the continuation of the residential area: an ancient roadway bordered by close-set houses and small shrines, notably the Amyneion, seat of a healing cult.

129. Lead curse tablet, cursing the metalworkers, Aristaichmos and Pyrrias, found in House D.

THE AGORA MUSEUM
IN THE STOA OF ATTALOS

All the finds from the excavations conducted in the Agora by the American School of Classical Studies since 1931 are now housed in the Stoa of Attalos (Fig. **130**). Some outstanding pieces found in the course of the earlier Greek excavations have been transferred to the Stoa from the National Museum, among them the statues of Apollo Patroos, the Iliad and the Odyssey, and a Corinthian capital from the Odeion of Agrippa (now on the site of the Odeion). The material from the excavations carried out by the American School on the North Slope of the Acropolis and on the Pnyx is also deposited in the Stoa. The following parts of the building are usually open to the public:

Terrace: various marbles, chiefly architectural.

Ground floor, colonnade: sculpture and inscriptions.

Ground floor, area of shops: main display, special exhibitions, sales room.

Upper floor: sculpture, inscriptions and models of the ancient city.

The Museum offices and workrooms are installed in the area of the ancient shops on the upper floor, with access through a door at the middle of the screen. The greater part of the archaeological material is shelved on the upper floor behind the screen and in magazines in the basement; students may be admitted on application at the Museum offices.

Washrooms and a drinking fountain are on the ground floor, north end.

TERRACE

Among the miscellaneous marbles assembled here from all parts of the excavation are gravestones, a marble sarcophagus of the archaic period, several fine cornice blocks and column capitals of the 5th century B.C., well heads, a bath tub from a circular bath house (p. 187), altars, inscribed statue bases, a series of poros crowning members from the enclosure wall of the Heliaia (Plan, **68**), a perirrhanterion.

130. Stoa of Attalos, plan of the Museum.

GROUND FLOOR

UPPER FLOOR

TERRACOTTA INDUSTRY

W.C.

W.C.

MUSEUM GALLERY

MARBLE SCULPTURE

MISCELLANEOUS MARBLES

RESERVED DISPLAY

WINE JARS

SALES INFORMATION

MEMORIAL ROOM

TERRACE

FOUNTAIN

EPHOR'S OFFICES

STOA MODEL

W.C.

W.C.

DARK ROOM

MENDING ROOM

DIRECTOR'S OFFICE

RECORDS

STUDY COLLECTIONS

STUDY

DRAFTING ROOM

STUDY

WINE JARS

MAGAZINES

AGORA MODEL

ACROPOLIS MODEL

N

GROUND FLOOR COLONNADE

Apollo Patroos* (S 2154) Fig. 39

To the right as one enters the building, against the ancient south wall, stands a colossal statue in Pentelic marble of Apollo. The head was inset and is missing; the arms are broken away. The god once held a kithara against his left side, and he wears the heavy formal dress (peplos and himation) habitual to him as god of music. A miniature ancient copy of the statue is exhibited in the museum gallery (p. 266). The statue was found in 1907 by Greek excavators on the west side of the Agora. It has been recognized as the cult statue from the Temple of Apollo Patroos (Plan, 23), a work attributed by Pausanias (I, 3, 4) to the artist Euphranor, one of the leading sculptors and painters at Athens in the middle of the 4th century B.C.

Statue Base Signed by Praxiteles* (I 4165)

The pedestal of white marble to the left of Apollo carried two statues, portraits of Spoudias and his wife Kleiokrateia; the statues were dedicated to Demeter and Kore. The couple were previously known as parties to an unseemly family quarrel with which the forty-first oration of Demosthenes is concerned. In modest lettering below the name of Kleiokrateia on the right side of the front of the base appears the signature of the most famous Athenian sculptor of the 4th century B.C.: Praxiteles. On the fragmentary left side of the front are scattered letters from the names of Spoudias and of another sculptor who did his portrait. The base was found to the north of the Temple of Hephaistos in a foundation of the early Roman period. It had probably stood in a sanctuary of Demeter seen by Pausanias (I, 2, 4) inside the Dipylon, where it must have suffered in the Roman siege of 86 B.C.

Original Base and Capital from the Interior Order of the Stoa of Attalos

Beside Interior Column I have been placed one of the original bases for this series of columns and a capital assembled from many fragments of the original. These members served as the basis for the restoration.

Ionic Capital of Periklean Date* (A 2973)

Against the wall between the doors of Shops A and B is shown an Ionic capital of Pentelic marble. A watercolor on the wall above records the painted decoration as it was recovered soon after excavation. This capital was extracted from the Post-Herulian Wall to the south of the Stoa of Attalos. With it were found the complete column now standing in Shop A and two shafts from the same series now lying in front of the Library of Pantainos. All come from an otherwise unknown building of the third quarter of the 5th century B.C. Masons' marks show that they had served some intermediate use before being incorporated in the 3rd century A.D. in the Post-Herulian Wall.

Statue Base Signed by Theoxenos the Theban* (I 5407)

On the terrace opposite Apollo is another marble pedestal that once carried portrait statues of a man and his wife dedicated by their son to Demeter and Kore. The name of the dedicator was Demopeithides, son of Physteus of Acharnai, and of his wife, Peisikrateia. The work is signed by the otherwise unknown artist, Theoxenos the Theban; the date is the second half of the 4th century B.C. The two blocks of Demopeithides' monument were found in the Eleusinion where the group had undoubtedly stood. Peisikrateia is perhaps to be recognized in the figure opposite Column 4 (p. 196).

Iliad and Odyssey* (S 2038, S 2039)

The robust female figures in armor opposite Column 2 are personifications of the *Iliad* and the *Odyssey*. The clue to the identification was given by the combination of figures on the armor of the smaller statue. Scylla occupies the cuirass; Aiolos, god of the winds, three sirens and a Polyphemos are shown on the upper lappets; all these recall scenes of the *Odyssey*. On one of the long lower lappets of this figure is the signature of the artist: Jason the Athenian. Traces of a sword on the right side of the companion figure are appropriate to the Iliad, who is also marked as the older sister by her larger size and greater maturity. The identification was confirmed by the discovery of the plinth of the Iliad, placed to the right of the statue. The plinth, which was cut from the same block as the statue, is inscribed with an epigram: "The Iliad, I that was both after Homer and before Homer, have been set up alongside him that bore me in his earlier years." In the same context as the plinth was found the left leg of the Iliad (not exhibited). The group may be restored with a figure of Homer, perhaps seated, flanked to right and left by the personifications of his two great works.

The statues came to light in 1869 at the southwest corner of the Stoa of Attalos; the inscribed base and the leg were recovered from a nearby Byzantine wall in 1953. Provenance, date (early 2nd century A.D.) and theme would all be appropriate for the association of the group with the Library of Pantainos (Plan, **48**). As yet, however, no suitable base has been found in the Library. Another possible location is suggested on p. 180. Pentelic marble.

Statue of a Goddess* (S 378)

The imperious female figure opposite Column 3, of well over life size and of Pentelic marble, was found in the Post-Herulian wall in the area of the Library of Pantainos. Head, right arm and right foot were all attached and are all missing. Above a tightly fitted chiton the goddess wears a mantle which is draped precariously over the left shoulder and the right thigh. The left hand rests with outspread fingers on the hip. The right arm was raised high as though to grasp a scepter or the like.

This sculptural type was widespread in the Hellenistic world. The statue from the Agora is one of the most monumental and probably also one of the earliest examples of its use. The type was employed for various divinities, certainly for Artemis, but also for Aphrodite as illustrated by a miniature example from the Agora (Museum, p. 266). In the absence of attributes the identification of the present statue is hazardous. It may be noted, however, that it was found in the Post-Herulian Wall close by the Aphrodite whom we shall meet shortly (p. 198) and in close association with elements from the ceiling of the Temple of Ares (Plan, **38**). There is some possibility, therefore, that we have here the two Aphrodites seen by Pausanias (I, 8, 4) in the Temple of Ares.

Portrait Statue of a Woman (S 1016)

The much battered statue in Pentelic marble of a woman of mature years opposite Column 4, heavily draped in chiton and himation, is of a type appropriate to the middle of the 4th century B.C. The statue was found just to the west of the Eleusinion (Plan, **56**), in which sanctuary it probably stood. The figure may be Peisikrateia from the pedestal once in the Eleusinion and now on the terrace of the Stoa (p. 195).

Herms Used as Supporting Figures* (S 33, S 198)

The priestess is flanked to right and left by Herms, both of which had served as supports at the side of major statues. That on the right, in which the god is bearded, bore the weight of a child in a group comparable with the Hermes and Dionysos at Olympia. The other figure represents the youthful, beardless Hermes; he retains over his head the bunched cloak of the major figure which stood beside the Herm. Both figures were found on the west side of the Agora and are to be rated as routine works of the early Roman period.

Stage Front of the Odeion of Agrippa*

Opposite Column 5 has been restored a section of the stage front of the Odeion of Agrippa (Plan, **41**); the restoration is based on ancient fragments found in the ruins of the building. The front was paneled with slabs of greenish marble from Karystos in Euboia set between Herms carved in white Pentelic marble; it was supported on a plinth of bluish Hymettian marble and surmounted by a crowning member in white marble delicately carved with interlacing lotus and palmette. Male and female heads were used, presumably in alternation. Both the heads and the carved ornament of the crowning member are good examples of the classicizing work of the Augustan period (ca. 15 B.C.).

Triton from the Odeion of Agrippa* (S 1214)

The head of a Triton on the wall above the stage front comes from one of six colossal figures, three Tritons and three Giants, carved about 150 A.D. to adorn the facade of the Odeion of Agrippa (Plan, **41**). The Tritons have been shown to be adaptations of the Poseidon of the west pediment of the Parthenon; as such they illustrate the classicizing tendency of the Antonine period. This head came to light at Eleusis, but the neck which joins the head was found in front of the Odeion.

Torso of a Youthful Divinity* (S 3109)

Against Column 6 stands a youthful marble torso about one half life size. Long ringlets descend over the shoulders. Across the back is a length of tightly drawn scarf the ends of which were draped over the forearms and attached to the thighs. Probably Dionysos, possibly Apollo is represented. Stylistically the piece is interesting since it was carved in Hellenistic times in the manner of the late archaic period. The statue, of Pentelic marble, was found beneath the floor packing of the Southeast Temple (Plan, **52**).

Tripod Base* (S 370)

Between Columns 6 and 7 stands the Pentelic marble base for a bronze tripod. The bowl of the tripod rested on top of the marble; its bronze legs were set against the thin edges of the marble in such a way as to enframe the sculptured panels. The tripod was presumably a prize won in a dramatic or dithyrambic contest. The nude male figure with knotted club has been identified as Theseus, Prince of Athens. He appears to have been the central figure, and so perhaps the hero of the successful piece. To the right he is flanked by a regal draped male (King Aigeus, father of Theseus?), to the left by a draped female figure with phiale (Medea, wife of Aigeus?). Dating probably from the 2nd century B.C., the base is an early and important example of the "Neo-Attic style." The highly mannered revival of such archaic features as patterned drapery, a mincing stride

197

and imperfect anatomy appear in startling contrast with contemporary realism in the rendering of Theseus' cloak.

The base was found standing upright in the middle of the principal room of the "Civic Offices" (Plan, **21**), surrounded by the debris from the destruction of the building in 267 A.D. Since there was no proper underpinning, this could not have been its original position.

Statue of Goddess* (S 1882)

The headless statue of a goddess of slightly more than life size opposite Column 6 has been reassembled from scores of fragments of Parian marble found in the Post-Herulian Wall near the southwest corner of the Library of Pantainos (Plan, **48**). In its flamboyance of figure and drapery combined with great delicacy of execution the statue recalls the parapet of the Nike Temple and the vase paintings of the Meidias Painter. A date about 420 B.C. is indicated. A goddess surely; Aphrodite almost certainly. Since many fragments from the marble ceiling of the Temple of Ares were found together with the statue, we may have to do with one of the two Aphrodites noted by Pausanias (I, 8, 4) in the sanctuary of Ares. See also p. 196.

Head of a Goddess* (S 2094)

From about the same period as the last torso, or slightly earlier (440-420 B.C.), is the female head, in fine-grained white marble, set against Column 8. This piece also comes from the Post-Herulian Wall. Beneath a low diadem the hair is swept back in soft wavy masses above the brow to be gathered into tighter, heavy rolls behind the ears; the back of the head is broken away. Perhaps Artemis.

"Nereid" Akroterion* (S 182)

Opposite Columns 7 and 8 we find ourselves before a female figure in Parian marble of life size and of singular grace. The thin and windswept chiton reveals the full beauty of the body, while a heavy outer garment gathered around the hips gives both real and aesthetic support to the lower part of the figure. The style, reminiscent of the Nike Temple parapet and of the Erechtheum frieze, points to the end of the 5th century B.C. The statue has been considered an early work of Timotheos who is known to have made one of the two sets of akroteria for the Temple of Asklepios at Epidauros a few years later. The pose of the Agora figure, in which the movement of the body toward the left is countered by the turn of the head toward the right, is appropriate for an akroterion on one of the outer corners of a gable roof. The heavy weathering on all sides of the figure is also characteristic of akroteria which were fully exposed to the elements. The only likely sources are the temples of Hephaistos and of Ares, and of the two the Temple of Hephaistos seems the more probable (p. 43).

Draped Female Figure* (S 37)

Opposite Columns 8 and 9 stands the lower part of a female figure in Pentelic marble clad in a very thin dress with a cloak bunched in front of the right thigh and draped over the extended left arm. Much of the front drapery was worked in a separate piece and inset, in consequence, no doubt, of some flaw that appeared in the marble as it was being worked. On top of the drapery over the left arm is the curved bedding for another patch. The back is unfinished. The style of the drapery and the high quality of the workmanship point to a date in the first quarter of the 4th century B.C. The statue had been built into a late foundation at the southeast corner of the Metroon (Plan, 14), and its freshness suggests that it stood somewhere in that area in a sheltered position. The identification is still obscure.

Draped Female Figure (S 210)

The upper part of a female figure of Pentelic marble set against Column 9 must have come from a statue with drapery like that of the last figure, and of equally fine workmanship. The now missing head was carved separately. This figure too is anonymous.

Two Statues of Goddesses* (S 462, S 473)

The two draped female figures of Pentelic marble opposite Columns 9 and 10 were found together with several more fragmentary statues built into a screen wall of the early Roman period around the little square to the south of the New Bouleuterion (Plan, **13**). There is good reason to regard them as victims of the Sullan siege of 86 B.C. which thus provides a convenient lower terminus for their date. The head of S 462 was inset, that of S 473 was cut in one piece with the torso. Both may be taken as characteristic Athenian products of the Hellenistic period: conservative in style, prosaic in workmanship. Each wears a tightly fitted chiton and a voluminous himation. Each is girt with a cord which encircles the chest below the breasts and is then carried over the shoulders. The remnants of Eros on the left shoulder of S 473 mark her as Aphrodite. She rests her left arm on a tree trunk, a motive inspired, no doubt, by the famous cult statue of "Aphrodite in the Gardens" of the late 5th century B.C. S 462 retains no attribute; she gives the impression of a dancing figure, hence perhaps a Nymph or Grace.

Votive Relief from a Sanctuary of Pan and the Nymphs* (I 7154) Fig. **131**

Between the statues of Aphrodite opposite Columns 9 and 10 is shown a Pentelic marble relief in which a number of divinities are gathered in a cave marked as a sanctuary by a rustic altar near its middle. From left to right the figures may be recognized as Demeter, Apollo (seated), Artemis, Hermes, three Nymphs (one seated), Pan seated on the rock filling his mug from a wine skin, and the horned river god Achelous of whom only traces remain at the extreme right. Above reclines Zeus who looks attentively at what is taking place near the altar. Here Hermes is delivering the infant Dionysos, newly born from the thigh of Zeus, into the hands of one of the Nymphs who will see to the young god's upbringing.

Pan, Achelous and the Nymphs are constant companions and are commonly found together in cave sanctuaries. It was probably in the well-known cave of Pan on the northwestern shoulder of the Acropolis that the relief was dedicated. Apollo and Demeter certainly and Zeus probably also had shrines on the North Slope of the Acropolis, hence a neighborly gathering.

The interest of the relief is enhanced by the name of the dedicator which appears on the base in front: Neoptolemos, son of Antikles, of

131. Votive relief of the Cave of Pan, second half 4th century B.C.

the township of Melite. This man is known to have been a very wealthy citizen in the second half of the 4th century B.C. who was commended repeatedly for his civic and religious benefactions. A date about 330 B.C. would suit the known career of the dedicator and the style of the relief.

The relief was found lying face down in the peristyle of the house of the Late Roman period on the north slope of the Areopagus (p. 160). The heads of all the figures have been deliberately mutilated, no doubt out of Christian zeal, and the key figure, the infant Dionysos, has suffered most grievously.

Standing Male Torso* (S 1313)

The torso of fine Pentelic marble and of about two thirds life size. against the wall opposite Column 11 lacks head, both arms and both legs below the knees. The figure is well finished all around and its surface shows little weathering. Despite its mutilated state the work impresses one by the beauty of its stance and modeling and by the sensitive finish of the marble. The weight was borne by the right leg; the left leg was thrust far back, the head was turned slightly to the proper left. In the absence of attributes identification would be hazardous. The statue is of interest, however, as an excellent example of the Athenian handling of a sculptural theme of which the most famous renderings were by Polykleitos. Stylistically the work could be as early as the 430's, and its technique indicates a date in the 5th or 4th century B.C. Found in a Christian tomb southwest of the Middle Stoa, original provenience unknown.

Standing Male Torso (S 502)

The still more fragmentary torso of classical date and made of Pentelic marble set against Column 11 came to light in two fragments in disturbed contexts near the middle of the Agora. There remains only the trunk of a figure of much the same scale and in much the same stance as the previous statue, but the head was slightly inclined to the proper right and the right arm was raised high as though the hand had rested on the head.

Group of Two Female Figures* (S 429)

On a high pedestal in front of the wall opposite Column 11 is a group in Parian marble comprising two mature female figures of about three quarters life size. The one carries the other high on her back as though rescuing a friend in distress. Both heads, all four legs and three of the arms are missing. The sculpture has been terribly battered, and the back has been heavily worn by foot traffic.

The two figures have been skilfully differentiated in the choice of dress and in the treatment of the drapery: the lower figure wears a peplos of heavy material, the upper has a chiton of thin, clinging stuff. The group was carefully finished all around, the back as well as the front. The execution is of high quality. The style indicates a date about 420 B.C.

The marble was found at a level of the Byzantine period in the filling of an ancient well on the slope of Kolonos to the east of the Temple of Hephaistos. In marble, scale and quality the group would be appropriate to one of the pedimental compositions of the Temple, probably, in view of its place of finding, the eastern. The meaning of the action is still enigmatic.

Statue of Athena* (S 1232)

In front of the wall opposite Column 11 and beyond the group just noted stands a small statue of Athena. Head and forearms were carved separately and attached; all are now missing. Missing too are the bronze heads of snakes that bordered the aegis, and the bronze ends of the girdle. The left arm hung down and probably rested on a shield at the side of the goddess; this would account for the summary treatment of the drapery on this side. The right forearm was bent forward, but we have no clue to what it held. The hair hung down the back in a heavy mass drawn together by a ribbon at its lower end. A bedding lightly worked on the hair shows that the helmet had a long pendent crest. In type the Agora statue is not far removed from the Athena Parthenos, but the easier stance and the treatment of the drapery, particularly rich on the right side, indicate a slightly later date, probably the late 430's. The quality of carving and the surface finish leave no doubt that this is a Greek original rather than a copy. The statue is of Pentelic marble, about two thirds life size. It was found in a context of late antiquity outside the southeast corner of the Agora.

Reclining Male Figure* (S 147)

Against the wall opposite Column 12 is the upper part of a male figure about two thirds life size, of Pentelic marble, reclining with the support of its left arm. The attitude recalls the "Ilissos" from the west pediment of the Parthenon, and the torso was at one time assigned tentatively to the corresponding position in the east pediment of the Temple of Hephaistos. But the emphatic modelling and the use of Pentelic rather than Parian marble appear to exclude it from the Hephaisteion. The torso may derive from a reclining Herakles of Hellenistic date. It was recovered from a modern foundation to the east of the Temple of Hephaistos.

Fragment of a Monument for a Victory in an Equestrian Contest* (I 7167) Fig. 132

On a square pedestal opposite Column 12 is a fragment from the lower left corner of a two-sided marble relief. The obverse preserves in whole or in part five horsemen. The riders are youthful, smooth-faced, bare-headed, clad in knee-length chitons. The commanding officer, who rides at the outer end of the line, is more mature: he is bearded and wears a helmet. Drilled holes in the appropriate places indicate that each of the men carried a single spear, made separately of bronze. The officer carried in addition a sword, the hilt of which appears above his left hand. The reins must have been rendered in paint, if at all.

On the reverse is the inscription: "The Tribe Leontis won the victory." To the left there remains a leg and the tail of a lion, a punning allusion to the name of the tribe. We infer that the event was a contest among the ten tribes; hence the riders on the obverse are to

132. Reconstruction of equestrian victory monument, early 4th century B.C.

204

be regarded as a tribal contingent led by their tribal cavalry commander (phylarch). There is nothing to indicate in which of the many possible contests the victory was won.

The relief was carved close to the time when Xenophon was writing his essays "On the Cavalry Commander" and "On Horsemanship," i.e. about 365 B.C. One feels that Xenophon would have approved both the style of the riders of Leontis and the rendering by the anonymous sculptor: "This is the attitude in which artists represent the horses on which gods and heroes ride, and men who manage such horses gracefully have a magnificent appearance" (*On Horsemanship*, XI, 8).

The relief is of Pentelic marble and was found reused in a late foundation to the west of the Royal Stoa, close to the site of the Bryaxis base (p. 114). That base, now in the National Museum, also came from a monument commemorative of victories won in equestrian contests; but whereas the present monument is a tribal dedication, the Bryaxis monument was of a more private nature, honoring as it did a man and his two sons all of whom had led their teams to victory in the Anthippasia.

Head of Nike* (S 2354)

The very fresh head of Pentelic marble, slightly over life size, set against Column 12, is a copy, carved probably in the 2nd century A.D., of a work of the second half of the 5th century B.C. The prototype was very similar to but not quite identical with the Nike of Paionios at Olympia. It was found in the Late Roman villa on the Areopagus slopes.

Reliefs from the Temple of Ares* (?) (S 676, S 679, S 870, S 1072)

The four female figures exhibited against the wall opposite Column 13 are selected from a group of forty or more fragments sufficiently uniform in scale and style to be attributed to a common source. All are of Pentelic marble, in high relief and of the finest quality. The style indicates a date in the 430's. Much of the frieze must have been occupied by quietly standing figures. Among the fragments not exhibited are several heads including one of a bearded male, a seated figure and a piece with the heads of sheep, presumably sacrificial victims. The full height of the standing figures was about 0.85 m. In characterizing his figures the designer has introduced variety of many sorts: in the stance (en face, profile, three-quarter poses), in the choice of garments and in the way they are worn, and in the headdress.

The fragments have been found widely scattered throughout the excavation, but with many concentrated around the Temple of Ares.

Statue of "Venus Genetrix" Type* (S 1654)

The small, headless torso of Aphrodite that stands against Column 13 is an adaptation made in the Roman period of a famous Athenian original of the late 5th century B.C., the so-called "Venus Genetrix." The surface has suffered from proximity to a cesspool. The goddess wears a thin chiton which has slipped down over her left shoulder and breast; her back is covered by a himation that was held up by her (now missing) right hand. In the left hand is a water pitcher, replacing an apple in the original. The statue was found in front of the Nymphaion (Plan, **60**) for which it was doubtless made; the date should therefore be the middle of the 2nd century A.D.

Torso of Athena* (S 654)

Opposite Column 14 stands the upper part of a torso of Athena carved in Pentelic marble. The aegis is here reduced to the proportions of a diagonal strap to support the head of Medusa. The snakes' heads that bordered the aegis were of bronze, and have been wrenched from their sockets; on the back of the figure the writhing serpents are worked in the marble. The right arm of the goddess was extended, presumably to hold her spear; the left hung down, probably to rest on her shield. The style points to a date about 420-410 B.C.; the scale and admirable workmanship of the statue attest to its importance.

The torso was found in a Byzantine wall 18 meters to the south of the Temple of Ares. It may be the statue of Athena seen by Pausanias in the sanctuary of Ares and attributed by him (I, 8, 4) to "a man of Paros, Lokros by name." This sculptor is otherwise unknown.

Prytany Decree* (I 1024)

The marble inscription set against Column 15 has never been separated from its ancient base. It illustrates the normal way in which these tall stelai were secured with molten lead in a slot cut in the top of a heavy block of rough stone which was let down into the earth almost to its full depth. The text records votes of thanks to the prytaneis, i.e. to the members of the Council of Five Hundred who had served as presiding officers in the past year, and to various officials of the Council. The inscription was found just to the east of the Tholos, the headquarters of the prytaneis; it dates probably from 260/59 B.C.

Standing Female Figure* (S 339)

The life-size female torso of Pentelic marble opposite Columns 15 and 16 is clad in chiton and peplos. The long "kolpos" and overfold permit a rich treatment of the drapery front and back. The left leg thrust well forward and the right knee slightly bent suggest a striding movement toward the spectator. Since the hair falls in a broad heavy mass down the very middle of the back, the head must have looked straight forward. The head itself, now missing, was worked separately and set in a socket. Both forearms also were cut separately and attached by dowels of which only the sockets remain; in both cases the arms were thrust forward. The upper part of the statue is heavily weathered from long exposure. The style points to a date in the first half of the 4th century B.C. The high quality of the carving and the heavy weathering leave no doubt that the statue is an original work rather than a copy of Roman times.

The statue was found in the Great Drain west of the Temple of Ares. Like the statue of Hadrian (Plan, **16**), this figure also had been reused in late antiquity as a cover slab on the drain.

Pedestal for a Prize in Chariot Racing* (S 399)

The low base of Pentelic marble opposite Columns 16 and 17 once carried a prize won in the apobates race at the Panathenaic Festival by the man whose name appears in the top band: Krates, son of

Heortios, of Peiraeus. In the top of the block is a square socket for the post that held the prize, and two smaller rectangular sockets for additional objects. The event itself is illustrated in the relief: the armed passenger was required to dismount and mount again while the chariot was in full motion. Harking back to the days of Homeric warfare, this event was accounted by Athenian tradition the earliest in the roster of the Panathenaic games. This will in part account for its prominence in the Parthenon frieze. The race was run on the Panathenaic Way in the Agora with the finish near the Eleusinion, and the victor's monument may be supposed to have been set up near the course. The style of the sculpture and of the lettering points to a date in the early 4th century B.C.

The base was found in the Post-Herulian Wall south of the Stoa of Attalos and a little below the Eleusinion.

Annual Report of the State Auctioneers* (I 5509)

A perfectly preserved inscription standing against Column 16 contains the report of the board of eight public auctioneers (poletai) for the year 367/6 B.C. Their activities comprised the sale of a confiscated house and the leasing of seventeen mining properties in the Laureion area.

Record of Arbitration* (I 3244)

This long and complete inscription on Pentelic marble set against Column 17 records the decisions handed down by a board of five private arbitrators in the year 363/2 B.C. The matter at issue was the administration of sacrifices made to various divinities and heroes by two branches of the clan of Salaminioi. The document is very illuminating not only for the "mechanics" of ancient religious practice but also for the process of arbitration, an important part of Athenian justice. The stele was to be set up in Athens in the Sanctuary of Eurysakes, one of the principal heroes of Salamis; it was found to the south of the Temple of Hephaistos where the Eurysakeion was located (p. 45).

208

Herodotus* (?) (S 270)

The bald and bearded head set against Column 18 is obviously a portrait of some distinguished intellectual of the classical period. The features correspond closely with inscribed portraits of Herodotus, although the baldness would be unusual; this may nevertheless be a likeness of the "Father of History." Copied from an early original in the 2nd century A.D., perhaps to adorn a library.

Statue of a Goddess from the Royal Stoa* (S 2370) Fig. 133

Against the wall opposite Column 18 is a female torso of Pentelic marble about 1 1/2 times life size. The head, now missing, was worked separately and set in a socket. The left forearm was likewise cut from a separate piece and secured with a dowel. This forearm is missing, as also the whole of the right arm and the legs below the knees. The figure rested its weight on the left leg; the left forearm was thrust forward. The goddess wears a sleeved chiton of thin and crinkly material. Her girdle, a thin cord, is looped over each shoulder, crossed behind and tied in front. Above the chiton is a voluminous himation thrown over the left shoulder and drawn diagonally across the front of the figure to be held between left forearm and waist. The outer garment is readily distinguished by its heavier, smoother fabric and by occasional fold marks. The statue is fully finished behind. A date in the third quarter of the 4th century is made probable by the proportions of the figure, the massing of the drapery, the treatment of the crinkly chiton and by the high quality of the carving.

For the restoration of the figure the best evidence is provided by the Themis from Rhamnous, a work of the third century B.C. by the local artist Chairestratos. The most likely explanation for the dependence of the Rhamnountine statue on the Athenian in its sculptural type is an identity of subject. As we have seen above (p. 84), our statue stood in front of the Royal Stoa, and for this position there could have been no more appropriate choice than the goddess who was the very personification of law and at the same time the protectress of oaths.

133. Colossal statue of an allegorical figure, probably Themis, possibly Demokratia, found in front of the Royal Stoa, 2nd half 4th century B.C.

Base from a Statue of Karneades* (IG II² 3781)

The low base of Hymettian marble against Column 19 once supported a seated statue of bronze; note the two holes in its top for dowels to secure the feet. The inscription on the front reads:

> *Attalos and Ariarathes of the township*
> *of Sypalettos dedicated (this statue of)*
> *Karneades of the township of Azenia.*

The man honored was the head of the New Academy, the leading philosopher in Athens of the 2nd century B.C. While serving as head of a delegation sent by the Athenians to plead a case before the Roman senate in 156-155 B.C. Karneades had given a series of lectures on Greek philosophy which made a lasting impression on the intellectual life of Rome. This is possibly the statue of Karneades which was seen and commended as a good likeness by Cicero (*de Finibus* V, 2, 4).

Portrait Bust of Antoninus Pius* (S 2436)

Opposite Column 19 is a marble bust slightly over life size, of the Emperor Antoninus Pius (138-161 A.D.). The Emperor wore armor (as shown by the epaulettes), below it a chiton, over it a heavy fringed cloak. This is a very good likeness of the Emperor in his later years.

White marble with large and widely spaced crystals. The bust was found in a well in the house of the Late Roman period on the north slope of the Areopagus (Plan, **58**).

Standing Male Portrait Statues* (S 850, S 936, S 1604)

Opposite Column 20 are exhibited two examples of a type of male portrait statue common in Greece in the Roman period. The figure wears a chiton or undergarment which is almost entirely concealed beneath a voluminous himation or mantle. Beside the left ankle of S 936 are the remains of a book box (scrinium). These and five other statues of the same period (three standing, two seated) were found to the east of the Odeion (Plan, **41**); they were probably set up at the time of the reconstruction of the Odeion about 150 A.D. and may well have carried portrait heads of some of the men of letters associated with the Odeion when it was used as a lecture hall. All are of Pentelic marble.

The head of a middle-aged man inset by the excavators in S 850 is of later date (about 300 A.D.).

Votive Offering from a Cobbler* (I 7396) Fig. **134**

The tall pillar of blue marble set against Column 20 has a slot in its top which once supported the offering proper, probably a marble relief with a cult scene. Our monument is exceptional in that even the top panel of the pedestal is decorated with a scene in low relief. Here

211

134. Cobbler's workshop, votive stele dedicated by the shoemaker Dionysios to the hero Kallistephanos, 1st half 4th century B.C.

we have a glimpse into the shoemaking shop of Dionysios, the dedicator. There are in all five figures of whom one at least is bearded and elderly, one is a young man and one a child. All sit on high-backed chairs except for the child who must be content with a stool. All are evidently engaged in the making of shoes, and a varied display of their products hangs from pegs set into a cleat on the wall above their heads.

The text, which begins on the band beneath the relief and continues on the shaft below, records first the dedication of the offering by

Dionysios and his children to the hero Kallistephanos (Well-crowned) and his children, in terms that recall scenes of worship on many reliefs dedicated by families to Asklepios and his children. Then in hexameter verse Dionysios relates that in response to a vision in his sleep he is now doing honor to the hero and to the hero's children. In return he asks the hero for wealth and good health. A date in the second quarter of the 4th century B.C. will suit the style of the relief and the letter forms. The hero Kallistephanos is otherwise unknown. The relief is a welcome addition to the few known illustrations of the classical period showing tradesmen at work. The shaft was found to the southeast of the Stoa of Attalos.

Portrait Head of Lucius Aelius Caesar* (?) (S 335)

The bearded male portrait head in Pentelic marble and of heroic scale opposite Column 22 is an outstanding work of the early Antonine period. The scale and quality are worthy of someone of importance. The head has been conjecturally identified as Lucius Aelius Caesar. Adopted by the Emperor Hadrian with a view to becoming his successor, Aelius died too soon (January 1, 138 B.C.). The head was found in the wheel pit of the watermill to the south of the Stoa of Attalos.

Portrait Head of Trajan* (?) (S 347)

That high rank in the subject did not always elicit outstanding quality in a portrait is demonstrated by the large head of Pentelic marble wreathed in laurel at the extreme northeast corner of the colonnade. The very generalized expression makes identification difficult, but the head may represent the Emperor Trajan (98-117 A.D.). The marble was found in the ruins of the watermill to the south of the Stoa of Attalos (Plan, 50). It is possibly to be associated with a statue base of Trajan found in the south colonnade of the road leading to the Roman Agora (I 7353).

Portrait Statue of a Magistrate* (S 657)

The stolid male figure against the north wall of the Stoa to the left of the alcove wears undertunic, overtunic and toga in the formal manner proper to a high civic official of late imperial times. The marble is Pentelic, the scale life size. Head, hands and feet are missing; but the battering to which the statue has been subjected does not detract from what was undoubtedly its chief point of sculptural interest, viz. the patterned and largely linear quality of the drapery which recalls the beginnings of Greek monumental sculpture in the early archaic period. Our piece in fact completes the cycle of sculptural development in Greece; dating from the 5th century A.D., it is one of the latest statues in the round surviving from ancient Athens.

Found near the northeast corner of the Late Roman "Palace" (Plan, 41).

Nike: an Akroterion from the Stoa of Zeus* (S 312)

We may end this section with the statue of Nike (Victory) in Pentelic marble set against the north wall of the Stoa. This statue came to light in front of the Stoa of Zeus (Plan, 25). Since the type and the heavy overall weathering are appropriate to an akroterion, we may suppose that the statue stood on the roof of the building, probably at the left-hand angle of the south wing. Figural akroteria are unusual on stoas, but this stoa was dedicated to Zeus, and Nike, as messenger to the gods, was frequently associated with Zeus.

The flamboyant style which was developed to such perfection at Athens in the generation after the Parthenon pediments was never more effectively employed than here. The akroteria, as the latest elements in the Stoa of Zeus, will date from the turn of the 5th and 4th centuries. Many fragments of the wings of this figure and various parts of other Nikai were found in front of the Stoa.

North Alcove and Original Flooring of the Stoa of Attalos

Before leaving this part of the building we may note the alcove beneath the staircase. The marble bench at the foot of its walls commands a pleasing view of the colonnade with its two very different series of columns and a prospect of the distant hills. Beside the northernmost interior column has been preserved a sample of ancient flooring that was found in this part of the building. It was made of marble chips imbedded in mortar. A similar type of flooring has been used in the restoration.

Fortune (S 1030)

The doorway in the north wall of the Stoa toward its front gave access to the north stairway. Behind the grille one may see a small statue in Pentelic marble of the Goddess of Fortune or Chance (Tyche). She had her normal attributes: a steering oar of which traces remain at her right side and a cornucopia on her left arm. Coarse work of the 2nd or 3rd century A.D.

GROUND FLOOR: AREA OF SHOPS

Of the twenty-one shops on the ground floor of the Stoa three at the south end and one at the north end have been restored to their original form. Ten shops have been thrown together to form a continuous museum gallery. We begin at the south end.

Stairwell

The first shop is now largely occupied by a restoration of the stairway of the Roman period designed to provide access to the upper floor. The walls of the room are for the most part ancient; in their faces are many small sockets presumably for the support of shelving. The Ionic column now standing in the stairwell is one of three found in the Post-Herulian Wall near the southwest corner of the Library of Pantainos. A second capital from the same series is shown to the left of the doorway of Shop A (p. 194). Note the traces of ancient paint on the capitals. These columns, close in scale to those in the north porch of the Erechtheion but a quarter of a century earlier, come from an otherwise unknown building of the 5th century B.C.

On the south wall of the Stoa, to the right of the doorway of Shop A, is a man's head rudely incised.

On the floor of the room are exhibited several large terracotta jars (pithoi), the normal receptacles for the storage of food in the ancient world. For stability and convenience of access the jar was set well down into the floor which normally was of clay. These specimens range in date from about 2000 to about 500 B.C.

Memorial Room

Three bronze plaques on the back wall commemorate the excavation of the Agora, the rebuilding of the Stoa of Attalos and the landscaping of the area. The record includes the names of those who participated in the work and of those who contributed money.

A bronze medallion on the right wall honors John D. Rockefeller, Jr., (1874-1960) as the first and principal donor.

Photographs on the left wall illustrate the state of the Agora area before excavation and of the Stoa of Attalos before restoration.

The mosaic floor is entirely modern; it is the kind of flooring that might have been found in such a room in late Greek times.

Sales Room

Guide books, picture books, postcards, color transparencies and replicas of certain objects are on sale. For other photographs and for the scientific publications relating to the Agora, application should be made at the Museum Offices on the upper floor of the Stoa.

Exhibition of Ancient Wine Jars* (If closed, apply to guards for key)

For the transport of wine the Greeks used a terracotta jar (amphora) that commonly held as much as a man could conveniently carry, i.e. 5 to 8 gallons. The bottom of the jar was pointed and shaped to fit the hand; a stout handle on either side facilitated lifting and pouring. The jar was stoppered by means of a terracotta disk secured with plaster, occasionally by a cork. While the clay was still soft a seal was commonly impressed on the top of the handle. The occurrence of the

216

names of magistrates as well as of manufacturers in these seals is a reminder that in those Greek states in which wine was a significant article of commerce the trade was rigorously controlled by the government. Frequently the stamps also indicate the place of origin, either explicitly by word, e.g. Knidian, Thasian, or by a familiar symbol, e.g. the rose of Rhodes.

The Agora excavations have yielded some 800 jars more or less complete (Fig. **135**) and over 20,000 stamped handles (Fig. **136**). Since in most cases the country of origin is now known, and since the dates can normally be fixed to within a half century, the wine trade has become the best documented chapter in the history of ancient commerce. The jars found in the Agora come from many parts of the Aegean, especially from Thasos, Chios, Rhodes, Kos and Knidos, but also from as far afield as the Black Sea, Italy and Spain. The range in time is from the 6th century B.C. to the 6th century A.D. On the shelves of the left-hand side of the room the jars are arranged in chronological sequence, beginning below with the plump and well-rounded shapes of the archaic period, progressing through the crisply profiled forms of Hellenistic times, and ending at the upper right with some "dagger-shaped" jars of late antiquity.

On the right-hand side of the room the arrangement is by place of origin. Here are represented all the famous wines of Greek antiquity. The most distinguished, and most costly, were those from Chios and Thasos; cheaper and much more common were the Rhodian and Knidian. Each of the important producing centers early adopted a characteristic shape of jar and clung to that shape for centuries as jealously as the makers of famous liqueurs and spirits of our day. Note for instance the bulging neck of the Chian jar, the ringed toe of the Knidian and the double handle of the Koan.

In the table case are exhibited characteristic specimens of the stamped handles. In several instances the symbol that appears on the jar can be matched on the coins of the producing state: the rose of Rhodes, the sphinx of Chios, Herakles the favorite hero of Thasos. The importance of the wine trade to some of these states is further attested by the appearance of wine jars of characteristic local shape on their coins. An especially rich series of stamps is that from the north Aegean island of Thasos.

Photographs on the back wall illustrate the use and handling of wine

217

*135. Wine jars
(amphorae) in
storage in the
basement of the
Stoa of Attalos.*

jars in antiquity. Here too is a map with an indication of the principal
centers of wine production and of wine consumption.

The exhibition has been mounted with the aid of a contribution from
the Achaia Clauss Wine Company in Patras, Greece.

The cuttings in the threshold and jambs of the doorway in Shop D are
particularly illuminating for the working of the ancient doors. Note
the cuttings for the single bar used for fastening the original doors
that were set in the line of the inner face of the wall. Later, after the
insertion of a mezzanine floor, the doors were moved to the outer
edge of the threshold; in this period there were cuttings for six bars

136. *A Rhodian amphora stamp with the head of Helios and the name Sostratos.*

on the inside and for one on the outside. The wear on the threshold shows that one normally entered on the right. Carved at eye level on the face of the right-hand jamb as one enters is the figure of Hermes, god of commerce: a clear indication of the use of this room.

MAIN GALLERY

The exhibition runs in a chronological sequence beginning at the south with the Neolithic and finishing at the north with the Turkish. We enter at the south end of the gallery (Fig. **130**).

NEOLITHIC AND BRONZE AGES*

About 3200-1100 B.C.

1. Wall Case. Vases of the Neolithic, Early and Middle Bronze Ages

The two plump jars of red burnished ware on the top shelf (P 14871, 14872) are among the earliest complete vases known from Athens; they date from the end of the Late Neolithic period, about 3200-2800 B.C., and come from a series of twenty early wells on the northwest slope of the Acropolis (Fig. **1**). A number of sherds from the same source, also on the top shelf, illustrate some of the finer fabrics of this period: red and black, burnished and incised, all shaped by hand. The Early Bronze Age, designated in mainland Greece as Early Helladic and dated about 3000-2000 B.C., is very sparsely represented in the Agora. A few characteristic sherds have been laid out on the stand at the middle of the middle shelf. They show that many of the old ceramic techniques persisted from the Neolithic period: burnishing, incising, mottling. Among the innovations is the use of a very thin, dull paint (Urfirnis) on which simple geometric designs may be overpainted (P 13957 in upper right). Among the most characteristic shapes of the period are the bowl with incurved rim (P 27031 in the middle) and the sauceboat (P 14844 in lower right with cream-colored paint).

For the Middle Helladic period (about 2000-1550 B.C.) the material is more abundant. Most of it, again, comes from wells, five of them on the northwest slope of the Acropolis, but domestic deposits of the period have been found also on the lower slopes of the Areopagus and beneath the Royal Stoa (Plan, **26**), while a sprinkling of sherds of this period has been observed over much of the area. The two lower shelves contain specimens of the most characteristic wares of the time: Gray Minyan and Matt-painted. Among the Gray Minyan note especially the two-handled cup (P 13968): perhaps an imitation of silver. In the Matt-painted vases simple geometric designs have been rendered in dull black paint on a light ground. Especially pleasing is the two-handled spouted bowl on the middle shelf (P 10521). The long-spouted, one-handled bowl on the bottom shelf was decorated in white against the red ground of the clay (P 10522). In shape both of these vessels show the influence of Minoan Crete; for their decoration note the watercolors on the wall to the right.

2. Small Freestanding Case. Neolithic Figurine (S 1097)

In the small case opposite the entrance is a marble figurine of a reclining woman whose chest is turned at an angle of 90° to her hips; the head is missing. Dating from the end of the Middle Neolithic period, this is one of the earliest pieces of stone sculpture known from Athens. It has close affinities with still earlier statuettes in Anatolia. The figurine was found in an unstratified context in the area of the Eleusinion.

3. Wall Case. Vases of the Mycenaean Period

The more extensive material of the Mycenaean or Late Helladic period (1550-1100 B.C.) comes almost exclusively from burials the positions of which are indicated on the plan on the wall between Cases 1 and 3. Forty-seven burial places of this period have been found up to 1987 (Figs. 1, 137). The sequence begins with Late Helladic II (15th century B.C.) and is continuous into the Early Iron Age. The pottery of Athens, as also Athenian metal work and jewelry, shares in the remarkable uniformity characteristic of Mycenaean culture on the southern mainland. Most of the Athenian vases would be hard to distinguish from those of the Argolid whether in clay, shape or decoration, and some of them are undoubtedly imports from that area.

In Case 3 are shown a number of characteristic vases. The two-handled goblet on the top shelf right in both shape and color is clearly an imitation of a gold vase (P 21262). The three large wine pitchers in the middle of the case with their strap handles and trough spouts also show the influence of metal work, bronze in this case. On one of the three pitchers an octopus has been applied with great feeling for its decorative possibilities (P 21246). The large mixing bowl on the bottom shelf middle (P 21564) is decorated in an unusually delicate pictorial style; in the middle of its wall is a horned altar on which stood a double axe. The two-handled open bowl on the bottom shelf right (P 21200), with the fish and duck swimming ceaselessly round

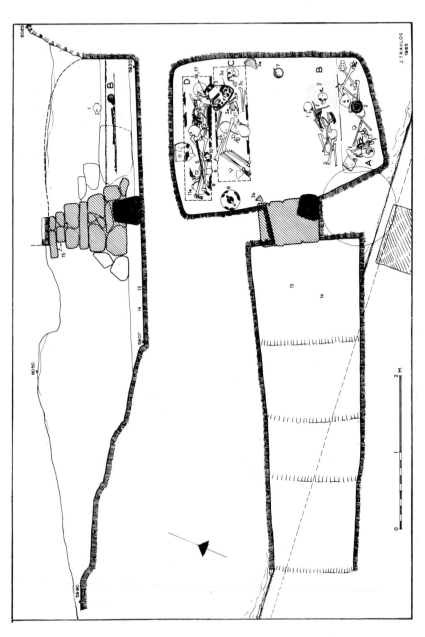

137. A typical Mycenaean chamber tomb, with four separate burials.

the margin of the pool, and the large one-handled mug (P 19211) are shown by their thick walls and coarse workmanship to be among the latest Mycenaean (Late Helladic III C).

On the bottom shelf left have been grouped some characteristic offerings from children's graves. The five vases are miniature and include a spouted feeding bottle. The terracotta figurines with their highly schematic shapes were also commonly placed in children's tombs, perhaps as playthings, more probably as symbolic nurses on the journey to the other world.

The gold ring on the middle shelf right (J 5) is from a grave of Late Helladic III A date (14th century B.C.). A male figure with staff in hand is leading two long-skirted female figures rapidly to the right. In the field above is a small flying figure, perhaps a butterfly; on the extreme left is a column-like object. No convincing interpretation has yet been proposed for this vivid little scene.

4. Wall Case. Offerings from Mycenaean Tombs

On the top shelf are ten vases from a child's grave of Late Helladic II B date (15th century B.C.). Here again the vases are for the most part small in keeping with the tender years of the deceased. Particularly pleasing in this group is the bowl (P 21300) with lilies on its wall and with three suspension loops on its rim.

The two lower shelves contain the furnishings of a chamber tomb on the Areopagus. Three burials had been made in the tomb in fairly rapid succession within the Late Helladic III A period (first half of the 14th century B.C.). The latest burial was that of a young man; on a blue-painted table at his side were laid his rapier (B 778), dagger (B 781) and razor (B 782), all of bronze. The rapier is a good example of the developed Mycenaean type, its narrow blade strengthened with a prominent mid-rib, the shoulders projecting in long horns; the wooden hilt has vanished leaving only the gold-headed bronze rivets by which it was fastened. On the floor of the tomb lay also a number of beads of steatite, and gold rosettes pierced for stitching to the shroud. On the plain vases of the middle shelf are traces of the coating of tin by which they were covered; these vessels were presumably intended for the grave and were so treated to make them look like silver.

5. Freestanding Case. Offerings from a Mycenaean Chamber Tomb

The case is devoted to another chamber tomb on the Areopagus (Late Helladic III A; early 14th century B.C.). A model shows the rectangular tomb chamber bordered to right and left by benches for offerings; in one corner is the burial pit with its stone lid. The doorway was found as it had been walled up after the funeral services. The burial pit had been opened, however, and the body removed, presumably in consequence of the collapse of the roof. The offerings comprised eight vases of various shapes, several ivory hair pins and a bronze mirror, a long-handled copper lamp and two ivory jewel boxes. On the floor of the tomb and in the burial pit were found many of the familiar shroud ornaments: thin gold plates of various shapes all pierced for stitching.

Noteworthy among the offerings are the two ivory boxes, both richly carved in low relief. On the wall and the lid of the larger box (BI 511; Fig. **138**) griffins pull down deer (drawing on nearby wall); the smaller (BI 513) has an allover nautilus design. These boxes rank

138. Ivory pyxis with griffins attacking a deer. 15th century B.C.

among the finest known examples of Mycenaean ivory carving; the ivory was imported from Egypt or Syria.

Another witness to foreign trade found in this tomb is the large pointed amphora of coarse reddish clay exhibited on a stump of ancient wall to the south of Case 4 (P 15358). This jar is of a type known to have been made in Canaan and exported widely around the eastern Mediterranean; it presumably contained some product of the land where it was made: incense, myrrh, spices (?).

As the largest and most richly furnished burial place of the Mycenaean period yet found in Athens, the chamber tomb on the Areopagus must be assigned to one of the principal Athenian families of the period.

EARLY IRON AGE*

11th-8th Centuries B.C.

The material for the study of this period also comes chiefly from graves, though the grave furniture is supplemented in a steadily rising proportion by objects of household use from wells (Fig. 2). Most abundant is the pottery.

Toward the end of the Bronze Age, i.e. in the 12th and early 11th centuries, the craft of the potter had declined: the fabric became coarse, the shapes lifeless, the decoration was reduced to the simplest linear patterns. In the latter part of the 11th century a revival set in; the potter, taking more pride in his work, took greater pains in preparing clay and glaze, put new life into some of the traditional shapes, devised some new shapes, achieved crisper outlines and more pleasing proportions. Multiple compasses were devised for drawing the groups of concentric circles and semicircles that had previously been done freehand. A few new decorative motifs were introduced: checkerboard, hatched panels, sawtooth, and narrow bands effectively grouped. This early phase of the new movement (about 1050-900 B.C.) is known as the Protogeometric period because of the incipient fashion for geometric designs.

The increasing predilection for the geometric was marked by the introduction about 900 B.C. of the meander pattern and the swasti-

ka. Over the next two centuries geometric patterns were the rage. The individual motifs were refined, and gradually a logical syntax of decoration was evolved. Both the individual motifs and their combination were clearly borrowed by the vase painter from the basket maker. Some of the commonest vase shapes of the period were also derived from basketry, e.g. the pointed and flat pyxis and the hemispherical bowl. Birds and animals were now occasionally admitted in a geometricized form. On vases made for the grave funeral rites began to be represented. Battles by land and sea were occasionally depicted. Finally, specific incidents from mythology were shown in a recognizable form. This marked the beginning of the humanistic and narrative tendencies which were to characterize Greek art of the classical period. These developments occurred within the so-called Geometric period (9th and 8th centuries B.C.).

9. Freestanding Case. Cremation Burial of a Warrior Craftsman* (Fig. 139)

Here is illustrated the normal method of adult burial in the Protogeometric and early Geometric periods. The body was burned on a pyre. Vases with offerings of food and drink were thrown on the fire. After the fire the ashes were gathered into an urn which was set down into a small pit; in and around the urn were stacked other offerings, in this case tools and weapons of iron and terracotta vases. Finally, a mound of earth was heaped up to mark and protect the burial place. Among the sweepings from the pyre in this burial were charred figs and grapes. A long sword had been bent into a hoop and placed like a wreath over the urn. Beside the urn were two spearheads of different sizes, two small knives, a narrow chisel, an axehead together with a whetstone, and two sets of horse bits. The bits, extremely rare in Greek lands, find their best parallels in central Europe.
This burial, to be dated about 900 B.C., came to light at the northwest foot of the Areopagus.

10. Freestanding Case. Grave of a Girl*

The case contains the grave of a girl found beneath the north end of the Stoa of Attalos. The date is about 1000 B.C. In a stone-lined

226

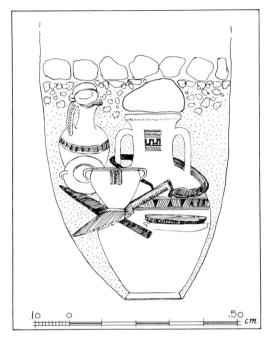

139. Cremation burial of a warrior, ca. 900 B.C.

trench the body was laid on its back. On the shoulders were found the long bronze pins for fastening the cloak, on each wrist a bronze bracelet, on a finger of the left hand a bronze ring. The offerings, four oil flasks and a wine jug, are all decorated in the Protogeometric style and all are small in keeping with the age of the deceased.

11. Freestanding Case. Protogeometric Vases

In Case 11 are shown characteristic grave furnishings of the 11/10th centuries B.C.: the large vessels (amphorae and hydriae) held the ashes of the cremated body; the offerings were chiefly wine pitchers, drinking cups and oil flasks such as the deceased would have used in this world and might be expected to need on the journey to the next. Note also the infant's feeding bottle with spout (P 6836).

227

12. Small Wall Case. Waste from a Potter's Workshop

The case contains waste from a potter's workshop of the early Protogeometric period (about 1000 B.C.) recovered from a well beneath the middle of the Agora. This is the earliest evidence for the making of pottery in the district that came to be known as the "Potter's Quarter" (Kerameikos). The fragments shown are trial pieces: bits of pottery daubed with paint which were placed in the kiln along with the whole pots and then pulled out at intervals to enable the potter to check the progress of the firing.

13. Freestanding Case. Pithos Burial of an Infant*

The exhibit illustrates the common method of burying infants throughout antiquity. The body was placed in a large storage jar (pithos) together with an assortment of small vases. The jar was set down in a pit dug in the soft bedrock and its mouth was closed with a stone slab; beside it was placed a large cooking pot blackened by fire. This burial was made at the northwest foot of the Areopagus. The late Geometric style of the vases points to the third quarter of the 8th century B.C.

14, 15. Wall Cases. Burial Offerings*

These cases contain the offerings from two richly furnished adult burials of the fully developed Geometric period. The first (Case 14), dating from late in the 9th century, was found on the north slope of the Areopagus; the second (Case 15), of the mid-8th century, belonged to a family burial plot south of the Tholos (p. 54). In both cases, as commonly in adult burials of this period, the corpse was laid on the floor of a pit cut down into the bedrock; the offerings were placed on or beside the body and the grave was then covered with rough stone slabs.
Prominent among the offerings are lidded boxes of terracotta (pyxides). In the earlier grave is a single example of a top-shaped pyxis, an early and rare type. The rest are of the more flat variety, perhaps patterned on baskets: the handles are knob-shaped, or, occasionally, in the form of horses, perhaps already a symbol of a noble status in

life and of a heroic status after death. The use of pyxides whether top-shaped or flat is restricted to graves. They presumably held food offerings to supplement the drink offerings attested by the wine jugs and drinking cups.

16. Small Wall Case. Offerings from a Funeral Pyre*

In the case on the opposite wall of the gallery is displayed a group of small vases and terracotta figurines found on the ancient road just outside the family cemetery to the south of the Tholos (p. 54). All the objects are broken and discolored by fire. They are to be regarded as offerings made in connection with one or other of the burials in the neighboring plot. The date is late in the 8th century B.C.

Funerary associations are especially evident in the case of the largest vase, an amphora (P 4990). On the neck is shown the corpse laid out on a bier and surrounded by mourners who tear their hair in grief. In a circular course around the body of the vase is a chariot race, the principal event in the funeral games of Homeric heroes. The snakes on shoulder, rim and handles speak also of the grave. Among the other vases are two two-handled bowls on tall stands: miniature copies in clay of the large bronze cauldrons that were given as prizes at funeral games. The standed incense burners (thymiateria) and the two-handled saucer on the wall will also have served in funeral rites. More familiar grave offerings are the wine pitcher and drinking cup, the small oil and unguent flasks. Noteworthy at this early date are the terracottas in the round: a bird and two quadrupeds, a divinity (?) seated in a throne perhaps holding a pomegranate in the right hand (T 762), a chariot group (T 751).

17. Freestanding Case. Grave Group of about 850 B.C.* (Fig. 140)

All the material in this case comes from the grave of a wealthy woman who died at the age of about 30 in the middle of the 9th century B.C. The grave was excavated in 1967 at the northwest foot of the Areopagus. The splendid early Geometric amphora on the left held the ashes of the body which had been burned on the spot (Fig. 140). In the amphora had also been deposited the woman's more precious jewelry; this had not gone through the fire. The large

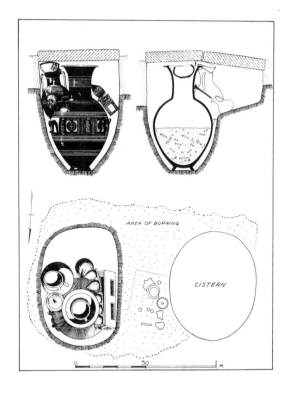

140. Cremation burial of a rich Athenian lady, ca. 850 B.C.

vase was closed with a mug and set down in a pit in the bedrock; around its shoulder were heaped a number of vases in fresh condition. The mouth of the pit was closed with a large brick. Among the ashes around the pit were many fragmentary vases and terracotta beads that had been thrown on the pyre.

The medium-sized amphora with a mug in its mouth on the upper shelf stood close by the great urn. Note the very delicate geometric decoration on the smaller vases. The small, open-work vessel is a miniature wool basket. More remarkable is the terracotta model of a linen chest surmounted by a row of five top-shaped granaries each with a trapdoor near its peak and with a pair of holes at its base perhaps for securing a wooden ladder (Fig. **141**). The symbolism is obvious: an abundance of food and of household furnishings whether in this world or the next.

141. Pyxis with model granaries (?) on lid, ca. 850 B.C.

The jewelry was remarkable for its period in both quantity and quality. The large terracotta beads, which were probably designed for funerary use, had gone through the fire. The unburned jewelry deposited in the urn included four long bronze pins, two bronze fibulae and a bronze ring (not exhibited). From the urn came also the necklace of glass paste with the banded glass pendant. Finally, the gold: three narrow rings, three broad hoops with geometric ornament, and a pair of massive earrings each comprising a trapezoidal plate with filigree and granular ornament with three pendants in the form of pomegranates.

Noteworthy also are the two small pyramidal seals of ivory, the attributes of a responsible housekeeper.

18. Freestanding Case. Geometric Vases

On the top shelf are the offerings from a woman's grave of about 900 B.C. found at the northwest foot of the Areopagus. Generous provision was made by the family for her journey to the other world: eight vases of assorted shapes, a terracotta pendant, earrings of electrum (alloy of gold and silver) and two pair of heavy traveling boots modeled in clay.

The wine jug (oinochoe) on the bottom shelf of Case 18 (P 4885) is interesting for both its structure and its decoration (Fig. **142**). Two tubes were inserted transversely through the body of the vase. The most probable explanation of this curious arrangement, otherwise unknown, is that it was a device for cooling the contents. When the jug, full of wine, was set in a basin of cold water or let down into a well the water would circulate through the tubes, and thus cool the wine more quickly. The vase is decorated with battle scenes: in a band around the body men fight on foot and from chariots; on the neck is a file of heavily armed men; note the plumed helmet and the figure-of-eight shield, the long heavy sword and the pair of spears reminiscent of those shown in Case 9. The weapons and the method of fighting are those described by Homer. It has been conjectured, indeed, that the scene represents a particular incident described in the *Iliad* (XI, 670-761), viz. the fight between the people of Pylos and the Epeians among whom were twin brothers, sons of Molione, who share the great square shield below the handle of the vase. If correctly interpreted this scene ranks among the earliest representations in Greek art of a specific incident.

On the same shelf is a small bowl of the late Geometric period which was evidently made by pressing a clay lining into a basket (P 17189); beside the ancient bowl is a modern basket of the same type.

142. *Roll-out watercolor of the Geometric oinochoe showing a battle scene from the Iliad, one of the earliest representations of myth in Greek art, late 8th century B.C.*

ORIENTALIZING PERIOD*

Late 8th and 7th Centuries B.C.

The material shown in Case 19 will illustrate some of the developments which occurred in Athens in the formative period of classical Greek art. Vase shapes become more varied and more specialized for different household needs: eating, drinking, cooking, washing, storage. Many of the vases betray the influence of metal work in the thinness of their walls, in their angularity and in the use of strap handles. The more liberal use of color (white and red in addition to the traditional black), was undoubtedly inspired by Near Eastern textiles. These textiles will also have been the principal medium by which the Athenian painter learned many new motifs: exotic animals such as the lion, hybrid creatures like the sphinx and siren, truncated figures in which only the forepart or the hindpart of an animal is shown, schematized floral designs based especially on the palmette and lotus. The same influence stimulated the development of a freer and more naturalistic style. But the most significant of all things learned by the Greeks from the Near East at this time were the Phoenician letters which in the second half of the 8th century began to be used in Athens on vases to label the figures or to name the owner. The occurrence in most deposits of this period of a significant sprinkling of vases imported from other parts of Greece, and even from Italy, marks the revival of commerce within the Greek world as well as between the Greeks and their neighbors.

19. Freestanding Case. Material from Two Wells

Case 19 contains representative objects from the filling of two wells of the second half of the 7th century; they are important in giving a picture of the normal household pottery of the time. Note the imports: the alabastron from Corinth (P 23425), the lamp from Asia Minor (L 5101), the pair of chalices from the island of Chios (P 23458, 23459), the fragment of a bucchero kantharos from Etruria (P 23454). The splendid lion's head on the wine jug (olpe) (P 22550) is a striking example of eastern influence, while the delightful pair of horses on the amphora (P 22551) was probably inspired by imports from the Greek islands. The woman's head painted in outline on the fragmentary amphora (P 17393) has the bigness of conception and the sure rendering that mark contemporary Attic sculpture, the first monumental statues in marble. Here too are more imports. A fragment from a large vase preserving two pair of human legs (P 576) is Argive; it comes from the debris of a sanctuary. The two-handled cup (kantharos) (P 7014) bears the owner's name painted by the maker on the rim: "I belong to ...ylos."

21. Small Wall Case. Offerings from a Shrine*

This group of material takes us out of the home to a sanctuary, the earliest yet known in the area of the Agora (middle of the 7th century B.C.). The material exhibited is a small selection from a large dump found at the northwest foot of the Areopagus. The shields of terracotta, the models of tripods in terracotta and in bronze, the warriors and chariot groups of terracotta, the painted terracotta plaques pierced for suspension, the drinking cups are all appropriate as offerings to the heroized dead. The most striking object in the group is a plaque showing an elaborately draped female figure with arms raised, evidently the epiphany of a goddess. The prominence of snakes to either side of the figure attests to connection with some of the early tombs on the slopes of the Areopagus.

ARCHAIC PERIOD

Late 7th - Early 5th Centuries B.C.

From the late 7th into the early 5th century the arts and handicrafts in Athens show a steady development, stimulated by growing prosperity and encouraged, through much of the period, by the enlightened patronage of the leading family, the Peisistratids. Since the Agora as yet boasted few substantial public buildings and no great sanctuaries, its excavation has naturally yielded little in the way of major sculpture or pottery of first quality. The finds have nevertheless contributed in various ways to a better understanding of the age.

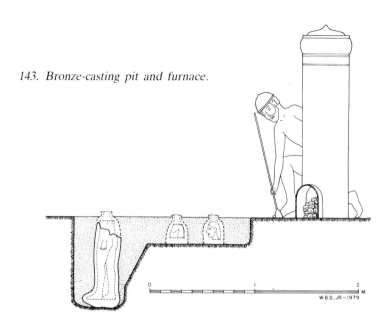

143. Bronze-casting pit and furnace.

W.B.D., JR – 1979

23. Freestanding Case. Mould for a Bronze Statue* (Fig. 143)

The mould for the making of a bronze statue of Apollo was assembled from debris found in a pit at the west edge of the Agora, just to the south of the Temple of Apollo (Plan, **23**). The casting was undoubtedly done by the lost-wax process. A core of clay was covered by a layer of wax, and this was then enveloped in an outer mould built up of three successive layers of clay. Metal skewers having been inserted to keep core and mould in their proper relative positions, the wax was melted out. The mould was planted upright in a pit in the bedrock and packed firmly with earth. Bronze brought to the melting point in a nearby furnace above was poured through a funnel-like opening at the top. On cooling, the mould was stripped away, the surface of the bronze was smoothed and the completed statue was set up in the nearby temple. Dating as it does from the middle of the 6th century B.C., this little establishment illustrates the effective simplicity of technical procedure at a time when Greek artists were just beginning to cast statues of hollow bronze.

Elsewhere in the excavations have been found fragmentary moulds and casting pits for the making of statues datable to the 5th, 4th and 2nd centuries B.C. and to the 5th century A.D.

24. Wall Shelf. Heads from Herms* (S 2452, S 2499, S 3347) (Figs. 49, 50)

Since Athens was noted for the number of Herms that stood in both public and private places it is not surprising that many should have come to light in the excavation of the Agora. Three typical heads of various types are exhibited here.

S 2452. A casualty of 415 B.C. is this slightly smaller than life-sized head of Parian marble which came to light among the votives of the late 5th century B.C. in the crossroads enclosure (Plan, 27, Fig. 49). Hermes here wears a full beard and moustache. A broad, flat head band rises to a peak in front and is tied behind with cords. The band divides the hair into two parts: the front hair is swept back in a naturalistic way into voluminous masses above the ears; behind the band the hair is combed in fine regular ridges that radiate from the crown and descend down the back under the band to end in a slight flourish at shoulder height. The lower lip is inset, presumably because of some mishap in the carving. The style of the head, combined with its fresh condition, indicates that it had been made only a few years before its destruction.

S 2499. This slightly larger than life-sized head of Pentelic marble was found in a context of the 4th century A.D. in the Double Stoa just to the west of the Royal Stoa; it was undoubtedly one of "the Herms" (Fig. 50). In type our head belongs to a large group of replicas that are connected by two inscribed examples with the Athenian sculptor Alkamenes (active about 430-410 B.C.). Characteristic are the three rows of corkscrew curls arched over the forehead; also the finely combed hair radiating from the crown and falling in a heavy mass down the back with a single ringlet brought forward from behind the ear to descend over the shoulder. A twisted band encircles the head. Beard and moustache are luxuriant; lips full. At the back of the neck is a socket for a large patch. Second century A.D.

S 3347. Life-sized herm of white marble, with corkscrew curls over forehead, full beard and moustache. Though somewhat battered, the almond-shaped eyes and upward-curving, deep-set mouth allow this head to be dated around 510-500 B.C., making this one of the earlier Herms found in Athens. From Byzantine fill on the west foundations of the Stoa Poikile.

24A. Wall Shelf. Archaic Heads* (S 1295, S 1071, S 2476)

S 1295. The small head of Herakles wearing the scalp of the Nemean lion as a helmet was found in a late antique context to the southwest of the Agora; the figure probably adorned a temple that may have stood in that district, Melite, in which was a famous sanctuary of Herakles. The piece is both charming and intriguing. Most elements of the style can be traced to the beginning of the 5th century B.C., but the treatment of eyes and mouth, and the use of Pentelic rather than island marble call for a date perhaps in the later 5th century B.C.

S 1071.* This life-sized head of island marble was found in a context of late antiquity above the Eleusinion; it probably comes from a statue of a maiden (*kore*) dedicated on the Acropolis. The hair is held by a diadem: in front are bangs ending in a double row of snail-shell curls; behind are long crimped tresses. She wears large disc earrings. The late archaic style points to a date at the beginning of the 5th century B.C.

S 2476. This small head of Parian marble about half life size was found in the crossroads enclosure (Plan, 27) in a context of the late 5th century B.C. The face is boldly modelled, the eyeballs bulge, the crinkly hair is confined by a diadem which allows a mass to fall down behind while three locks fall over either shoulder in front. She wears disc earrings. The sculptural style of our head, which finds close parallels on the Athenian Treasury at Delphi, points to the early years of the 5th century B.C.

CLASSICAL PERIOD: CIVIC LIFE

5th-4th Centuries B.C.

The excavation has yielded many objects associated with the various departments of civic life that were centered in the Agora: legislation, administration, the judiciary, finance, war memorials, etc. Most of this material dates from the great period of Athens: late 6th to late 4th century B.C., and constitutes a valuable supplement to the ancient authors. As these objects are unique to the Agora and illustrate the functioning of the Athenian state, they make up the most important part of the museum collection.

25. Stand. Inscriptions on Marble*

The Agora, as the most frequented part of the city, was the commonest place for setting up inscriptions that were meant to be read by many people. The excavations have in fact yielded over seven thousand inscriptions on marble. A few pieces of outstanding interest are shown here.

The small fragment on the left (I 3872) comes from the base of the statues of Harmodios and Aristogeiton who struck down Hipparchos, son of the tyrant Peisistratos, in 514 B.C. The first part of the epigram, which is preserved in a late Greek grammarian, reads "A great light shone for the Athenians when Harmodios and Aristogeiton slew Hipparchos." Part of the name of Harmodios can be made out. The piece was found in the northern part of the Agora where Pausanias saw the statues in the 2nd century A.D. and not far from the spot where the deed occurred.

Next comes a fragment from a list of the magistrates, the eponymous archons, who gave their names to the Athenian years (I 4120). The names here preserved, dating from 527/6 to 522/1 B.C., are ...eto..., Hippias, Kleisthenes, Miltiades, Kalliades and Peisistratos. The list was set up about 425 B.C., and was intended no doubt for the convenience of administration.

Third from the left is a fragment from the heading of the tribute list of the Athenian Empire for the year 418/17 B.C. (I 4809a). The greater part of these lists is to be found in the Epigraphical Museum in Athens. At the lower right of the fragment begins the entry of the amounts paid into the treasury of the goddess Athena from the tribute collected from the region of the Hellespont.

The inscription on the right (I 2729) (Fig. 91) comes from the Library of Pantainos (Plan, 48). On it are engraved library regulations dating from about 100 A.D.: "No book shall be removed since we have

238

taken an oath to that effect. Open from the first hour till the sixth." On the other side of the stand, to the left, are two non-joining fragments of a monument erected in memory of Athenians who fell fighting the Persians (I 303). The inscription consists of two epigrams, the first written on a smooth top margin, the second added on a specially dressed panel below. The general sense is certain: according to the first epigram the fallen, fighting both by land and sea, had saved Greece from slavery; the second records the preservation of Athens from burning at the hands of the Persians. The second poem in all probability relates to the Battle of Marathon (490 B.C.), but the relation between the two epigrams is uncertain. The upper epigram was copied in the Hellenistic period, and of the copy a fragment is shown to the right (I 4256).

(To continue with the public antiquities, move back and across to Case 20.)

20. Freestanding Case. The Athenian Army and Sokrates in the Agora*

On the top shelf is displayed material from the Athenian army. B 1373 is a spear-butt, which would be attached to the end of the wooden shaft of a spear to counterbalance the heavy metal point (Fig. **144**). It carries the incised inscription: "The Athenians from the Lesbians (dedicated this) to the Dioskouroi." It should date to 428/7 B.C., therefore, when the Athenians suppressed a revolt of their allies on the island of Lesbos (Thuc. Book III). The lead tablets and round stamped clay tokens are part of a cavalry archive found in the crossroads well at the northwest corner of the Agora (Fig. **145**). The lead strips, which were found rolled up, carry the name of a man and the color, brand, and value of his horse. Horses of the Athenian cavalry were apparently inspected and registered on a regular basis. The clay tokens are stamped with the name of an official: "Pheidon, the Hipparch (cavalry commander) in Lemnos" (Fig. **66**). The same officer is known as a trainer of young cavalrymen according to a fragment of the comic poet Mnesimachos: "Go forth, Manes, to the Agora, to the Herms, the place frequented by the phylarchs, and to their handsome pupils, whom Pheidon trains in mounting and dismounting." Presumably the tokens were used in a messenger

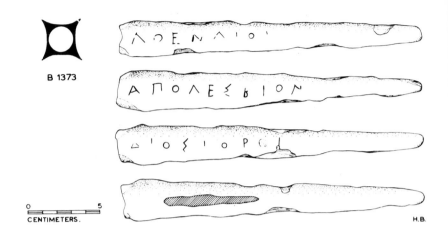

B 1373

0 ————— 5
CENTIMETERS.

H.B.

144. Bronze spear-butt taken from the Lesbians in 428/7 B.C., dedicated to the Dioskouroi.

5 CMS.

145. Lead tablet describing a horse from the Athenian cavalry: Belonging to Konon, a chestnut with a centaur brand, worth 700 drachmas.

240

system or as passports of some sort. The two rectangular clay tokens (SS 8080, MC 1245) are similarly official, used by Xenokles the Peripolarch, the border commander.

The small round lead tokens were also used by the army, apparently for the issuing of armor (Fig. **146**). Each disk is stamped on one side with a letter of the alphabet, while the other side has a representation of a piece of armor: helmet, breastplate, greaves, and shields are all represented.

Other material comes from buildings associated with the life and death of Sokrates. The hollow bone eyelets for laces and the iron hobnails used for shoemaking come from a 5th century house which lay just outside the Agora, right by the boundary stone near the Tholos (p. 57, fig. **25**). The fragment of black-glazed drinking cup was found nearby and presumably identifies the owner of the cobbler's shop as Simon. Xenophon, Diogenes Laertius and Plutarch

146. Lead tokens used for the issuing of pieces of armor: helmet, greaves, and breastplate.

tell us that Sokrates, when he wished to meet those students too young to enter the Agora would meet them at the house of Simon the cobbler, which lay nearby.

The rest of the material in the case comes from the building lying southwest of the main square, tentatively identified as the State Prison (Plan, **72**), where Sokrates was put to death. Thirteen small medicine bottles found in a cistern in the building represent a remarkable concentration of this rare shape, and the small marble statuette of Sokrates (S 1413) himself was found in the building as well.

26. Wall Case. Public Antiquities*

A set of official weights and measures is known to have been kept in the Tholos. The law required that weights and measures to be used in commerce should first be checked against these standards. The excavations around the Tholos have brought to light official examples dating from the 6th, 5th and 4th centuries B.C., and a few others have been found elsewhere in the area; these provide welcome evidence for the absolute values of the ancient units. Numerous weights and one measure of the type used in commerce have come to light in the ruins of houses and shops; they show greater deviations from the standard than would be tolerated today.

On the bottom shelf, left, is a set of three bronze weights of about 500 B.C. found in a well near the Tholos. All are inscribed "official property of the people of Athens." On each weight the denomination is indicated both by writing and by a symbol:

stater = knucklebone (810 grams)
quarter (stater) = shield (199.5 grams)
sixth (stater) = tortoise (127.5 grams)

The lead commercial weights shown to the right are also marked both in writing and with symbols:

2 staters = wheel (1792.5 grams)
stater = knucklebone (841.5 grams)
mina = dolphin (455 grams)
third (stater) = amphora (301 grams)
quarter (stater) = tortoise (231 grams)
sixth (stater) = half amphora (156.5 grams)
eighth (stater) = half tortoise (105 grams)

At the middle of the floor of the case is a tall cylindrical measure of terracotta found in a well on the north slope of the Acropolis (AP 1103); its date is the third quarter of the 5th century B.C. The Y-shaped bar in the mouth was intended to facilitate leveling, from which it is clear that the vessel was a dry measure. Its official character is indicated by the inscription painted around the middle: "official" *(demosion)*, and by the owl stamped on the wall just below the lip. The capacity is 3.2 liters, i.e. 3 ancient *choinikes*.

Next to the right is another cylindrical dry measure, likewise inscribed "official" (demosion) and stamped on the wall with the head of Athena and a double-bodied owl (P 3559) (Fig. **147**). This specimen, dating from the 4th century B.C., was found near the Tholos. Its capacity is about 1.7 liters, the equivalent of 1 1/2 choinikes.

For an official measure in bronze see Case 41.

On the extreme right is a third dry measure, more coarsely made and with its wall bent out to form a wide rim (P 14431) (Fig. **147**). It comes from the ruins of a house and is to be dated about 100 B.C. On the outer end of a mass of lead set through the wall is stamped a figure of the seated Dionysos. The capacity is about 1.7 liters, i.e. 1 1/2 choinikes. The vessel conforms to the specifications in an Athenian law of the late 2nd century B.C. for the measure to be used in the sale of various fruits and nuts. The lead seal was applied by the officials in the Tholos after checking against a standard measure. On the shelf above is a small pitcher *(olpe)* of about 500 B.C. with

147. *An assortment of official dry measures for grain and nuts, 5th to 2nd centuries B.C.*

the painted ligature ⟨Æ⟩ for demosion, i.e. "official" (P 13429). This then will have been a standard liquid measure; it contained 0.252 liters, the capacity of the ancient kotyle (1/12th of a chous).

Beside the olpe is a small black drinking cup (kylix) of the second quarter of the 5th century B.C. (P 5117). Scratched on its floor is the same ligature meaning "official." The cup, found in a well below the Stoa of Zeus, may have been used in some nearby public dining hall. The marble wash basin of which a fragment is shown at the left end of the upper shelf also served a public body (I 4869). According to the inscription on its rim it belonged to the Bouleuterion or Council House. It was found just south of the Old Bouleuterion (Plan, **14**) and may be dated from its letter forms in the early 5th century B.C. The three little terracotta plaques in the middle of the shelf each with one end cut in a jagged line are symbola, i.e. "things to be fitted together" (MC 820-822). They were made in the shape of dominoes and inscribed on both faces. On one side, above, was written the name of a township; below appears the abbreviation for an office, pol--, probably for poletes, an official auctioneer. On the other side across the middle was written the name of a tribe. Before baking, the plaque was cut through the middle in a jagged line. After baking, the parts were presumably distributed and subsequently reunited, possibly in connection with allotment to a township office, or to establish the identity of a messenger. The tablets were found in a deposit of the third quarter of the 5th century B.C. behind the Stoa of Attalos.

27. Freestanding Case. Equipment from the Law Courts*

Here is shown a unique example of the water clock *(klepsydra)* used for measuring speeches in the law courts (P 2084). By the ancients themselves it was regarded as the most characteristic feature of the courts. Shaped like a modern flower pot, but with two handles, the vessel has a small, bronze-lined outlet at the bottom, and a larger hole under the rim to allow the vessel to be filled to exactly the same level each time (Fig. **148**). The lower hole was closed with a stopper until the speaker began; the plug was then withdrawn and the speaker might continue as long as the water ran, in this case 6 minutes. The capacity is indicated by the XX on the wall, i.e. two choes (6.4 liters). Also on the wall are faint traces of the word

148. Models of the terra-
cotta water clock in use.

"Antiochis," the name of one of the ten tribes of Athens. The water
clock was found in a well of the late 5th century B.C. at the southwest
corner of the Agora (p. 56).

To the left of the water clock are several wheel-shaped objects of
bronze some of which are inscribed "official ballot" *(psephos de-
mosia)* (Fig. **149**); they correspond with Aristotle's account of the
ballots used by the Athenian jury-men for recording their votes (*Ath.
Pol.*, 68). The ballots with solid axles were for acquittal, the hollow
for condemnation. The six solid ballots shown here were found
together in the ruins of a building of the 5th and 4th centuries B.C.

149. Official inscribed ballots ("public vote") from the Lawcourts, found in
the container under the Stoa of Attalos (fig. 78).

245

beneath the north end of the Stoa of Attalos (Plan, **44**); they are good evidence for identifying the building as a law court.

The unglazed lid of a cooking pot or echinos (P 28470) carries a painted inscription which, though fragmentary, seems to list documents stored and sealed in the pot until their presentation at a trial (Fig. **150**). It dates to the 4th century B.C. and was found in the northeast area of the Agora.

To the right of the water clock also shown are a number of the bronze identity tickets (pinakia) carried by all citizens eligible for jury service (Fig. **151**). On each was incised the name of the bearer, his father and his township (demos), and each bore an official stamp: an owl or a gorgoneion. The stamped letter indicates the bearer's jury section. Some of the pinakia retain traces of letters from an earlier use. These pinakia figure largely in Aristotle's account of court procedure, beginning with their use in the allotment machine (kleroterion) of which a specimen is shown against the wall of the gallery to the right.

The small bronze ball shown with the identity tickets was also used in the allotment machine.

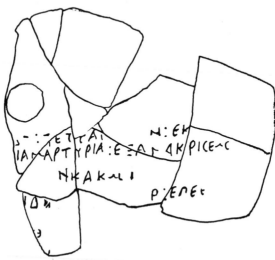

150. Lid of a small pot used to hold evidence until the time of a trial, probable reading: "Of the written copies, the following four are inside: testimony from the arbitration, law on the abuse of heiresses, challenge of testimony, oaths of litigants. Antenor put the lid on." 4th century B.C.

151. *Official jurors' identification tags. At top, "Demophanes the son of Phil..., of the township of Kephisia." Bronze, 4th century B.C.*

28. Wall Pedestal. Allotment Machine* (I 3867) (Fig. 152)

The allotment machine *(kleroterion)* consisted of a marble stele in the front of which were one or more columns of slots of a size to receive the identity tickets of the jurors. The number of columns varied according to the function of the machine; in this case there were eleven columns. At the left edge are cuttings for the attachment of a vertical bronze tube. The allotment machines stood at the entrances to the law courts. The slots were filled with identity tickets. Bronze balls, some black and some white, were poured into the tube

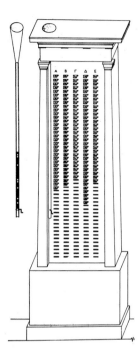

152. Restored drawing of an allotment machine (Kleroterion) used to pick jurors for a trial.

and released at the bottom one by one. Depending on whether a black or a white ball came out, the citizens represented by one whole row of name plates were either retained or rejected for jury service on that day. This machine, like all that have survived, is of the Hellenistic period; in the 4th century B.C. they were movable and so presumably of wood.

Decree against Tyranny* (I 6524) (Fig. **153**)

Next stands a complete marble stele inscribed with a law passed by the people of Athens in 336 B.C. The law, proposed by Eukrates, son of Aristotimos of Peiraeus, was intended to discourage attempts to set up a tyranny, i.e. a dictatorship: "If anyone rise up against the people with a view to tyranny, or join in establishing tyranny, or overthrow the People of the Athenians or the Democracy in Athens, whoever kills him who does any of these things shall be blameless."

248

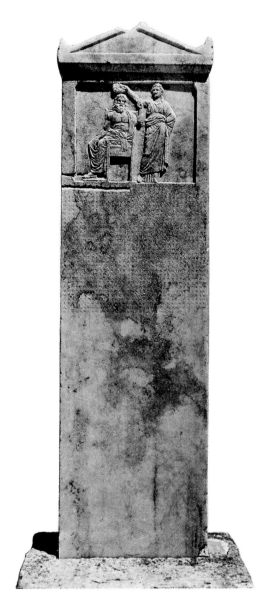

153. *Decree against tyranny, 336 B.C., with a relief showing the People
(Demos) of Athens being crowned by Democracy.*

If, however, a tyranny were to be established, the law prohibited the Council of the Areopagus, which was still looked upon as the guardian of the constitution, from meeting. In this way a tyrant who had achieved power *de facto* was prevented from gaining *de jure* recognition. Two copies of the law were to be engraved on marble stelai and set up, one near the entrance to the meeting place of the Council of the Areopagus, the other in the meeting place of the Assembly. A sum of 20 drachmai was appropriated for the making of the stelai. The text is illustrated by a relief in which Democracy places a wreath on the head of the People of Athens.

The law was passed a few months after Philip II of Macedon had broken the power of Thebes and of Athens at Chaironeia (338 B.C.); it was directed, no doubt, against the possibility of a pro-Macedonian revolt in Athens. The effective life of the law, however, was short. In 322 B.C. the Macedonians occupied Athens. Eukrates, the proposer of the law, is reported to have perished miserably. The marble copies of his law were presumably pulled down; the surviving stele was discovered in the building fill of the Square Peristyle that was under construction in the late 4th century at the northeast corner of the Agora (Plan, **44**).

29. Freestanding Pedestal. Kneeling Boy* (P 1231) (Fig. 154)

The terracotta figure of a kneeling boy represents an athlete in the act of binding a ribbon, symbol of victory, about his head. The ribbon is restored, but its existence is attested by the position of hands and fingers and by the analogy of contemporary vase paintings. The figure is hollow and is topped by a vase mouth proper to an oil flask such as were carried by athletes to hold their rub-down. Sculptural quality combined with delicate execution makes this figure a little masterpiece of the mature archaic art of Attica (540-530 B.C.).

30. Wall Case. Black-figured and Red-figured Vases*

In the long wall case to the right are shown some characteristic specimens of black-figured and red-figured vases of the archaic period.

In the right side of the case, top shelf, among the numerous oil flasks

154. *Vase in the form of a kneeling boy, ca. 540-530 B.C.*

(lekythoi) note especially the large specimen on the extreme right (P 24104). It bears a particularly interesting version of an ever popular theme: the introduction of Herakles into Olympos.

On the middle shelf right is a good example of the "Siana" type of drinking cup (P 20716, about 570 B.C.); on the floor medallion a running warrior, on the exterior on either side a grazing horse. On the same shelf is a fine specimen of the miniature painting in vogue in the middle of the 6th century B.C.: a perfume bottle *(alabastron)* decorated by the Amasis Painter with a frieze of quietly standing divinities (P 12628). The three drinking cups *(skyphoi)* of generous proportions on the bottom shelf are all works of the Theseus Painter of about 500 B.C.; note especially the middle piece on which boys riding pickaback engage in the game called ephedrismos (P 1546). The left-hand side of the case is devoted to red-figure. On the top shelf, right, are three small and one medium-sized drinking cups *(kylikes)* (P 1272-1275). The first three are of the Group of Acropolis 96; the fourth, P 1275, is related. They date around 500 B.C. All four vases were found to the northeast of the Temple of Hephaistos in a deep shaft which had been used as a dumping place by neighboring potters of whom this master was one. All four cups have single figures in their floor medallions: an athlete with jumping weights (P 1272), a castanet player (P 1273), a man playing kottabos (throwing wine at a target from a drinking cup) (P 1274), a boy hurrying along with two wine jars on a shoulder pole (P 1275).

The kylix on the top shelf left (P 2698) is of technical interest, being a good example of the intentional combination of black and red glaze, a fashion in vogue in Athens especially in the late 6th and early 5th centuries B.C.

On the middle shelf are further instances of the finding together of works by the same Athenian vase painter. The two cups by Epikte-tos, one (P 24110) with boxers on its floor medallion and the other with a satyr on a donkey (P 24114), were found in a well beneath the south end of the Stoa of Attalos. From the same well come three of the four cups attributed to the Chairias Painter and shown to the left on the same shelf: a lyre player (P 24115), maenad (P 24116), hetaira at an altar (P 24102). The fourth cup by the Chairias Painter, with a woman washing (P 23165), was found in a well near the southwest corner of the Agora. The date is ca. 500 B.C.

The red-figured wine jug *(chous)* (P 15210) at the middle of the bottom shelf is probably to be connected with the spring festival called the Anthesteria. The spirit of revelry has invaded even a bronze foundry: a slave bearing an offering tray approaches the head of the establishment who stands in holiday attire in front of his smelting furnace.

On the floor of the case to the left is a selection from a deposit of slender red-figured pitchers *(oinochoai)* found on the north slope of the Acropolis. The shape is unusual and the painted scenes still more so. On the body is a four-horse chariot with Athena at the reins and a groom at the horses' heads. In two cases Athena appears also on the neck of the vase, as Promachos. The goddess is rendered in an archaistic style comparable with that of the Panathenaic amphorae. On the front of the vase a pair of breasts stand out in high relief. The style of painting points to the closing years of the 5th century B.C. The prominence of Athena and the place of finding suggest some sacred or civic use, perhaps in connection with the Panathenaic Festival.

31. Small Freestanding Case. Krater by Exekias* (AP 1044)

We turn back to a small case below one of the rear windows to find a mixing bowl (krater) by Exekias, the leading black-figure painter of the middle of the 6th century B.C. The vase was found in a well high on the north slope of the Acropolis; it had perhaps been dedicated on the Acropolis and subsequently discarded. That it was esteemed in antiquity is shown by the ancient mending. The vase is the earliest known example of its shape: the calyx krater. On one side rages the battle over the body of the fallen Patroklos; on the other side is preserved the front part of the procession that accompanied Herakles to his deification on Olympos. In a lower zone on either side is a little picture of lions pulling down a bull, clearly inspired by pedimental compositions. On the handle side we have an oblique allusion to the festive purpose of the vessel: above the handle a maenad sits in the shade of a grape vine unaware as yet of the long-tailed satyr who hurries up from below.

32. Freestanding Case. Red-figured and White-ground Vases*

The four small vases in this case are all of choice quality. In the medallion of the white-ground cup (P 43) a youth tunes his lyre while his pet hare listens attentively; in the field the love-name "Erinos" (ca. 480-470 B.C.) On a fragmentary bobbin at the other end of the case (P 5113), also white-ground, Helios the sun god rises with his winged horse above the white-crested waves. The two red-figured cups in the middle of the case (P 24113 and 24131, both of the late 6th century) come from a well beneath the Stoa of Attalos. The one to the left nicely illustrates the range of subject matter popular with Athenian vase-painters of the time: on the exterior, A: the duel between Achilles and Memnon in the presence of their mothers; B: a Dionysiac revel; in the floor medallion a youth bearing a hare presumably as a love gift. In the field of the medallion is the signature, "Gorgos made me"; on the outside of the cup is the love-name "Krates." The other red-figured cup is by another well known vase-painter, Epiktetos. Only the medallion is painted: a naked girl hurries away from a foot-bath carrying her shoes in her hands; in the field is the love-name "Hipparchos."

33. Small Freestanding Case. Sphinx Amphora* (P 1247)

The amphora near the window (P 1247), adorned on either side by a somber figure of a crouching sphinx, in the earliest black-figure technique, is a work of the Nettos Painter of 620-610 B.C. The vase was intended no doubt to be placed on a grave, and its much weathered state suggests that it was for long exposed to the elements. At about this same time the Athenians began the practice of placing sphinxes carved in the round from stone or marble on top of their tombstones to guard the tombs.

34. Wall Case. Spartan Shield from Pylos* (B 262) (Figs. 60, 61)

The shield is of the type normally carried by a heavy-armed warrior *(hoplite)* in the 5th century B.C. Its border is adorned with a rich braid pattern. The metal has the thickness of blotting paper and may have been lined with leather or some other material.
Punched through the bronze in large letters is the inscription: "The Athenians from the Lakedaemonians from Pylos." Since the letter forms are of the late 5th century B.C., the shield may be identified as one of those carried by the 292 Spartans captured by the Athenians at Pylos in 425 B.C. The spectacle of Spartans surrendering alive made a great impression on the Greek world. The Athenians proudly hung the Spartan shields in the Painted Stoa where some were still seen by Pausanias in the 2nd century A.D. Our example for some reason was

removed earlier; it was later used as the lid of a cistern to the south of the Temple of Hephaistos and was buried when the cistern was abandoned in the 3rd century B.C.

34A. Leg and Sword from a Bronze Equestrian Statue*

The bronze leg and sword in the case below the Pylos shield came from a large gilded bronze statue of a figure on horseback, probably of Demetrios Poliorcetes, Macedonian ruler of Athens late in the 4th century B.C. The pieces were found discarded in the public crossroads well (p. 86) in a level dating to ca. 200 B.C., a time of strong anti-Macedonian feeling. The leg is hollow-cast, the sword solid bronze; note the traces of gilding. Another gilded bronze may be seen in Case 36.

36. Pedestal. Bronze Head of Victory (Nike)* (B 30)

The head, about one half life size, comes from a winged Nike. The V-shaped termination below was designed to fit into a socket in the bust. The topknot, drawn up and tied pony-tail style, has been lost; it was cast separately and attached to the peg at the crown of the head. See the illustration on the side of the stand. The eyes, also missing, were made in separate capsules and inset. Channels encircle the head just below the hair; they also run up to the top of the skull from front and back and down the neck on either side. Traces of earlier channels, now packed with bronze, may be detected on the back of the neck and on the sides of the skull. In the channel above the forehead is a piece of sheet silver; behind the ears are small masses of gold above silver. It appears that the head (as also the torso) was once covered with sheets of silver and above the silver with gold fastened in such a way that the precious metal could be removed. The figure is probably to be identified as one of the "Golden Nikai" which are known from the ancient authors and inscriptions to have served as repositories for the state's gold reserve in the 5th and 4th centuries B.C. Made about 420-415 B.C., our statue was twice stripped of its precious metal to help meet financial crises, first toward the end of the 5th century and again at the beginning of the 3rd. The bronze was found in a well of the late 3rd century B.C. at the west side of the Agora.

35. Small Freestanding Case. Child's Commode* (P 18010)

Near the next window is shown a contrivance for purely domestic use: a child's chair of the early 6th century B.C., gaily decorated with birds and beasts. The use is assured by the picture on a cup in Brussels (see photograph on the wall).

38. Freestanding Case. Ostraka and Graffiti* (Fig. 155)

In Case 38 are shown representative examples from the collection of some 1200 ostraka found in the Agora. These potsherds, called "ostraka" by the Greeks in both ancient and modern times, were used as ballots in the 5th century B.C. in the process of ostracism which took its name from the ballots. At times when there was fear of a tyranny a vote was held in the Agora. Each citizen wrote on his ballot the name of the man whom he feared. If as many as 6000 ballots were cast the proceeding was valid and the man whose name

155. A selection of ostraka (sherds) used in votes to exile prominent politicians in the 5th century B.C.

256

appeared most frequently was exiled for a period of ten years. Sherds of all sorts were used for the purpose: scraps of figured, black-glazed and plain vases, roof tiles, well-heads, etc. The writing too shows great variety even among ballots cast on the same day, and there are not a few errors in spelling. The name of the man is normally accompanied by that of his father or township or both. Very occasionally the voter has given more precise expression to his feelings, as in the case of an ostrakon with the name of Xanthippos, father of Perikles (P 16873; translation O. Broneer):

> Xanthippos, son of Arriphron, is cursed for his rascality;
> Too long he has, the potsherd says, abused our hospitality.

On one side of the case are shown ostraka from the Agora proper on which appear the names of all the famous men known to have come up for ostracism from the earliest instance of its use (487 B.C.) to the latest (417 B.C.). Those on the opposite side of the case are part of a hoard of 190 ostraka found in a well on the north slope of the Acropolis. All bear the name of Themistokles and all are probably of the year 482 B.C. They must have been prepared in advance, presumably by some political club for the convenience of illiterate voters; but they seem not to have been used. Note the careful writing; numerous pieces are by the same hand.

On the end of the case are a number of less formal documents on potsherds: messages, lists, the alphabet, etc. The most numerous category records an owner's name.

37, 40, 39, 41. Cases. Household Pottery of the Classical Period*

The two long wall cases, nos. 37 and 39 on the back wall, and the freestanding Cases nos. 40 and 41 near the front wall together afford a very good picture of the kitchen and table ware used in an Athenian household of the classical period.

We start with Case 37. On the floor of the case, left, are examples of the three types of vessel most commonly used for handling water: the large jar *(kados)* with two handles through which a rope could be run for drawing water from the well, the large three-handled jar *(hydria)* for carrying the water from well to house, and the small pitcher *(chous)* for table use. These water vessels, made of a micaceous brown clay with extremely thin walls which added little to the burden of the carrier, continued to be shaped by hand long after most other vases were regularly turned on the wheel. Near the middle of the floor is a chamberpot *(amis)* (P 2352). To the right are a couple of one-handlers, the most common bowl in this period for table use. The large spherical jug (P 20786) still retained a cork in its mouth when found; dating from about 480 B.C. this is the earliest known cork stopper. The jug had been lowered into a well to keep its contents cool. The two-handled basins *(lekanai)* to the right, fully glazed inside, banded outside, will have served a great variety of household needs.

On the two upper shelves of Case 37 are illustrated some of the most common shapes of table ware. All are covered with the black glaze which maintained its glossy quality through the 6th, 5th and 4th centuries. Most prominent are the vessels for holding and drinking wine. Toward the upper left are three examples of wine-coolers *(psykteres)*, their bodies drawn in below so that they could be let down into bowls of cold water. Beneath them is a wine pitcher *(chous)*, similar in shape to the plain water pitcher below, but glazed to prevent seepage; the garland painted on the shoulder of the jug reminds one of the common use of garlands at Greek symposia. On the top shelf are also deep two-handled drinking cups *(skyphoi)* of a type borrowed by the Athenians from Corinth; the shape was popular through the 6th and 5th centuries. Farther right are stemless drinking cups *(kylikes)* that had a long vogue from the 7th into the 4th century since they were more practical than their high-stemmed figured contemporaries. Closer examination will show that some of the black vases are decorated with geometric and floral designs stamped or incised before the clay had hardened. Two elegant examples of kantharoi of the second half of the 5th century are shown on the middle shelf, left; the plainer specimens to the right illustrate the most common type of drinking cup of the 4th and early 3rd centuries B.C.

In Case 40 is shown a selection from a great mass of household debris recovered from a well near the south end of the Stoa of Attalos. The group affords an idea of the furnishing of an Athenian house of the second quarter of the 6th century B.C., the early years of Peisistratos. Note the wide variety of shapes for different household uses, and the diversity also in the finish: plain, black, semi-black and black-figured. As usual in such household deposits the figured vases form a small minority of the whole. Among the black-figured is a mixing bowl (krater) by the painter Lydos (P 24943): in a body zone on one side a wild goat, on the other side swans. Of interest also are the comic figures on the fragmentary amphora (P 24944) and the small oinochoe (P 24945); in spirit as in date, they are close to the poros sculpture on the Acropolis. Among other objects of household use is a wooden comb (W 39), a couple of loom-weights (MC 1002, 1003), a primitive lamp much blackened from burning (L 5218), and a stylus of bone for writing on waxed tablets (BI 746).

With the long wall Case 39 we move into the kitchen. The equipment comprises a wide range of devices for cooking, all made of a coarse, brown fire-resistant clay, without paint or decoration of any sort. On the floor of the case are illustrated the principal types of brazier in vogue in the classical period designed to hold round-bottomed cooking pots. At the right are a couple of braziers consisting each of a shallow round basin with broad flat rim supported on a low stand (P 4869, 21956). These were evidently designed for grilling with a slow fire of charcoal. One of them indeed has long lugs on its rim to support spits for making the equivalent of the modern shishkebab. The bell-shaped devices shown here may also have served as portable ovens, the dough set beneath, the coals heaped around.

On the shelf above are illustrated grills, round-bottomed cooking pots, frying pans, and a strainer.

In Case 41 is shown a small selection from the contents of a well near the southeast corner of the Agora. The well had gone out of use and was filled with a vast mass of debris about the year 400 B.C. On the floor of the case are shown the characteristic trefoil-mouthed water pitchers (choes), some wheel-made and black-glazed, other hand-shaped and unglazed. Four of these unglazed pitchers bear pictures painted in pastel-like pigments of various colors (white, black, pink, green) with scenes relating to comedy; one of the four is exhibited (P 23900) while watercolors of all are shown nearby on the wall. Anticipating as they do the phlyax vases of South Italy, the Athenian pitchers are important documents for the history of the theater. On the upper shelves appear typical drinking vessels of the period: skyphoi, two-handled and one-handled mugs. Here too are tiny pitchers, terracotta lamps, powder boxes, terracotta figurines, a small bone Herm, an ivory stylus for writing on wax, loom-weights, a whetstone, a terracotta copy of the lion-head terminal of a bracelet. Among the red-figured vases a pitcher (chous) showing a child among his playthings (P 23877) is of the type carried by children at the "Festival of Pitchers." Two other pitchers of similar shape have scenes relating to victories: on one (P 23896) a prize tripod is flanked to right and left by Nikai, on the other (P 23850) a boy leading a horse holds a victor's wreath in his hand. Another noteworthy object from this well is a bronze measure (B 1082), cylindrical in shape and inscribed "official property of the people of Athens"; it holds about 0.111 liter, probably an ancient hemikotylion. Compare the terracotta measures in Case 26.

42. Small Wall Case. Coins*

Here are shown a very few of the total of some 75,000 identifiable coins found in the excavations. The great majority are of bronze and of small denominations. The silver numbers approximately 300 pieces. The collection also includes a 5th century Kyzikene stater of electrum (an alloy of gold and silver) and several gold coins: a Persian daric (465-425 B.C.), a posthumous stater of Alexander the Great struck at Sardis about 321 B.C., a Venetian ducat (1694-1700 A.D.), three Turkish pieces of which only one, dating from 1574 A.D., is shown, and a 20-franc piece of Napoleon III (1854 A.D.). The exhibition illustrates briefly the history of Athenian coinage from its beginnings in the first half of the 6th century B.C. to its end at the time of the barbarian sack of A.D. 267. Also shown are specimens of coins minted in other Greek cities, a series of Roman coins beginning in the time of Sulla, and a small sampling of the coinage of the Byzantine empire, of the Frankish overlords, of the Venetians and the Turks who dominated Athens in turn.

43. Freestanding Case. Painted Marble Lintel* (A 818)

This fragmentary marble is shown by the decoration on its soffit and by the inclination of its preserved end to be part of a lintel. In a panel on the vertical face was painted a lioness striding right; the figure appears to have been rendered in a light color against a blue ground.

The soffit panel was filled with a diamond pattern; its vertical surround bears a lotus-and-palmette border. The style points to the third quarter of the 5th century B.C. The fragments were found in the Post-Herulian Wall overlying the Eleusinion (Plan, **56**), but the original use of the block is unknown. It is important, nevertheless, as a rare example of figure painting on marble in the classical period.

HELLENISTIC PERIOD

Late 4th - 1st Century B.C.

The long period between the death of Alexander the Great (323 B.C.) and the sack of Athens by Sulla (86 B.C.) is represented in the Museum chiefly by pottery and terracotta figurines. We look first at the pottery.

By the last quarter of the 4th century B.C. the old red-figure style had died a natural death. It was succeeded by various other techniques for the decoration of vases. One innovation was the use of thinned clay and white paint for the application of floral and geometric designs: the so-called "West Slope Style" named from the discovery of much of this ware on the West Slope of the Areopagus in the 1890's. In this period too moulds were used commonly to achieve an imitation of metal vessels with decoration in low relief, especially the so-called "Megarian Bowls," once mistakenly believed to have originated in Megara. The old black-figure technique still occurred sporadically, notably on the Panathenaic prize amphorae. The technical quality of the pottery declined after the 4th century, in part no doubt because metal vessels came to be more commonly used by those who could afford them while the less affluent were satisfied by imitations of metal in clay.

44. Freestanding Case. Hellenistic Pottery and Jewelry*

Here are exhibited several good specimens of the West Slope technique. Two of the tall-stemmed drinking cups *(kantharoi)* on the floor of the case are inscribed with a toast to friendship *(Philia)*. The

261

enormous kantharos (P 6878) bears a dedication by one Menokles to Dionysos and Artemis; on the better preserved side (shown in watercolor on the nearby wall) is a hunting scene with a little shrine of Artemis, goddess of the hunt, in the middle. The fragment of a Panathenaic amphora (on the floor) is one of many such found in the Agora (P 1893); the practice of giving jars of olive oil at the Panathenaic Festival persisted through the Hellenistic and Roman periods. Interesting too is the occurrence in Athens of an imitation of a "Hadra hydria" (P 6313) of the type used as ash urns in the Hadra cemetery of Alexandria.

On the upper shelf of this case are shown several examples of the lagynos, a type of wine jug with tall slender neck and with either a globular or an angular body, popular in the Hellenistic period. Those with a creamy white wash were imported to Athens, probably from Asia Minor. From Asia Minor too will have come the wine mixing bowl *(krater)* of gray clay at the inner end of the case (P 3155). Note that the figures on the neck (satyrs, maenads, etc. appropriate to the festive use of the bowl) were moulded separately and applied. Both they and the handles are clearly derived from metal originals.

Here too, is displayed assorted pieces of gold jewelry recovered from the crossroads well (p. 86). Note especially the earrings in the form of winged Erotes.

45. Freestanding Case. Hellenistic Miscellany

The neighboring case contains a medley of characteristic products of Hellenistic craftsmanship. The manufacture of Megarian Bowls, an active industry in Athens from the last quarter of the 3rd to the middle of the 1st century B.C., is illustrated by moulds and by stamps for the making of moulds. Some of the earlier bowls with purely floral decoration in very delicate, crisp relief must be close to metal prototypes. These are followed by a category with figured decoration, miscellaneous but chiefly idyllic in its themes. About the middle of the 2nd century B.C. a calyx-like scheme of long petals came into favor and persisted to the end. Terracotta lamps of the period often share the relief decoration of the Megarian Bowls; other lamps were modeled in the round in the shape of heads: Negroes, bulls, etc. The spindle-shaped unguent bottles of gray clay are found on virtually all sites of the Hellenistic period in the eastern Mediterranean. They and their contents must have originated in some common center, but the characteristic vase form was sometimes copied elsewhere, as in Athens, and adorned in the West Slope technique. Tiny containers of medicines and ointments are also widespread in this period; they may be of terracotta or of lead and they are commonly stamped with the name of the drug and of the producer. Especially numerous are the thimble-sized lead containers of lykion, a popular purgative.

The massive ivory crossbar from a sword hilt (BI 457) is a rare and noteworthy object.

MINIATURE SCULPTURE OF VARIOUS PERIODS

In two small cases on the back wall (49, 50) is shown a selection of the innumerable little figures of bronze and terracotta that have come to light in the Agora. Some of the terracottas were found, together with the moulds for shaping them, in the ruins of the modest shops of their makers, the coroplasts. One or two small groups are of types suitable for dedications at sanctuaries, e.g. the sanctuary of Demeter.

49. Wall Case. Terracottas*

In Case 49, upper left, is exhibited a mould of the 4th century B.C. for a figure of a reclining woman together with a modern cast (T 3879). The bearded head on the floor of the case, a silen or possibly Sokrates, is not mouldmade but very delicately fashioned by hand; it served perhaps as a positive prototype for the making of moulds (T 313).

In the upper right is shown a clay impression taken from a piece of fine metalwork, one half of a belt clasp (T 3393). Beside the ancient impression, which is in the negative, is a modern cast in the positive. Note the imprint of the cord by which the metal was attached to a leather backing. The seated warrior has been recognized as Odysseus accompanied by the armor of Achilles which had been awarded to him on Achilles' death. Odysseus grieves, probably for the impending fate of his great rival, Ajax, who may well have been represented on the other half of the clasp. The impression, made by a craftsman perhaps to record the figure for future adaptation, illustrates the extraordinary skill and delicacy of Athenian metalwork in the late 5th century B.C.

On the floor of the case, left, a few figurines with religious themes are grouped around an altar. The seated figure in the background echoes a cult image of a goddess. Prominent in terracotta and in bronze, as also in marble, are the so-called Herms: abbreviated representations in which a realistic head is supported by a schematic trunk. The divinity most commonly so treated is Hermes himself, either youthful or bearded; but occasionally goddesses also appear as in the tall terracotta to the right. Approaching the altar are three women; the pig no doubt is intended for sacrifice; in the far corner of the little sanctuary squats a sleepy slave boy.

On the floor of the case, right, are figurines relating to the theater, a large category among the terracottas of Athens. The group of four figurines on the lower level, dating from the 4th century B.C., shows slaves in attitudes characteristic of Middle Comedy: sitting in insolent security on altars, carrying a huge wine jug, leering at some (now missing) girl. The tall thin figure to the right, with arms akimbo and wearing shaggy trunks, is a rare and interesting example of a character from a satyr play (PN T 139). At the back are characteristic masks: a slave, a hetaira, an old man. In the middle is a group of two figures on a couch: a female reclining and a man seated (T 2404). The inscription below (in Latin characters) tells us that the female is a personification of Comedy, the male is Pylades, presumably a famous comic actor of that name. The piece dates from the 3rd century A.D.; replicas are known from Ostia.

The flying Victory (Nike) in the middle of the case is a splendid creation of the 3rd century B.C.; note the cuttings for wings in the shoulders (T 2309). She is flanked by Erotes, also in flight.

50. Wall Case. Terracottas, Bronzes, Ivories*

The neighboring case to the left is more miscellaneous. The period extends from the 1st century B.C. to the 5th century A.D. The figures of the early Roman period, Aphrodite and Eros in both bronze and terracotta, are little more than miniature echoes of famous old sculptural types. More interesting for the history of art are the crude yet vigorous terracottas of the 4th and 5th centuries A.D.; here the coroplast is working more independently. He is no longer concerned with delicacy of modelling, but depends largely on incision and paint. Note especially the bearded head in the lower right (T 3055), the toy dog in the lower left (T 1510) and the seated woman suckling a child in the upper left (T 511): a type that stands midway between the Isis and Horus of Egypt and the Virgin and Child of Christian art. In the late Roman period the coroplast devoted much of his talent to the making of plastic lamps and of children's playthings, both well represented in this case. The baroque satyr's head on the back of the case (middle) is a good example of ivory carving of the 2nd century A.D.; the ivory must have adorned some piece of furniture.

The bronze serpent with human head and flowing locks on the left upper shelf is one of the few known representations of Glykon, a reincarnation of the god Asklepios which was brought about by a magician in Anatolia in the 2nd century A.D. (B 253).

On the floor of the case to the right are some gaming pieces: besides the dice there are some knucklebones of sheep (astragaloi) which were favorite playthings of Greek children, especially of girls.

On the back wall of the gallery between Cases 49 and 50 are hung two life-sized terracotta masks of the 3rd century A.D. They must be patterned closely on the masks, presumably of lighter and tougher material, used in the theatre. The one (T 478) represents the leading slave of comedy; the other (T 1818) is taken from a figure of tragic pantomime.

46, 47. Wall Shelves. Small Copies of Famous Statues*

The excavations have yielded many of the simplified miniature copies of popular old statues that were turned out by Athenian sculptors in the Roman period. They were intended, no doubt, for the adornment of private houses.

The weary Herakles (S 124) on Shelf 46 goes back to an original of the 4th century B.C. probably by Lysippos. The type is best known from a colossal copy, the "Herakles Farnese" now in Naples, which is signed by an Athenian sculptor, Glykon. The little image of the triple

Hecate (S 852), goddess of crossroads and of entrances, echoes remotely a famous work of Alkamenes on the Acropolis. The miniature Aphrodite (S 1192), on whose right shoulder Eros once perched, is of the same type as a colossal statue that now stands in the colonnade of the Stoa (p. 196). Note the ancient paint.

On Shelf 47 are two statuettes inspired by cult images in sanctuaries of the Agora. In the little shrine (S 922) sits the Mother of the Gods with phiale, tympanum, lion and attendants much as she must have appeared in the Metroon (Plan, **14**, Fig. **30**). The heavily draped Apollo with kithara (S 877) is a copy at 1/10 scale of Euphranor's statue of Apollo Patroos now standing in the colonnade (p. 193). The multifigured relief on Shelf 47, an original of the 4th century B.C. (S 1251), shows a family of worshippers approaching a group of Eleusinian divinities: Demeter seated, Persephone standing and Iakchos with the infant Wealth on his arm.

48. Freestanding Pedestal. Ivory Apollo* (BI 236) (Fig. 156)

The foot-high ivory statuette of the resting Apollo once held a bow or lyre in the outstretched left hand. This is a miniature replica, made in the 2nd or 3rd century A.D., of a work of the 4th century B.C. that stood in the Lyceum Gymnasium in Athens. The common attribution of the original to Praxiteles is not certain, but its fame is attested by the number of extant replicas. The ivory was found in a well shattered into more than 200 fragments. (See photograph on the right-hand side of the pedestal.)

52. Table Case. Terracotta Lamps*

From the 5800 terracotta lamps found in the excavations enough have been displayed to illustrate the development of this common household article. The series starts at the upper left with a hand-shaped open saucer of a type borrowed by the Greeks from the Near East along with many other things in the 7th century B.C. The form was gradually improved and made more practical: the rim was bent in to prevent spilling, a nozzle was devised to hold the wick more firmly, a handle was added, and glaze was applied to make the clay more

156. Apollo Lykeios, ivory statuette of the 2nd/3rd centuries A.D.

impervious to oil. From the 6th into the 3rd century B.C. lamps were
turned on the potter's wheel.

In the Hellenistic period the lamp was normally made with a pair of
moulds, one for the upper and one for the lower part (one such
mould is shown). The new technique speeded production and
permitted the addition of some plastic ornament similar to that found
on the contemporary Megarian Bowls.

In the 1st century B.C. the top of the lamp (discus) began to be
treated as a field for a circular relief in which were represented a
great variety of themes. In the Athenian shops technical skill reached
its climax in the 2nd and 3rd centuries A.D. Thereafter invention
failed; moulds were made from lamps and lamps from moulds with

267

the same theme until it became a coarse caricature of the original. By the 6th century the Athenian lamps were utterly degenerate both artistically and technically; when the industry revived in the Byzantine period the cycle began afresh with an open saucer form.

In all periods the fuel used was vegetable oil, chiefly olive. It was fed through a fabric wick like that still in place in one of the lamps in the case. Such lamps will burn for one to two hours giving as much light as a candle.

60. Wall Case. Miscellany of the Roman Period*

Here have been assembled a few characteristic products of Greek craftsmanship of the Roman period both local and imported.

In the Roman period, in contrast with earlier times, a considerable proportion of the fine pottery used in Athens was imported. This was due in part to losses suffered by the potters in the sack of Athens by Sulla in 86 B.C. On the floor of the case is a bowl of the latter part of the 1st century B.C. made at Arretium, in north Italy (P 17219). The large plates of thin red fabric, one with figures in low relief, shown to right and left are also imported, perhaps from North Africa; they are of the 3rd century A.D. (P 15179, 21649). Local, however, are the flower pots in the middle of the floor; they are two of many found in place in planting holes around the Temple of Hephaistos (Plan, **1**); they date from the 1st century A.D. (P 7051, 7261) (Fig. **16**).

On the middle shelf are shown several glass vessels of the 2nd and 3rd centuries A.D. Note here also a terracotta bowl with the head of the Emperor Augustus in high relief on its floor (P 22351); the bowl dates from the 3rd century A.D. Christian symbols first come into common use in Athens in the 5th century A.D.; several are shown here: a water pitcher with the Christian monogram and the incised inscription "of the Virgin" (P 25133), a fragment from the floor of a red-ware plate with the head of an unknown martyr bearing his cross (P 197), a lamp on which St. Peter is shown at full length also with his cross of martyrdom (L 4754). A fragment from the disc of a lamp bearing the head of St. Paul is shown among the lamps in Case 52 (L 1153).

On the top shelf are pitchers of the 3rd century A.D. moulded in the shape of boys' heads (P 10004, 11939) to be compared with the contemporary marble portraits, and two wine jugs decorated in relief, one of the 1st century A.D. with applied clay (P 10714), the other of the 3rd century by the use of moulds (P 17877). In the middle is a lamp discus of the 3rd century A.D. illustrating the story of Hero and Leander (L 4251): Leander, vigorously swimming the Hellespont, is guided shoreward by the lamp which Hero holds out from a window high in her tower.

The semicircular bone plaque attached to the back wall of the case once adorned the end of a small casket of the 4th or 5th century A.D. (BI 288). In the middle stands a voluminously draped figure holding a pair of spears in the left hand, a plumed helmet in the right. In the field to the left are a couple of bundles, to the right an amphora. The identification of the figure is problematic.

61. Wall Case. Well Group of the 1st to 10th Century A.D.*

In the large wall case at the north end of the gallery is shown a small selection of the objects recovered from a single well in the Agora. This well happens to be one of the deepest (35 m., i.e. 115 feet), but it is typical in the wide variety of objects that had been dropped or thrown into it. The stratified deposit runs from the 1st into the 6th century A.D.; after a break marking the Dark Age in Athens, the record resumes for a short period in the 10th century. A few characteristic pieces have been laid out by centuries starting with the earliest at the lower right. One can observe the changes in fashion in table ware through the ages. The numerous complete lamps attest to many a night journey to the well. The walnuts and peach stones are interesting indications of diet. Among the playthings are shown a pair of dice, also some attractive sea shells, and terracotta figurines.

Most numerous are the vessels for water. They include many pitchers for carrying water from the well into the house. The medium-sized jars with basket handles will have been used for drawing water on the end of rope. There is shown also a lead pail (IL 563) that will have served the same purpose, and two wooden buckets made of staves (W 6, 14); these are of the 4th century A.D.

On the end wall of the gallery above Case 61 is a section of mosaic floor from a room in a large house of the 4th century A.D. outside the southwest corner of the Agora. The design for the whole floor is shown in the watercolor on the adjacent wall to the left. The figured scene that must have occupied the square panel has been almost entirely destroyed; there remain only the elaborate geometric borders worked out in strong colors with tesserae of marble, limestone and glass.

A watercolor on the wall of the gallery to the left of the door shows the Doric order from the facade of the Stoa of Zeus (Plan, **25**), late 5th century B.C. The painting was made while the ancient colors were still fresh on the stone.

SCULPTURE OF THE ROMAN PERIOD*

A number of particularly fine portrait busts and heads are shown on brackets toward the north end of the gallery. Note especially, on the front wall (Shelf 53), the head of an Egyptian priest dating from the 1st century B.C.; his profession is shown by the shaven skull and head band (S 333). On the opposite wall (Shelf 55) is a strikingly beautiful bust of a young man of the Julio-Claudian period (early 1st century A.D.), perhaps a member of the imperial family (S 356). Slightly later is the head of a young woman (Shelf 56) whose distinctive coiffure points to the time of Tiberius (14-37 A.D.). The three other portraits (Shelves 47, 54, 58) should all date to the early 2nd century A.D. (Fig. **157**).

Facing the door (Base 62) is a youthful satyr holding a goat at his left side; in his right hand was a Pan's pipe (S 221). The porcelain finish of the flesh parts, contrasting effectively with the rough surface of hair and hide, is characteristic of the Antonine period (mid-2nd century A.D.). Note the traces of ancient paint on hair and eyes.

63. Wall Case. Byzantine and Turkish Periods*

The case contains a selection of the finer pottery found in the ruins of the houses that overlay much of the Agora from the 10th to the 12th centuries. Most of these wares were imported into Athens.

On the top shelf are illustrated some of the techniques in vogue in the earlier part of the period: plain glaze laid over the smooth surface of the clay; solid glaze above ornament impressed in low relief while the

157. Roman portrait of a man, perhaps Pantainos, found in the Library of Pantainos, ca. 100 A.D.

clay was still soft; polychrome designs in matt colors (black, yellow, pink) applied to a light-colored biscuit and then covered with thin glaze. In the middle of the shelf are shown two glazed chafing dishes each with a small compartment for a charcoal fire to keep the food warm (P 3075, 10147).

Most of the vessels on the middle shelf, dating from the 11th and 12th centuries, are decorated in the sgraffito technique. A dark colored clay was overlaid with a thick slip of creamy white. When the slip became firm the designs were incised through it into the dark clay, and parts of the background were scraped clear of slip so as to make the design stand out in light against dark. The whole of the decorated surface was then overlaid with a protecting coat of thin, almost colorless glaze. Birds and animals appear commonly in the medallions which are surrounded by elaborate geometric ornament and occasionally by imitations of Arabic writing (so-called Kufic). In a coarser and slightly earlier ware, illustrated by the large bowl in the middle, the design, instead of being incised, has been painted in matt colors (green and black) over a light slip and then protected as before by a transparent glaze.

The fragments of sgraffito plates and bowls on the floor of the case illustrate some of the exploits of Digenis Akritas, the Herakles of the Byzantine period. Note especially the middle piece (P 8623) in which Digenis, in keeping with the songs of the epic cycle, is killing a dragon with five arrows.

The majolica plate with the portrait of a Venetian doge, made in the 16th century in North Italy (P 5673), reminds one that Venetian traders were active in the eastern Mediterranean even when Athens was in Turkish hands.

The water pitcher (lower right) with the lion drawn in blue outline on a creamy white ground (P 1902) represents the Turkish period (1458-1831 A.D.). This specimen dates from the 16th or early 17th century; it was made locally under the influence of Italian majolica. Potters' kilns of the Turkish period have been found in the middle of the Agora above the classical floor level just as preclassical potters' shops have been found below.

Upper Floor, Colonnade*

Stairways lead up to the upper floor at each end of the Stoa. Additional antiquities are on display upstairs, though the area in recent years has not been open to visitors on a regular basis. Of especial interest are the models of the Akropolis, Pnyx, Agora, and Stoa of Attalos. Also on display are two Ionic capitals of the 5th century B.C. The one in the south stairwell, from an unknown building, shows traces of its original painted ornament. The second comes from the temple of Athena at Sounion and was reused in the Agora in the Southeast Temple (Plan, 52) in the Roman period. Set against the south wall is an inscribed record of the sale of confiscated property of Alcibiades and others in 415/4 B.C. following their conviction for parodying the Eleusinian Mysteries and for mutilating the Herms of Athens. Ten such stelai originally stood in the Eleusinion. The remaining display is made up largely of statues, herms, and portraits of the Roman period.

BIBLIOGRAPHICAL NOTES

The bibliography is not complete; it is intended merely to facilitate reference to some of the more significant publications of Agora material. The three basic works to consult are: R. E. Wycherley, The Athenian Agora, Volume III, Literary and Epigraphical Testimonia, Princeton 1957, H. A. Thompson and R. E. Wycherley, The Athenian Agora, Volume XIV, The Agora of Athens, Princeton 1972, and J. M. Camp, The Athenian Agora, London 1986.

19 History of the Area

Agora XIII, passim (Prehistoric Period); *Agora VIII* (8/7th century B.C.); *Agora XIV,* 1-24 (general), *Agora XXIV* (late antiquity).

35 History of the Excavation

E. Capps, *Hesperia* 2 (1933) 89-95; *Agora XIV,* 220-224.

39 Hephaisteion

H. Koch, *Studien zum Theseustempel in Athen,* Berlin (1955) (general); W. B. Dinsmoor, *Hesperia* Supplement V (1941) (results of recent exploration); S. Karouzou, *Ath. Mitt.* 69-70 (1954-55) 68-94 (cult images and pedestal); C. H. Morgan, *Hesperia* 31 (1962) 210-219 (metopes); 221-235 (friezes); 32 (1963) 91-108 (pediments, akroteria, cult images); H. A. Thompson, *AJA* 66 (1962) 339-347 (sculptural program); B. Schlörb, *Untersuchungen zur Bildhauergeneration nach Phidias,* Waldsassen/Bayern (1964) 61f. (sculpture in general); A. Delivorrias, *Attische Giebelskulpturen und Akrotere des funften Jahrhunderts,* Tübingen (1974) 16-60 (pediments, akroteria); W. B. Dinsmoor, Jr., *AJA* 80 (1976), C. N. Edmonson and W. F. Wyatt, Jr., *AJA* 88 (1984) 135ff. (roof and ceilings); D. B. Thompson, *Hesperia* 6 (1937) 396-425 (garden); A. Frantz, *Dumbarton Oaks Papers* 19 (1965) 202-205 (conversion to Christian use); J. Travlos, *Pictorial Dictionary of Ancient Athens,* London (1971), 261-273; *Agora III,* nos 281-295; *Agora XIV,* 140-149; J. Camp, *The Athenian Agora,* pp. 82-87.

45 Arsenal (?)

G. R. Edwards, *Hesperia* 26 (1957) 334-337; *Agora XIV,* 80f.; R. Pounder, *Hesperia* 52 (1983) 233ff.

45 Demos and the Graces

J. Travlos, *Pictorial Dictionary,* 79-81; *Agora III,* nos 125-132; *XIV,* 223.

45 Eurysakeion

W. S. Ferguson, *Hesperia* 7 (1938) 1-74; *Agora III,* nos 246-255; *XIV,* 40f.

47 Tholos

E. Vanderpool, *Hesperia* 4 (1935) 470-475 (Tholos and Prytanikon); *Hesperia* Supplement IV (excavation report); J. Travlos, *Pictorial Dictionary,* 553-561; *Agora III,* nos. 589-609; *XIV,* 41-46; J. Camp, *The Athenian Agora,* pp. 76-77, 94-97. Building F: T. L. Shear, Jr. in *Athens Comes of Age,* Princeton (1978), pp. 5-7.

54 Early Cemetery
Hesperia Supplement II.

54 Civic Offices to South of Tholos
Agora XIV, 72-74.

56 House of Simon
D. B. Thompson, *Archaeology* 13 (1960) 234-240; *Agora XIV*, 173f.

58 Boundary Markers
Hesperia 8 (1939) 205f.; 37 (1968) 61-63; *Agora III*, nos. 713f.; *XIV*, 117-119.

59 Drains
Picture Book 11; *Agora XIV*, 194-197.

62 Bouleuterion and Metroon
H. A. Thompson, *Hesperia* 6 (1937) 115-127; *Hesperia* Supplement IV, 148-151; *Picture Book* 4, *passim*; *Agora III*, nos. 387-433, 465-519; *XIV*, 25-38.

66 Statue of Hadrian
T. L. Shear, *Hesperia* 2 (1933) 178-183; *Agora I*, no. 56; *Picture Book* 5, no. 14.

68 Q. Trebellius Rufus
J. H. Oliver, *Hesperia* 10 (1941) 72-77; 11 (1942) 80.

68 Bronze Stelai
R. S. Stroud, *Hesperia* 32 (1963) 143.

68 Altar of Zeus
R. Stillwell, *Hesperia* 2 (1933) 140-148; H. A. Thompson, *Hesperia* 21 (1952) 91-93; *Agora III*, nos. 379-386; *XIV*, 160-162.

69 Eponymoi
R. Stillwell, *Hesperia* 2 (1933) 137-139; T. L. Shear, Jr., *Hesperia* 39 (1970) 145-222; *Agora III*, nos. 229-245; *XIV*, 38-41.

72 Southwest Temple
W. B. Dinsmoor, Jr., *Hesperia* 51, (1978) 410-66.

73 Civic Offices and Tile Standard
G. P. Stevens, *Hesperia* 19 (1950) 174-188; *Agora XIV*, 79f.

74 Poros Benches on Kolonos
H. A. Thompson, *Hesperia* 6 (1937) 218-220; A. L. Boegehold, *Hesperia* 36 (1967) 111-120; *Agora XIV*, 71; J. Camp, *The Athenian Agora*, p. 100.

74 Apollo Patroos, Temple
H. A. Thompson, *Hesperia* 6 (1937) 77-115; J. Travlos, *Pictorial Dictionary* 96-99; *Agora III*, nos. 107-113; *XIV*, 136-139; C. Hedrick, *AJA* 92 (1988) 185ff.

77 Zeus Phratrios and Athena Phratria
H. A. Thompson, *Hesperia* 6 (1937) 84-90, 104-107; *Agora III*, p. 52; *XIV*, 139f; C. Hedrick, *AJA* 92 (1988) 185ff.

77 Stoa of Zeus Eleutherios

R. Stillwell, *Hesperia* 2 (1933) 110-124; H. A. Thompson, *Hesperia* 6 (1937) 5-77; J. Travlos, *Pictorial Dictionary*, 527-533; *Agora III*, nos. 24-46; *XIV*, 96-103.

79 Royal Stoa

T. L. Shear, Jr., *Hesperia* 40 (1971) 243-255; 44 (1975) 365-374; *Agora III*, nos. 4-23; *XIV*, 83-90; J. Camp, *The Athenian Agora*, pp. 53-57, 100-105. Emily Vermeule has made the very plausible suggestion that the lithos is from the lintel of a Mycenaean tholos tomb salvaged in antiquity and regarded as something both royal and sacred.

86 Crossroads Sanctuary

T. L. Shear, Jr., *Hesperia* 42 (1973) 126-134, 360-369; J. H. Kroll, *Hesperia* 46 (1977) 83ff., 114ff, 49 (1980) 86ff. (cavalry records).

88 Late Round Building

T. L. Shear, Jr., *Hesperia* 42 (1973) 125f. *Agora XXIV*, p. 60.

89 Tyrannicides

S. Brunnsaker, *The Tyrant-Slayers of Kritios and Nesiotes*, Lund (1955) (good general discussion); B. D. Meritt, *Hesperia* 5 (1936), no. 1 and *Picture Book* 10, no. 4 (inscription); *Agora III*, nos. 256-280; *XIV*, 155-160.

89 Orchestra and Ikria

A. Pickard-Cambridge, *The Dramatic Festivals of Athens*[2], Oxford (1968) 25-42; M. Bieber, *History of the Greek and Roman Theatre*, Princeton (1961) 54; N. G. L. Hammond, *Greek, Roman and Byzantine Studies* 13 (1972) 387-450; *Agora III*, nos. 524-528; *XIV*, 126-219.

90 Herms

T. L. Shear, Jr., *Hesperia* 40 (1971) 255-259; *Agora III*, nos. 301-313; *XI*, 108-117; *XIV*, 94-96.

93 Double Stoa on the Dromos

T. L. Shear, Jr., *Hesperia* 42 (1973) 370-382.

96 Altar of the 12 Gods

T. L. Shear, *Hesperia* 4 (1935) 355-358; H. A. Thompson, *Hesperia* 21 (1952) 47-82; M. Crosby, *Hesperia* Supplement VIII (1949) 82-103; *Agora III*, nos. 361-378; *XIV*, 129-136. D. Francis and M. Vickers, "Leagros kalos," *PCPS* 1981, pp. 97-136.

98 Basilica and Adjacent Buildings

T. L. Shear, Jr., *Hesperia* 42 (1973) 134-144.

101 Painted Stoa

Agora III, nos 47-98; *XIV*, 90-94; T. L. Shear, Jr., *Hesperia* 53 (1984) 1ff.; J. Camp, *The Athenian Agora*, pp. 68-72.

109 Gate

T. L. Shear, Jr., *Hesperia* 53 (1984) 1ff; J. Camp, *The Athenian Agora*, pp. 162-165.

109 Altar of Aphrodite Ourania
T. L. Shear, Jr., *Hesperia* 53 (1984) 1ff; C. N. Edwards, *Hesperia* 53 (1984) 59ff.

111 Panathenaic Way
J. Travlos, Πολεοδομική ἐξέλιξις τῶν ᾿Αθηνῶν (1960), 38ff., 66, 70; E. Vanderpool, *Hesperia* 43 (1974) 311-313 (equestrian displays); *Agora III*, nos. 729f.; *XIV*, 192f.; T. L. Shear, Jr., *Hesperia* 44 (1975) 362ff. (starting line).

114 Temple of Ares
W. B. Dinsmoor, *Hesperia* 9 (1940) 1-52 (architecture); M. H. McAllister, *Hesperia* 28 (1959) 1-64 (architecture); *Hesperia* 20 (1951) 57f. and 21 (1952) 94f. (frieze); P. N. Boulter, *Hesperia* 22 (1953) 141-147 (east central akroterion); A. Delivorrias, *Attische Giebelskulpturen und Akrotere,*Tübingen (1974) 94-161 (pediments, akroteria, frieze); W. B. Dinsmoor, Jr., *AJA* 78 (1974) 211-238 (sima from Sounion); *Agora III*, nos. 116f.; *XIV*, 162-165.

116 Sacred Repository
H. A. Thompson, *Hesperia* 27 (1958) 148-153; *Agora XIV*, 119f.

118 Late Roman Complex
H. A. Thompson, *Hesperia* 19 (1950) 134-137; *JRS* 49 (1959) 67f.; *Agora XIV*, 211f.; *XXIV*, 97, 109.

118 Odeion
H. A. Thompson, *Hesperia* 19 (1950) 31-141; J. Travlos, *Pictorial Dictionary*, 365-377; *Agora III*, nos. 520-523; *XIV*, 111-114; *XXIV*, 95-116.

124 Monopteros
W. B. Dinsmoor, Jr., *Hesperia* 43 (1974) 412-427.

125 Lawcourts
Agora XIV, 52-72; J. Camp, *The Athenian Agora*, pp. 107-113.

126 Shop Building under the Stoa of Attalos
Hesperia 19 (1950) 320; 21 (1952) 101; *Agora XIV*, 172.

127 Bema
Hesperia 7 (1938) 324; *Agora III*, no. 99; *XIV*, 51f.

130 Stoa of Attalos
Picture Book 2; J. Travlos, *Pictorial Dictionary*, 505-519; *Agora III*, nos. 99-102; *XIV*, 103-108; J. Camp, *The Athenian Agora*, pp. 168-175.

135 Street to the Roman Market
T. L. Shear, Jr., *Hesperia* 42 (1973) 144-146, 385-398; 44 (1975) 332ff.

140 Library of Pantainos
Hesperia 4 (1935) 330-332 (discovery); 18 (1949) 269-274 (sculptor's rooms); *Hesperia* 15 (1946) 233 and *Hesperia* Supplement VII (1949) 268-272 (dedicatory inscription); J. Travlos, *Pictorial Dictionary*, 432-435; *Agora III*, no. 464; *XIV*, 114-116.

142 **Post-Herulian Wall**
J. Travlos, Πολεοδομική ἐξέλιξις, 122-124; *idem, Pictorial Dictionary*, 161, 163, 179; *Agora XIV*, 209; *XXIV*, 5-11.

144 **Water Mill**
A. W. Parsons, *Hesperia* 5 (1936) 70-90; *Picture Book* 7, no. 2; *Agora XIV*, 214; R. Spain, *Hesperia* 56 (1987) 335-353; *Agora XXIV*, 80-81.

146 **Southeast Stoa**
Hesperia 29 (1960) 344-347; 35 (1966) 79-85; J. Travlos, *Pictorial Dictionary*, 436; *Agora XIV*, 109f.

147 **Southeast Temple**
Hesperia 29 (1960) 339-343; *Agora XIV*, 167f.; W. B. Dinsmoor, Jr., *Hesperia* 51 (1982) 410ff.

151 **Crossroads Shrine**
Hesperia 28 (1959) 95f.; 29 (1960) 333; *Agora XIV*, 169.

152 **Eleusinion**
Hesperia 8 (1939) 207-212 (discovery); 29 (1960) 334-338 (excavation); J. Travlos, *Pictorial Dictionary*, 198-203; *Agora III*, nos. 191-228; *XIV*, 150-155.

155 **Early Tombs on the Areopagus**
T. L. Shear, *Hesperia* 9 (1940) 274-291 and *Agora XIII*, 158-169 (Mycenaean chamber tomb); E. L. Smithson, *Hesperia* 37 (1968) 77-116 (burial of 9th century B.C.).

155 **House on the Areopagus**
T. L. Shear, Jr., *Hesperia* 40 (1971) 266-270; A. Frantz. *Proceedings of the American Philosophical Society* 119 (1975) 34-38; *Agora XIV*, 213-215; J. Camp, *The Athenian Agora*, pp. 202-211; *Agora XXIV*, 37-48.

160 **Church of St. Dionysios**
A. Frantz and J. Travlos, *Hesperia* 34 (1965) 157-202; *Agora XIV*, 218.

161 **Nymphaion**
Hesperia 24 (1955) 57-59; *Picture Book* 11, fig. 3; *Agora XIV*, 202f.; R. Ginouves, *Laodicée du Lycos, le Nymphée*, Quebec-Paris (1969), 149.

162 **Mint**
Hesperia 23 (1954) 45-48 (discovery); 24 (1955) 59; 29 (1960) 343f.; *Agora III*, pp. 160f.; *XIV*, 78f.; J. Camp, *The Athenian Agora*, pp. 128-135.

162 **Southeast Fountain House**
Hesperia 22 (1953) 29-35 (discovery); *Picture Book* 11, fig. 2; *Agora III*, nos. 434-455; *XIV*, 197-199; J. Camp, *The Athenian Agora*, pp. 42-44.

166 **Holy Apostles**
Picture Book 7, 46-58; *Agora XIV*, 216-218; *Agora XX*.

166 **South Stoa I**
Hesperia 22 (1953) 28f. (discovery); 23 (1954) 39-45; 35 (1966) 47; 37 (1968) 43-56; *Agora XIV*, 74-78; J. Camp, *The Athenian Agora*, pp. 122-126.

173 South Stoa II
Hesperia 6 (1937) 357f. (discovery); 29 (1960) 359-363; *Agora XIV*, 68.

176 East Building
Hesperia 22 (1953) 36f. (exploration); *Agora XIV*, 68-70.

177 Middle Stoa
Hesperia 5 (1936) 4-6; 21 (1952) 86-90; J. Travlos, *Pictorial Dictionary*, 234-239; 578f.; *Agora XIV*, 66-68; V. R. Grace, *Hesperia* 54 (1985) 1ff.

180 Heliaia
Hesperia 23 (1954) 33-39; *Picture Book* 4, 21; *Agora XIV*, 62-65.

181 Water Clock
Hesperia 23 (1954) 37f.; J. Armstrong and J. Camp, *Hesperia* 46 (1977) 147ff.; *Agora XIV*, 64f.

181 Southwest Fountain House
Hesperia 4 (1935) 360; 18 (1949) 213-214; 24 (1955) 52-54; 25 (1956) 52-53; 35 (1966) 42-43; *Picture Book* 11, fig. 25; *Agora XIV*, 200f.

184 Triangular Shrine
Hesperia 37 (1968) 58-60 and 123-133; *Agora XIV*, 120f.

185 State Prison
M. Crosby, *Hesperia* 20 (1951) 168-187; *Agora III*, pp. 149f.; *The Athenian Agora*, pp. 113-116; E. Vanderpool, *From Athens to Gordion*, Philadelphia (1980), 17-31.

187 Bath at Northwest Foot of Areopagus
T. L. Shear, Jr., *Hesperia* 38 (1969) 394-415.

187 Residential-Industrial Area
R. S. Young, *Hesperia* 20 (1951) 67-134 (burials), 135-288 (dwellings and shops); *Agora XIV*, 15f. (family cemetery), 173-191 (houses and shops).

193 Apollo Patroos, Statue
H. A. Thompson, Ἀρχ. Ἐφ., 1953/54, III, 30-44; S. Adam, *The Technique of Greek Sculpture* (1966), passim; G. M. A. Richter, *The Sculpture and Sculptors of the Greeks*[4] (1970), p. 222, fig. 785; Olga Palagia, *Euphranor*; J. Travlos, *Pictorial Dictionary*, 96, figs. 123, 124; *Agora XIV*, 139, pl. 69; C. Hedrick, *AJA* 92 (1988) 185ff.

193 Praxiteles Base
T. L. Shear, *Hesperia*, 6 (1937) 339-342; B. D. Meritt, *Hesperia* 26 (1957) 200-203; J. Marcadé, *Recueil des Signatures des Sculpteurs Grecs* II, Paris (1975), no. 115, pl. XLIV; *Picture Book* 10, fig. 27; *Agora III*, p. 85; XIV, 154f.

194 Ionic Columns
H. A. Thompson, *Hesperia* 29 (1960) 351-356; J. Travlos, *Pictorial Dictionary*, figs. 152f; *Agora XIV*, 166.

194 Theoxenos Base
B. D. Meritt, *Hesperia* 26 (1957) 203-206; *Agora XIV*, 153f.

194 Iliad and Odyssey
G. Treu, *Athenische Mitteilungen* 14 (1889) 160-169; *Hesperia* 23 (1954) 62-65; J. Travlos, *Pictorial Dictionary*, figs. 308-310; *Agora XIV*, 115.

195 Standing Goddess
T. L. Shear, *Hesperia* 4 (1935) 384-387; E. B. Harrison, *Hesperia* 29 (1960) 374; A. Delivorrias, *Attische Giebelskulpturen und Akrotere* Tübingen (1974), 96, Anm. 428.

196 Herms as Supports beside Statues
Agora XI, nos. 210-213.

196 Stage Front of Odeion
Hesperia 19 (1950) 64-68; J. Travlos, *Pictorial Dictionary*, fig. 487.

197 Triton Head
Hesperia 19 (1950) 106; *Agora XIV*, 113, pl. 61.

197 Apollo or Dionysos
Agora XI, no. 109.

197 Tripod Base
T. L. Shear, *Hesperia* 4 (1935) 324, 387-393; W. Fuchs, *Die Vorbilder der Neuattischen Reliefs*, (1959), pp. 46, 128 note 61, 166 note 8, 168, 171; *Agora XI*, no. 128; C. M. Havelock, *Hellenistic Art*, Greenwich, Conn. (1971), no. 162; *Agora XIV*, 79, 126.

198 Aphrodite
E. B. Harrison, *Hesperia* 29 (1960) 373-376; S. Adam. *Technique of Greek Sculpture*, 16, 52, 75, 81.

198 Head of a Goddess
E. B. Harrison, *Hesperia* 29 (1960) 369-370.

198 Nereid
T. L. Shear, *Hesperia* 2 (1933) 527f.; B. Schlörb, *Timotheos* (1965) 53, 93; A. Delivorrias, *Attische Giebelskulpturen und Akrotere*, 45-47; S. Adam, *Technique of Greek Sculpture*, 53, 93.

199 Draped Female
T. L. Shear. *Hesperia* 2 (1933) 175-178; B. Schlörb, *Untersuchungen*, 53, pl. 9, 2; S. Adam, *Technique of Greek Sculpture*, passim.

199 Two Statues of Goddesses
Hesperia 6 (1937) 168; A. Delivorrias, *Antike Plastik* VIII, 3, 26 (S 473).

200 Nymphs Relief
T. L. Shear, Jr., *Hesperia* 42 (1973) 168-170; *Opuscula Romana* IX (1973) 183-192; H. A. Thompson, *Journal of the Walters Art Gallery* 36 (1977) 73-84.

201 Herakles (?)
H. A. Thompson, *Hesperia* 18 (1949) 233f.; H. v. Heintze, *Rom. Mitt.* 72 (1968) 19, 36ff.; *Agora XIV*, 148, no. 152.

202 "Ephedrismos"
H. A. Thompson, *Hesperia* 18 (1949) 235f.; A. Delivorrias, *Attische Giebelskulpturen und Akrotere*, 33-40; *Agora XIV*, 148.

203 Torso of Athena
H. A. Thompson, *Hesperia* 18 (1949) 234; *Agora XIV*, 148, n. 152.

203 Recliner
H. A. Thompson, *Hesperia* 18 (1949) 233; *Agora XIV*, 148, no. 152.

204 Horsemen Relief
T. L. Shear, Jr., *Hesperia* 40 (1971) 271f.; *Agora XIV*, 95, no. 72.

205 Head of Nike
T. L. Shear, Jr., *Hesperia* 40 (1971) 273; E. B. Harrison in *The Eye of Greece.*

205 Reliefs from Temple of Ares
H. A. Thompson, *Hesperia* 21 (1952) 94f.; B. Schlorb, *Untersuchungen*, 34-36; J. Travlos, *Pictorial Dictionary*, fig. 144; E. Harrison in *Archaische und Griechische Plastik*, II Mainz 1986, 109-117.

206 Water Carrier
Hesperia 22 (1953) 53f.; *Picture Book* 11, fig. 3.

206 Torso of Athena
T. L. Shear, *AJA* 40 (1936) 196, 198; B. Schlorb, *Untersuchungen*, 35; G. Despinis, *Συμβολή στήν μελέτη τοῦ ἔργου τοῦ 'Αγορακρίτου*, Athens (1971) 186ff.; *Agora XIV*, 164.

207 Prytany Decree
S. Dow, *Hesperia* Supplement I, p. 43, no. 9; *Agora XV*, no. 86.

207 Standing Female Figure (S 339)
T. L. Shear, *Hesperia* 4 (1935) 371-374.

207 Apobates Base
Hesperia 4 (1935) 379-381; J. Travlos, *Pictorial Dictionary*, fig. 26; *Agora XIV*, 121.

208 Poletai Stele
M. Crosby, *Hesperia* 10 (1941) 14; 19 (1950) 206; *Hesperia* Supplement IV, 59; Supplement IX, 94, 150-154; *Picture Book* 4, fig. 6.

208 Diaitetai Stele
W. S. Ferguson, *Hesperia* 7 (1938) 1ff.; *Agora III*, no. 254.

209 Herodotos (?)
Hesperia 4 (1935) 402; *Agora I*, no. 1; *Picture Book* 5, no. 2 (identification doubtful); G. M. A. Richter, *The Portraits of the Greeks*, I, London (1965), p. 146 (identification doubtful).

209 Themis
T. L. Shear, Jr., *Hesperia* 40 (1971) 270f.; O. Palagia, *Hesperia* 51 (1982) 410ff.

210 Karneades Base
IG II² 3781; *Hesperia* 19 (1950) 318f.; *Picture Book* 2, fig. 35; B. D. Meritt, *The Athenian Year*, Berkeley and Los Angeles (1961) 229f.; G. M. A. Richter, *Portraits of the Greeks*, II, p. 250; *Agora III*, pp. 46, 213; XIV, 107.

211 Antoninus Pius
T. L. Shear, Jr., *Hesperia* 42 (1973) 170.

211 Togati
Agora I, nos. 52, 57, 58

211 Shoemaker Relief
J. McK. Camp, *AJA* 77 (1973) 209; *The Athenian Agora*, pp. 146-147.

213 Lucius Aelius Caesar (?)
Agora I, no. 28; *Picture Book* 5, front cover, fig. 13.

213 Trajan (?)
Agora I, no. 17; *Picture Book* 5, fig. 11; C. C. Vermeule, *Roman Imperial Art in Greece and Asia Minor*, Cambridge, Mass. (1968) p. 387. Other identifications have been suggested; a Flavian priest, Claudius, Domitian.

214 Magistrate
Agora I, no. 64; *Picture Book* 5, fig. 19; A. Frantz, *Dumbarton Oaks Papers* 19 (1965) 193; *Agora XXIV*, pp. 65, 113.

214 Nike from the Stoa of Zeus Eleutherios
T. L. Shear, *Hesperia* 4, (1935) 374-379; H. A. Thompson, *Hesperia* 6 (1937) 37; J. Travlos, *Pictorial Dictionary*, fig. 671; *Agora XIV*, 99; A. Delivorrias, *Attische Giebelskulpturen und Akrotere*, pp. 124f., 137ff., 160.

216 Graffito on Wall of Stoa
Picture Book 5, fig. 43.

216 Wine Jars
V. Grace, *Picture Book* 6; V. Grace and M. Savvatianou-Petropoulakou in *Exploration Archéologique de Délos* XXVII, Paris (1970), ch. XIV, with bibliography pp. 287f.

220 Neolithic and Bronze Ages
For a full presentation of the Agora material from these periods see *Agora XIII*. For the burials see also *Picture Book* 13. For contemporary material from elsewhere in Athens cf. Maria A. Pantelidou, Αἱ Προϊστορικαί Ἀθῆναι, Athens, 1975.

225 Early Iron Age
Hesperia Supplement II; *Picture Book* 13; *Agora XIV*, 10-15.

226 Burial of a Warrior Craftsman
C. W. Blegen, *Hesperia* 21 (1952) 279-294; *Picture Book* 13, figs. 38, 39; *The Athenian Agora*, pp. 31-32

226 Protogeometric Burial
Hesperia 23 (1954) 58; *Picture Book* 13, fig. 35.

228 Pithos Burial
Hesperia 29 (1950) 330f.; *Picture Book* 13, figs. 52f.

228 Geometric Burial Groups
Hesperia 17 (1948) 158f. (Areopagus grave); *Hesperia* Supplement II, 76-78 (Tholos grave).

229 Funeral Pyre
Hesperia Supplement II, 55-67.

229 Grave Group of ca. 850 B.C.
E. L. Smithson, *Hesperia* 37 (1968) 77-116.

232 Grave with Shoes
R. S. Young, *Hesperia* 19 (1949) 275-197.

232 Geometric Wine Cooler
Hesperia Supplement II, 68-71; R. Hampe, *Frühe griechische Sagenbilder*, Athens (1936), 87f.; *Agora XIV*, 15.

233 Orientalizing Period
Agora VIII, passim; *Agora XIV*, 15; *The Athenian Agora*, pp. 32-34.

234 Offerings from a Shrine
D. Burr, *Hesperia* 3 (1933) 542-640; *Picture Book* 3, figs. 10-18.

235 Mould for Bronze Statue
Hesperia 6 (1937) 82f.; *Agora XIV*, 188-190; Carol Mattusch, *Hesperia* 46 (1977) 340-347; *Picture Book* 20.

236 Head of a Herm (S 2452)
T. L. Shear, Jr., *Hesperia* 42 (1973) 164ff.

236 Head of a Large Herm (S 2499)
T. L. Shear, Jr., *Hesperia* 42 (1973) 406f.

236 Head of a Herm (S 3347)
T. L. Shear, Jr., *Hesperia* 53 (1984) 40-43.

237 Head of Herakles (S 1295)
Agora XI, no. 97A.

237 Marble Head (S 2476)
T. L. Shear, Jr., *Hesperia* 42 (1973) 400f.

238 Tyrannicides' Base
Hesperia 5 (1936) 355-358; S. Brunnsaker, *The Tyrant-Slayers of Kritios and Nesiotes*, Lund (1955) 84-98, 154f.; *Picture Book* 10, fig. 4, *Agora III*, no. 280; *XIV*, 156f.

238 Archon List
B. D. Meritt, *Hesperia* 8 (1939) 59-65; D. W. Bradeen, *Hesperia* 32 (1963) 187-208; *Picture Book* 10, fig. 5.

238 Tribute List
Hesperia 8 (1939) 54-59; *Picture Book* 10, fig. 10; R. Meiggs and D. Lewis, *Greek Historical Inscriptions*, Oxford (1969), no. 75.

238 Library Rules
T. L. Shear, *Hesperia* 5 (1936) 41-42; A. W. Parsons, *Hesperia* Supplement VIII, 268-272; *Picture Book* 10, fig. 32; *Agora III*, no. 464; *XIV*, 115.

239 Epigrams on the Persian Wars
J. H. Oliver, *Hesperia* 2 (1933) 480-494; 5 (1936) 225-234; B. D. Meritt, AJP 83 (1962) 294-298; *Picture Book* 10, figs. 2, 3; R. Meiggs and D. Lewis, *Greek Historical Inscriptions*, no. 26.

239 Spear-butt
J. Camp, *Hesperia* 47 (1978) 192ff.

239 Lead Cavalry Tablets
J. Kroll, *Hesperia* 46 (1977) 83ff.

241 Clay Tokens
J. Kroll and F. Mitchel, *Hesperia* 49 (1980) 86ff.

241 Lead Armor Tokens
J. Kroll, *Hesperia* 46 (1977) 141f.

241 Sokrates Material
Simon: D. B. Thompson, *Archaeology* 13 (1960) 234-240; *The Athenian Agora*, pp. 145-147. Prison: M. Crosby, *Hesperia* 20 (1951) 168-187; *Agora III*, 149ff.; *The Athenian Agora*, pp. 113-116; E. Vanderpool, *From Athens to Gordion*, Philadelphia 1980, pp. 17-31.

242 Public Antiquities
Weights and Measures: *Agora X*; *Picture Book* 4, figs. 14-19; Symbola: *Hesperia* 20 (1951) 51ff.; *Picture Book* 4, fig. 8.

244 Dicastic Equipment
Picture Book 4, figs. 21-26; *Agora XIV*, 52-56; *The Athenian Agora*, pp. 107-113. A. L. Boegehold, *Hesperia Supplement XIX*, pp. 1-6.

247 Kleroterion
S. Dow, *Hesperia* Supplement 1, 198-215; *Harvard Studies in Classical Philology* 50 (1939) 1-34.

248 Decree against Tyranny
B. D. Meritt, *Hesperia* 21 (1952) 355-359; M. Ostwald, *TAPA* 86 (1955) 103-128; J. Pouilloux, *Choix d'Inscriptions Grecques* 32 (1960) 121-124; *Picture Book* 4, fig. 29.

250 Kneeling Boy
E. Vanderpool, *Hesperia* 6 (1937) 426-441; *Picture Book* 3, fig. 23; G. M. A. Richter, *Kouroi*³, London (1970) 77f.; *Agora XIV*, 186.

250 Black Figure and Red Figure
P 20716: E. Vanderpool, *Hesperia* 20 (1951) 61-63; J. D. Beazley, *Paralipomena* 25; P. 12628: E. Vanderpool, *Hesperia* 8 (1939) 247-266; J. D. Beazley, *Paralipomena* 64; skyphoi by Theseus Painter: E. Vanderpool, *Hesperia* 15 (1946) 289-291; J. D. Beazley, *ABV* 158; P 1275: E. Vanderpool, *Hesperia* 15 (1946) 280; J. D. Beazley, *ARV* 105; P 2698: E. Vanderpool, *Hesperia* 15 (1946) 285-287); Chairias Painter: L. Talcott, *Hesperia* 24 (1955) 72-75; P 15210: G. van Hoorn, *Choes and Anthesteria*, Leiden (1951) no. 227; oinochoai from North Slope: R. Green, *Hesperia* 31 (1962) 82-94; M. Moore and M. Z. Philippides, *Attic Black-Figured Pottery*, *Agora XXIII* (1986).

253 Exekias Krater
O. Broneer, *Hesperia* 6 (1937) 468-486; *AJA* 42 (1938) 445; J. D. Beazley, *ABV* 145, 19.

253 Red Figure and White Ground
P 43: L. Talcott, *Hesperia* 2 (1933) 224-230; J. D. Beazley, *ARV* 923; P 5113: L. Talcott, *Hesperia* 5 (1936) 333-335; P 24113: L. Talcott and B. Philippaki, *Hesperia* 24 (1955) 64-66; J. D. Beazley, *Paralipomena*, 2291; P 24131: L. Talcott and B. Philippaki, *Hesperia* 24 (1955) 63f.; J. D. Beazley, *Paralipomena*, Epiktetos no. 69 ter.

254 Sphinx Amphora
E. Vanderpool, *Hesperia* 7 (1938) 367-371; J. D. Beazley, *ABV* 5, 2.

254 Pylos Shield
T. L. Shear, *Hesperia* 6 (1937) 346-348; 'Αρχ. 'Εφ., (1937) A, 140-143; *Picture Book* 4, figs. 33f,; *Agora XIV*, 92.

255 Bronze Leg and Sword
T. L. Shear, Jr., *Hesperia* 42 (1973) 165-168; *The Athenian Agora*, pp. 162-165.

255 Bronze Head
T. L. Shear, *Hesperia* 2 (1933) 519-527; H. A. Thompson, *Harvard Studies in Classical Philology*, Supplement I (1940) 183ff.; D. B. Thompson, *Hesperia* 13 (1944) 173-209; *Agora XIV*, 190f.

256 Child's Commode
Hesperia 17 (1948) 184f.; *Picture Book* 12, figs, 39, 40.

256 Ostraka
E. Vanderpool, *Ostracism at Athens*, Semple Memorial Lectures, University of Cincinnati (1970); *Picture Book* 4, figs. 27f.; *Agora XIV*, 50f.

257 Household Pottery
Agora XII; *Picture Book* 1; B. Sparkes, "The Athenian Kitchen," *Journal of Hellenic Studies* 52 (1962) 121-137.

259 Pitchers with Comic Scenes
M. Crosby, *Hesperia* 24 (1955) 76-84; T. B. L. Webster, *Hesperia* 29 (1960) 261-263, 279, B 2-5; A. D. Trendall, *Phlyax Vases*[2] (1967), pp. 23f.: A. Pickard-Cambridge, *The Dramatic Festivals of Athens*[2], Oxford (1968), 212f.; A. D. Trendall and T. B. L. Webster, *Illustrations of Greek Drama*, London (1971), 120; *Agora XII*, 205.

259 Debris from a Well
H. A. Thompson, *Hesperia* 25 (1956) 57-61.

260 Coins
Agora II; Picture Books 15 and 18.

260 Painted Lintel
Hesperia 8 (1939) 221; G. P. Stevens, *Hesperia* 23 (1954) 169-184.

261 Hellenistic Pottery
Thompson, Thompson and Rotroff, *Hellenistic Pottery and Terracottas*, Princeton (1987); S. G. Miller, *Hesperia* 43 (1974) 194-245; S. Rotroff, *Hellenistic Pottery: Mouldmade Bowls*, Agora XXII; T. L. Shear, Jr. *Hesp.* 42, 1973, pp. 131-132 (jewelry).

263 **Terracotta Figurines**
D. B. Thompson, *Hesperia* 2 (1933) 184-194; Thompson, Thompson and Rotroff, *Hellenistic Pottery and Terracottas*, Princeton (1987); *Picture Book* 3, *passim*.

263 **Impressions from Ancient Metal Work**
D. B. Thompson, *Hesperia* 8 (1939) 285-316; Supplement 8 (1949) 365-372; 39 (1969) 242-251 (Mourning Odysseus); E. R. Williams, *Hesperia* 45 (1976) 41-66.

264 **Theatral Figures**
T. B. L. Webster, *Hesperia* 29 (1960) 254-284.

264 **Small Objects of the Roman Period**
Agora VI (Terracotta figurines and plastic lamps); *Picture Book* 3 (Terracottas, Ivories, Bronzes).

265 **Small Copies in Marble**
Herakles: *Hesperia* 17 (1948) 180; Hekate: *Agora XI*, 86-107; Aphrodite: *Hesperia* 10 (1941) 5; Mother of the Gods: *Agora XIV*, 31; Apollo; *Agora XIV*, 139; Eleusinian relief: *Hesperia* 17 (1948) 177f.

266 **Ivory Apollo**
T. L. Shear, *Hesperia* 6 (1937) 349-351; *Picture Book* 3, fig. 60.

266 **Terracotta Lamps**
Agora IV and *VII*; *Picture Book* 9.

268 **Miscellany of the Roman Period**
Agora V (Pottery); D. B. Thompson, *Hesperia* 6 (1937) 404-409 (flower pots); *Picture Book* 5, title page, figs. 3-6 (terracotta medallions).

269 **Well Group**
Agora V, 82-120.

270 **Sculptures**
For portraits: *Agora I* and *Picture Book* 5; for the satyr: T. L. Shear, *Hesperia* 2 (1933) 536-541.

270 **Byzantine and Later Pottery**
A. Frantz, *Hesperia* 7 (1938) 429-467 (Middle Byzantine); 10 (1941) 9-13 (Akritas); 11 (1942) 1-28 (Turkish); *Picture Book* 7, *passim*.

272 **Models of the Acropolis and Pnyx**
Acropolis: J. Travlos, *Pictorial Dictionary*, fig. 89; Pnyx: *Ibid.* pp. 466-475; *Picture Book* 4, fig. 2; *Agora XIV*, 48-50; H. A. Thompson, *Hesperia* Supplement XIX (1981) 133ff.

272 **Ionic Columns**
H. A. Thompson, *Hesperia* 29 (1960) 351-356; Agora XIV, p. 166.

272 **Column Capital from Sounion**
W. B. Dinsmoor, Jr., *Hesperia* 51 (1982) 410ff.

272 **Record of an Auction**
W. K. Pritchett, *Hesperia* 22 (1953) 225-299; 25 (1956) 178-317; A. Pippin, *op. cit.*, 318-328; D. A. Amyx, 27 (1958) 163-310; W. K. Pritchett, 30 (1961)

23-29; R. R. Holloway, 35 (1966) 84; B. D. Meritt, 36 (1967) 84-86; J. McK. Camp, 43 (1974) 319-321; R. Meiggs and D. Lewis, *Greek Historical Inscriptions*, no. 79; *Agora III*, no. 207; *XIV*, 153.

INDEX

Academy: 105, 108
Acropolis: 19, 22, 30, 191, 253:
    Excavation on North Slope 19, 253
Adyton: 75
Agora, primitive: 19
Agorakritos: 65
Agrippa, M. Vipsanius: 28, 122, 130
Aigeus: 197
Akroteria: 43, 78, 82, 115, 198, 214
Alaric: 31
Alexander the Great: 89
Alkamenes: 41, 236, 266
Alkibiades: 93, 152
Allotment machines: 247f.
Altars: 22f., 45, 63, 68, 77, 97, 100,
    109ff., 115, 154
Amphorae (Wine Jars): 216ff.
Amyneion: 190
Antenor: 89
Anthesteria: 252
Anthippasia: 113, 205
Antigonos and Demetrios: 71
Antiphon: 92
Antoninus Pius: 156, 211
Aphrodite 162, 195, 196, 198ff., 206,
    266;
    Hegemone 45;
    Ourania 109ff.
Apobates: 113, 207
Apollo:
    Lykeios 266;
    Patroos 23f., 31, 74ff., 193, 266
Apollonis: 130
Apuleius: 18
Aqueducts: 28, 108, 145, 151f., 161.,
    164, 173, 176, 183, 197
Archbishop's Palace: 160
Archeia (Public Offices): 54f., 73f.,
    171f., 198
Archives: 63, 65
Archon Basileus: 79, 85
Archons: 84, 238

Areopagus:
    Council 82, 159;
    Hill 22, 155ff., 201, 234
Ares, Temple of: 114f., 196, 198,
    205f.
Argyrokopeion (Mint): 162f.
Ariarthes: 210
Aristogeiton: 18, 89f., 238
Aristophanes: 71
Aristotle: 47, 68, 246
Arretine Pottery: 268
Arsenal (?): 45
Artemis: 198, 262;
    Eukleia 39
Assembly (Ekklesia): 22, 24, 47, 68,
    250
Astragaloi: 86, 265
Asylum: 96
Athena: 39f., 66, 105, 115, 203, 206,
    253;
    Phratria 77
Athenaeus: 18, 128
Attalos I: 71
Attalos II: 25, 130, 210
Augustus: 28, 115, 268

Ballots: 56, 245
Basileus: 79, 85
Basilica: 98f.
Baths: 122, 156, 187, 191
Bema: 127
Beule Gate: 142
Boule (Council): 19, 47ff., 61ff., 152,
    207
Bouleuterion: 61ff.
Boundary Stones: 184;
    Agora 38, 58f.
Bronze Casting: 77, 189, 235f., 255
Bryaxis Base: 113, 205
Building C: 66
Building F: 53

287

Mysteries of Demeter: 93, 107, 152

Neoptolemos: 200
Nesiotes: 89
Nikai: 78, 156, 205, 214, 255, 264
North Slope of Acropolis: 19, 152, 191, 200, 253
Nymphaion: 161f.

Odeion of Agrippa: 28, 118ff., 196f.
Omega House: 156ff.
Onesippos: 85
Orchestra: 90
Ostraka and Ostracism: 256f.
Ourania: see Aphrodite

Painted Stoa: 101ff.
Palace:
   Late Roman 118ff.;
   of Tyrants (Building F) 53
Panainos: 104
Panathenaic: 22, 93, 113f., 207, 253; Amphorae 262
   Way 32, 60f., 86, 111f., 124, 147, 151ff.
Pantainos: 28, 140, 271
Parian Marble: 39, 43, 58, 109f., 198
Parthenon: 39, 111, 123, 152
Paul: 159
Pausanius: 38, 74, 75, 78, 79, 82, 90, 93, 95, 104f., 109, 114, 123, 154, 164, 193, 206, 254
Peirene: 162
Peisianax: 104
Peisikrateia: 194, 196
Peisistratids: 19f., 53, 96, 165, 234, 238
Peloponnesian War: 24, 106, 152
Pentelic Marble Quarries: 109
Perirrhanteria: 59, 73, 97, 191
Persians: 22, 53, 66, 77, 79, 89, 96, 98, 105
Pheidias: 65, 111
Pheidon: 112
Philip II: 250
Philosophical Schools: 31, 105, 130
Philostratos: 123
Phosphoroi: 53
Photios, 90

Phratries, 75ff.
Pindar: 90
Plato: 90, 97, 186
Plutarch: 90, 97, 186
Pnyx: 22, 68, 191
Poikile, Stoa: 101ff.
Poletai (Auctioneers): 55, 208, 244
Polygnotos: 104
Portraits: 18
Post-Herulian Wall: 31, 33, 73, 123-4, 133, 135, 142ff., 148, 151f., 177, 194, 196, 198
Pottery Workshops: 27, 79, 181, 228, 272
Poulytion: 92f.
Praxiteles: 93, 193, 266
Prison (Desmoterion): 185ff., 242
Propylon (Gate): 61, 109, 135f., 154
Probus: 31
Prytaneis: 47, 62, 207
Prytaneion: 85
Ptolemy III: 71
Pylos: 105f., 254

Race Course: 112
Railway, Athens - Peiraeus: 35f., 45, 77, 79, 81, 88, 90, 96, 123, 146
Rhamnous, status of Themis: 209
Roads: north side of Agora 98, 100; south side of Agora 155, 169; at southwest corner 184
Rockefeller, John D.: 35
Roma: 45
Roman Market: 135ff.
Roof tiles: 73; of Tholos 53
Round Building, Late Roman: 88
Rufus, Quintus Trebellius: 68

Sacred Gate: 60
Sacred Repository: 117ff.
Salaminioi: 208
Sculptors' Workshops: 141, 155, 177, 181, 189
Sgouros, Leon: 33
Shear, T. L.: 135
Shields: 78, 105f., 234, 254ff.
Shops: 95, 100, 109, 127, 133, 135f., 138, 146, 151

291

NOTES

NOTES